THE RED WINES
OF
FRANCE

Margaret Rand

Consultant Editor
Joanna Simon

THE RED WINES
OF
FRANCE

Margaret Rand

Consultant Editor
Joanna Simon

a Salamander book

Published by Salamander Books Limited
LONDON • NEW YORK

A Salamander Book

Published by Salamander Books Ltd,
52 Bedford Row,
London WC1R 4LR,
United Kingdom

© Salamander Books Ltd 1987

ISBN 0 86101 273 9

Distributed in the UK by
Hodder & Stoughton Services,
P.O. Box 6,
Mill Road, Dunton Green, Sevenoaks,
Kent TN3 2XX

All correspondence concerning the content of this volume should be addressed to Salamander Books Ltd.

Credits

Editor:
Philip de Ste. Croix

Designer:
Roger Hyde

Colour artwork:
Ann Winterbotham and Stephen Seymour
© Salamander Books Ltd

Maps:
Sebastian Quigley
© Salamander Books Ltd

Index:
Jill Ford

Filmset:
SX Composing Ltd, England

Colour reproduction:
Melbourne Graphics Ltd, England

Printed in Italy

CONTENTS

Foreword 6
Grapes and Vines 8
Cultivation and Harvest 10
How Red Wine is Made 12
Ageing and Bottling 14
French Wine Laws 16

18 The Wine Industry
20 How to Read the Label
22 How to Buy
26 Serving Wine
28 Wine and Food
30 Vintage Charts

34
BORDEAUX

66
BURGUNDY

88
RHÔNE

106
LOIRE

112
SAVOIE AND JURA

114
THE SOUTH-WEST

*A*UTHOR: Margaret Rand is editor of *Wine & Spirit* magazine. After leaving Bristol University she worked in book publishing before taking up wine writing and tasting, in which she proved her expertise by winning *The Observer*/Rémy Martin Cognac tasting competition in 1985. She is a taster on many of the highly-respected panels of WINE magazine and writes frequently for it, as well as producing a regular column on wine for *The Daily Express.* She contributed the section on Spanish wines to *The Wine Lists* (Guinness, 1985). In January 1988 she will take over as editor of WINE magazine.

*C*ONSULTANT EDITOR: Joanna Simon has edited two of the foremost wine journals in the English language: *Wine & Spirit* magazine, which she joined as assistant editor in 1981, becoming editor in 1984, and WINE, which she edited between October 1986 and December 1987. She has travelled extensively in Europe and Australia, has tasted for a number of wine magazines, as well as *The Financial Times,* and has written for a wide range of trade and consumer publications on wine-related subjects. She is currently wine correspondent for *The Sunday Times*, and Contributing Editor of WINE and *Wine & Spirit.*

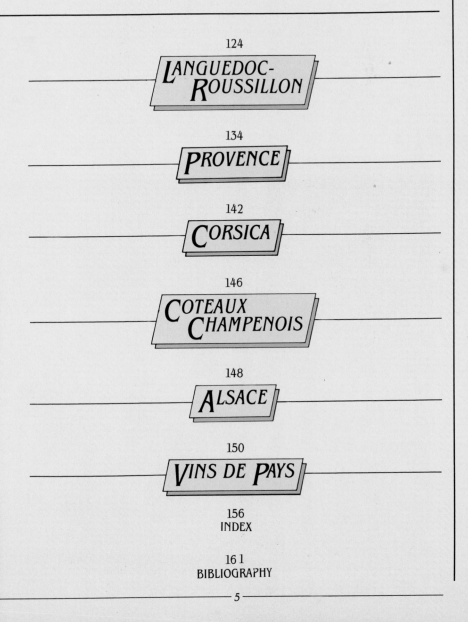

124
LANGUEDOC-ROUSSILLON

134
PROVENCE

142
CORSICA

146
COTEAUX CHAMPENOIS

148
ALSACE

150
VINS DE PAYS

156
INDEX

161
BIBLIOGRAPHY

FOREWORD

French wines, despite the meteoric rise of such winemaking areas as California and Australia, remain the benchmark for most wine drinkers. Fine claret and burgundy have set standards worldwide for red wines, and the concentration of serious Californian and Australian winemakers upon such French grape varieties as Cabernet Sauvignon has, if anything, helped to extend the range of French influence. These days, too, French winemakers are as keen to acquire their expertise in other continents as these comparative newcomers to the field are to visit French cellars.

But not everything in France is so international. The great château proprietors of Bordeaux may think nothing of jetting to the other side of the world to host a tasting, but in some parts of Burgundy a winemaker might think it just as much of an event if he travelled to the next village to taste. At some estates the visitor will be welcomed by a bilingual or trilingual guide; at others the owner himself will greet guests in rapid French – and take it for granted that they understand. Some of the world's finest wines, too, can be found in the latter cellars.

It is this that helps to make the variety of French wines so fascinating. The first part of this book looks in detail at the question of how wine is made – and in particular how red wine is made. For making red and white wine involves totally different techniques, not least because the desired results are so totally different. *The Red Wines of France* examines red grapes – how the vines are treated, how the grapes are picked, and what happens when they are crushed, fermented into wine and pressed. It discusses, too, why some wines need ageing and why some are best drunk young, and how the winemaker can influence the style of his wine and decide even before he picks his grapes whether he wants a light, fruity wine or a big, tough, mouthfilling one.

For not only is every conceivable style produced in France, but the winemakers can rise to just about any challenge the wine lover might throw at them. There is a French red wine to drink with chocolate, and one that goes superbly with salmon; both are listed in the wine with food section on page 29. This part of the book also looks at how to serve wine, and asks if it is really necessary to have a different sort of glass for every sort of wine. It looks at decanting, too, and

whether all (or indeed any) French reds are best drunk at room temperature.

The second part of the book travels round France region by region, and examines the lesser known areas as closely as many of the everyday names. And some of France's lesser-known wines are very obscure indeed. Where, for example, is Collioure? And where would you expect to find the Grolleau grape grown?

The classic regions, of course, are familiar to every wine drinker. Everybody has heard of Bordeaux and Burgundy. But what is less obvious are the factors that make some wines great and some just ordinary. Sometimes it is soil, sometimes climate, sometimes a winegrower who is convinced that he can produce the best and is determined to make the rest of the world believe it, too. Equally, there are estates that are not as good as they used to be, or whole appellations that are on the way up or in decline. In fact, France, familiar as it might appear to be, can produce as many surprises and as many wine finds as any New World wine region, or indeed any vinously less well-known European country. The trick is simply having the patience to look.

Metric/Imperial Equivalents

The French wine industry uses metric measurements to express volumes, weights, dimensions, etc. This book, therefore, also uses metric units for such measurements. For those readers unfamiliar with the metric system, or who are more comfortable thinking in Imperial units, listed below are the necessary conversion factors.

$$1 \text{ metre (m)} = 3.281 \text{ ft}$$
$$1 \text{ kilometre (km)} = 0.6214 \text{ miles}$$
$$1 \text{ hectolitre (hl)} = 100 \text{ litres} = 22 \text{ UK gallons or } 26.4 \text{ US gallons}$$
$$1 \text{ hectare (ha)} = 10,000 \text{m}^2 = 2.471 \text{ acres}$$
$$1 \text{ kilogram (kg)} = 2.205 \text{lb}$$
$$1 \text{ tonne} = 1,000 \text{kg} = 2,205 \text{lb}$$

Any description of the vines of France has to start right at the bottom – with the roots. These, nowadays, are largely of American origin. When the phylloxera insect rampaged through France (and indeed through the rest of Europe) towards the end of the last century, it laid waste to France's vineyards. Endless solutions were tried, but only one proved both practical and effective, and that was to graft the vulnerable but high quality European vines on to rootstock from the phylloxera-resistant American species. *Vitis vinifera*, the European vine, had fallen like ninepins before the onslaught of the aphid, which had probably arrived in Europe on vine cuttings. But all the North American species of *Vitis* – *labrusca*, *berlandieri*, *riparia* and *rupestris* being the most important ones – were found to be resistant in varying degrees to phylloxera. Hence the introduction of grafting, which undoubtedly saved the European vineyards from almost total destruction.

Choosing the right rootstock is not just a matter of picking the most resistant American species. The relative vigour of the rootstock and the graft have to be considered, as does the suitability of the rootstock to the soil in each vineyard, and the climate.

A simple answer would have been to re-plant Europe with American species, and plenty of experimental vineyards were set up in the last century. But not even the prospect of phylloxera-free ungrafted vines could make up for the taste of the resulting wines. The usual description is foxy, meaning pungent and unpleasant.

Phylloxera is only one of the thousand natural enemies of the vine. Just before it arrived in Europe there had been an epidemic of oidium (powdery mildew), the cure for which was found to be copper sulphate solution, or Bordeaux mixture. This remedy is still used today. Downy mildew or peronospera is another hazard, as is rot. On the right grapes at the right time, noble rot, or *botrytis cinerea*, produces great sweet white wines

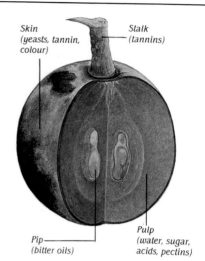

Above: *The pulp of a grape consists mostly of sugar, water, fruit acids and pectins. Tannins are concentrated in the skin and stalk. The bloom on the skin harbours the wine yeasts.*

Skin (yeasts, tannin, colour)

Stalk (tannins)

Pip (bitter oils)

Pulp (water, sugar, acids, pectins)

because it concentrates the sugar in the grape; on red grapes it can destroy the colour. Fungus diseases are worse where humidity is high, but can be controlled by spraying; insect pests like caterpillars or red spider can be controlled by insecticides. An often quoted cause of poor cropping, *coulure*, is not really a disease at all: it is the failure of the flower buds to set, and is caused by cold, damp weather during flowering. *Millerandage* happens slightly later, but the end result is the same: it causes the young fruit to drop after flowering.

Virus diseases, however, which serve to weaken vines and reduce the quality and quantity of the crop, cannot be dealt with by

Below: *Vines in the Côte d'Or in Burgundy. Clonal selection can improve the quality and size of the yield.*

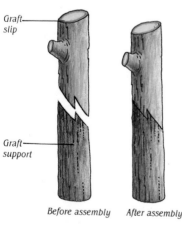

Graft slip

Graft support

Before assembly   After assembly

Above: *This diagram shows the English type graft which is widely used in France. Grafting French slips on to American rootstock was introduced as a remedy to the phylloxera crisis.*

Above: *Planting young vines in Beaujolais. At this stage the vines show just a single stick above the ground and are at their most vulnerable to harsh weather conditions. Caring for them can be back-breaking work.*

spraying. Even after a vineyard has been uprooted, the soil will have to be fumigated to eradicate the virus. So, increasingly, virus-free clones are being produced, and clonal selection of vines is an increasingly important factor in planting a vineyard.

It also means that the grower can decide whether to plant clones that are heavy cropping, perhaps at the expense of quality, or to go for a smaller, higher quality crop. The former choice has often been made in Burgundy. Clonal selection also opens up the possibility of having a whole vineyard ripen at precisely the same time, which is fine if the weather is good that week, less satisfactory if it rains. Such practices all emphasise that the potential for controlling the way vines behave is greater now than ever before.

However, what cannot be controlled so far is the basic suitability of a vine to an area. Some vines ripen earlier than others, the onset of ripening being taken to be the moment when the grapes start to change colour: the *veraison*. After this time, the sugar content of the grape increases, and the balance of malic and tartaric acid changes. The whole question of the suitability of vines to particular areas is crucial to winemaking: it is examined in detail overleaf.

The sort of environment a vine might choose for itself, and the environment that might be chosen for it with a view to producing the best possible wine are by no means the same. Vines, like most of us, like an easy life; plenty of water, plenty of sun, plenty of space to spread their branches. And not too much work: left to itself, a vine will produce grapes in quantity, but the mere fact of producing them in quantity will tend to mean that wine made from them will be weak, light and characterless.

Enter the wine grower. First of all he selects the right soil – well drained, to make the roots plunge deeper in search of water and nutrients. The best soil in each region may be gravel, as in the Haut-Médoc, or granite, as in the Rhône, or schist, or even clay, as in Pomerol. Here the cool temperature of the soil can slow the ripening process and produce reds with more flavour and depth. Conversely, in the Southern Rhône, the large stones that cover the vines absorb the heat during the day and reflect it back on to the grapes at night, thus ensuring round-the-clock ripening.

Increasingly it is thought that it is the physical make-up of the soil, rather than its chemical composition, that is crucial to the production of fine wine, because a vine can get the nutrients it needs from most soils.

Linked inextricably with soil is climate, and, more specifically, microclimate. A microclimate is the combination of climatic factors that affect the immediate vicinity of the vine, something that can change almost metre by metre. One side of a vineyard may be more sheltered from the prevailing wind, or less prone to frost, or may catch the sun for an hour or two longer, than another side. On a larger scale, the west-facing slope of a hill can gain from the warm afternoon sun in the critical autumn ripening period. A range of hills, or nearby woods in the right place, can protect quite a large area from cold winds; the sea, and large rivers, too, have a moderating effect on the overall climate of an area.

Above: *Although often unsuitable for other crops, well-drained, stony soil often produces the best vines.*

Guyot simple

Guyot double

Above and above right: *Guyot simple and Guyot double are variations on the same classic theme. Both involve training the vines along two (or more) wires, the top to support the foliage, the bottom to bear the weight of the grapes.*

Alsace

Gobelet   *Bush*

Above: *In the Gobelet and bush training methods, the vine is cut back to a few spurs which produce fruit-bearing canes.*

Above: *The Alsace method of high training, though mainly used for white grapes, may also be used for Pinot Noir.*

Vine Cultivation: The Annual Cycle

January
Pruning and general repairs to wires, stakes, walls.

February
Pruning; taking of cuttings for new graftings.

March
End of pruning. Some fertiliser applied. Preparation for planting new vines; bench grafts started.

April
New vines planted: bench grafting completed; one-year old grafts planted in vineyard. Canes of pruned vines tied to wires. Frost protection.

May
Weed control by cultivation. Frost protection. Spraying against disease: the main hazards are oidium (powdery mildew), rot and other fungus diseases.

June
Flowering. Spraying against disease before and after flowering; not during.

July
Spraying against disease. Weed control. Some long (non-fruiting) shoots cut back.

August
Tying up of shoots; spraying; (at end of month) long shoots trimmed so vine concentrates on producing fruit, not leaves.

September
Spraying against *botrytis* (for red vines). Net against bird damage.

October
Harvest: this can be by hand, or by machine where the terrain is not too steep or irregular.

November
Winter ploughing; heaping of earth at base of vines to prevent frost damage.

December
Winter ploughing; some fertiliser applied, pruning.

Too much rain and too little sun can spoil a whole year's work for the grower. Ideally, winters should be cold, to give the vines a chance to rest, but in the summer an average temperature of 22°C or more is best, with at least an average of 15°C at the time of flowering. But the most devasting damage of all can be from frost or hail. Frost, or even deep snow, in the winter, is fine; as long as the vine is dormant, which is roughly from November until March, temperatures as low as -28°C can usually be withstood. Once the sap has begun to rise, however, the story is different, and if the vines have begun to shoot, not only can the crop be put in jeopardy, but next year's crop as well. Vines can even be killed by a severe frost occurring during a late phase of the growing cycle.

Hail causes considerable damage at other times. Once the grapes are formed, swelling nicely and looking promising, then the grower should beware. A short, sharp hailstorm will slash through grapes and leaves alike, stripping the fruit from the branches and bruising the wood so that the following year's harvest is affected as well. The cheapest form of protection against hail is to stretch nets over the vines (they work against birds, too). Rockets can be fired into hail-bearing clouds to bring the hail down harmlessly on non-vine bearing land, but this solution is expensive and not always practicable.

To combat frost, smudge pots can be seen in many vineyards in France. These are small stoves, that stand between the vine rows and are lit on frosty nights to warm the air. Another effective measure against frost is simply to spray the vines with water when a frost looks imminent. It sounds hazardous but is not: the water freezes on the buds and the layer of ice protects the shoots from even lower temperatures.

Below: *Snow on the Côte d'Or. Vines are seldom harmed by such weather in deep winter; it is after the sap has started to rise that damage can be done.*

The process of winemaking really starts in the vineyard. But assuming the right vines have been planted in the right place, on the right soil, the weather has been good, and the pickers sent into the vineyard at the optimum moment, the moment of truth comes when the grapes arrive at the winery. The next few weeks are critical, and all depends on the winemaker's judgement.

Getting the grapes in to the winery as quickly as possible is the first important step. Autumn temperatures can be high, and juice from broken grapes can oxidise before the crop even gets to the cellars. Grapes that are too hot can also lead to lack of aroma in the wine, if they are not chilled on arrival.

Once there, red grapes go into a crusher, which may remove the stalks at the same time as crushing (but not pressing) the grapes. Attitudes to stalks vary throughout the regions of France, as well as according to each winemaker's personal view: in Bordeaux few or none are left in the juice; in the Rhône all are usually left on. Where mechanical harvesters are used, the decision has already been taken, since this method of harvesting ensures that the stalks are left on the vine.

Stalks have their uses in winemaking. They add tannin, and make pressing easier, as well as helping to aerate the fermenting mass of skins and juice. On the debit side, too many of them can give an astringent, "stalky", taste to the wine. They can reduce the colour, too, and just take up valuable space.

The pulpy mass of crushed grapes is passed to the fermentation vats. Traditionally these were of oak, and of varying sizes, and were used year after year. Provided that they were kept clean, they were a perfectly safe and neutral environment for the new wine. Nowadays the fermentation vat is more likely to be of stainless steel, or in less modern regions, cement, or glass-fibre.

The temperature of the must (as the unfermented grape juice is called) can rise high and fast, if it is not watched carefully. Hot weather outside and furious bubbling inside the vat can easily lead to temperatures of well over 30°C. Temperature control of some sort is therefore vital, and the most advanced stainless steel vats have the facility for either cooling or heating the must, should the latter be necessary.

Cultivated yeasts are often used to start the fermentation, in which case the wild ones naturally present on every grape skin will have been stunned beforehand with a dose of sulphur dioxide, the all-purpose antiseptic for wine. If the wine is to be chaptalised, sugar is also added before the fermentation starts, but this is forbidden in the South.

Once the fermentation is under way, the skins will be pushed to the top of the vat by all the bubbling carbon dioxide (given off as the yeast converts the grape sugar into alcohol) beneath them. Here they form a solid cap (known as the *châpeau*) which needs to be broken up, partly so that the wine can gain

How Red Wine is Made

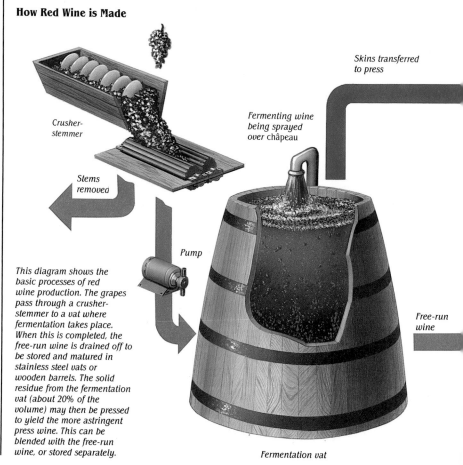

Crusher-stemmer

Stems removed

Skins transferred to press

Fermenting wine being sprayed over châpeau

Pump

Free-run wine

This diagram shows the basic processes of red wine production. The grapes pass through a crusher-stemmer to a vat where fermentation takes place. When this is completed, the free-run wine is drained off to be stored and matured in stainless steel vats or wooden barrels. The solid residue from the fermentation vat (about 20% of the volume) may then be pressed to yield the more astringent press wine. This can be blended with the free-run wine, or stored separately.

Fermentation vat

colour from the skins, and partly to prevent the cap becoming a target for bacteria. Traditionally it was either pushed down into the vat with poles, or men jumped in and waded about in the vat. But neither method is possible with modern steel or cement vats. So the wine is usually pumped out from the bottom of the vat and sprayed back over the cap.

Below: *Georges Duboeuf and his son with their 1985 Beaujolais vintage. The "whole berry" fermentation method is often used in Beaujolais (see pp 84-5).*

How long it is necessary to do this depends on how long the skins are kept in contact with the must. Too long a time, and the wine will gain too much tannin and be tough and unyielding to the taste for too long. Too short a period, and the wine will be light in colour and without enough tannin to age. Fermentation may take up to four weeks to complete, but the trend in the less classic regions is to run the must off the skins before the fermentation is complete.

Once the fermentation is over, which is when all the sugar has been converted to alcohol, or when the alcohol level has reached 17° to 18°, whichever is the sooner, it will stop of its own accord. Wine yeasts cannot operate in too alcoholic an environment, which is why fermentation can be stopped by the addition of alcohol.

The next stage is to run the wine off the skins and press the latter. The free-run wine will be lighter and more delicate, but the *vin de presse*, which is very dark and tannic, will be mixed with it in the right quantities to give the final wine its balance. The type of press chosen depends largely on the type of wine that is desired. The hydraulic basket press is common, and based on the most traditional sort of press: a plate at the top descends on to the packed skins and wine is forced out through the slatted sides. A variant is the horizontal bladder press, in which an inflatable rubber bag inside the press exerts gentle pressure on the skins all round it.

Horizontal basket press

Storage of press wine

Press wine blended with free-run wine

Storage vat

Wine maturing in wood casks or bottles

After the wine has been run off the skins, and the *vin de presse* extracted from them, the wine is still not quite ready to settle down to ageing. The malolactic fermentation has yet to be undergone. In the past, this transformation of the sharp-tasting malic acid to the smoother lactic acid used to take place naturally in the spring following the harvest, but now it is more likely to be induced straight after the alcoholic fermentation or even at the same time. An injection of the relevant bacteria may be needed to set it off, but often simply raising the temperature of the *chai* is enough to start the process.

If the wine is of a type intended to be drunk young and fresh, it can now be fined, filtered and bottled. If, however, it is a fine wine, then there is more in store for it. If wine is to be aged before bottling, it will often be matured in wood. Storing wine in concrete or steel vats does not mature the wine in the same sense, because what is crucial is the slow interaction of air and wine that brings added complexity. Too much air and you get oxidation, but just enough speeds up the ageing process far more than can happen in bottle. Oak barrels that are several years old will do just that, and nothing more, but new oak will give extra flavours, such as that of vanilla from vanillin in the wood, and more tannin, to the wine. The most aggressive oaky flavour comes from brand new barrels, which is why only the very biggest, richest wines go entirely into new oak. Partly it is a question of economics, as well. New barrels are expensive, and only the finest estates can afford them. What often happens in good but not great Bordeaux estates is that half or one third of each year's crop goes into new wood, so that when the final blend is made the effect on the wine is subtly perceived.

Bordeaux *barriques* of 225 litres capacity are the biggest that can easily be moved by one man, but they also happen to have the best volume-to-surface area ratio, which in turn is the best for ageing the wine. If air can permeate through the wood, it follows that wine can evaporate, and so constant topping up in the first period of ageing is essential. In a Bordeaux first-year *chai*, the barrels are loosely stoppered with glass bungs; it is not until they are moved to the second-year *chai* that wooden bungs are hammered tightly in, and the barrels turned so that the stoppers are roughly at a 2 o'clock position.

All this time, the tiny particles of solid matter that are in suspension in the wine are gradually falling to the bottom of the cask. Much is removed by fining, which involves pouring egg whites (or isinglass, gelatin, blood, or one of several other harmless substances) into the wine. The egg white drops slowly to the bottom, collecting with it solid particles that are too light to fall by themselves. The solids that fall to the bottom of the cask are known as the lees, and several times a year the young wine is run off and transferred to another barrel, leaving the lees behind. This is known as racking.

Above: *New barrels in Burgundy. New oak imparts tannin to the wine, and only the biggest reds can stand up to being kept entirely in new barrels.*

If a wine in its final form consists of a blend of several grape varieties, these varieties will almost certainly have been fermented and aged separately. When the blend is made, the cellar master must take into account not only the taste he wants, but also factors like the characteristics of the year and the capacity of each individual *cépage* (or blend) for ageing.

Before the wine is finally bottled it will probably be filtered. Not all wine is filtered, though standard commercial brands usually are because it removes the chance of consumers complaining about sediment in the bottle and, more importantly, the chance of bacteria harming the wine. The finer the filter, the smaller the particles it will catch – and the greater the chance of the flavour being slightly dulled, too. Sometimes it is worth the risk of a slight sediment for the sake of that extra flavour.

Wine may also be pasteurised, which means heating it very briefly to a temperature of around 85°C. This treatment ensures that the wine is absolutely stable, but because at the same time it restricts the future development of the wine it is not (with the odd exception) used for fine wines. This is not the same as hot bottling, a common method of making sure once and for all that standard quality wines do not referment in bottle. In this process the wine is heated to around 55°C at the time of bottling.

Another way of ensuring stability is to fill the bottle first with an inert gas like nitrogen. This then takes the place of air in the small space between the cork and the surface of the wine. Fine wine intended for ageing, however, needs that small amount of air: the maturation process that began in oak barrels will be continued, over the years, by contact with that air.

Left: *The cooper's workshop at Château Margaux. The 225l* barrique *has the ideal volume-to-surface-area ratio from the point of view of ageing the wine.*

*T*he French *Appellation Contrôlée* (AC) system, introduced in 1932, has provided a model not just for similar legislation in other European wine-producing countries, but a potential model for the rest of the world as well: places like Australia and California debate at length the reasons why they should or should not introduce similar controls, and it is always the French system that provides the benchmark.

French wine law provides for four tiers of wine, with the regulations being administered by the *Institut National des Appellations d'Origine* (INAO) in Paris. At the bottom there are *vins de table*, which may not state their region's origin on the label. Above them are *vins de pays*, country wines from well over 150 different designated regions ranging in size from the huge to the minute. Then come *Vins Délimités de Qualité Supérieure* (VDQS). These are governed by the same type of rules that apply to AC wines, and acceptance by a tasting panel is necessary. Many VDQS wines have been promoted to full AC status, and more will follow this path.

Fully-fledged AC wines are regulated at all stages of their production from vineyard to bottle. To begin with, the actual area of land in which vines may be planted is delimited. If a piece of land within the region has soil which is considered wrong for the wines of the region – too rich, perhaps, like the alluvial marshland of the Médoc – it will not be included in the AC. The varieties of vine which may be planted are listed in the regulations. The principle here is of course to ensure that only suitable vines are planted, but also to maintain the character of any particular wine. Cabernet Sauvignon, for example, can be grown successfully in many regions outside Bordeaux, but if grown in too high a proportion in, say, the Midi, the nature of those wines would change and no longer be typical.

The yield per hectare is also governed, though admittedly the rules are a little elastic here. The *rendement de base*, or basic yield, is generally around 40hl/ha (hecto-litres per hectare) sometimes more, cer-tainly less for the finest AC. This can be increased if the vintage warrants it (or re-duced, but somehow this never seems to happen) by recourse to the *rendement annuel* (yearly yield). Even further increases are possible: with the aid of the *plafond limite de classement*, all except the very top wines can have up to 20 per cent again added to what they can produce. This question of yields is treated rather more expediently than perhaps it should but it has to be said that attempts to get round the law as it stands, and to obtain an even greater yield per hectare classified as AC are not regarded favourably. A grower's entire crop from a particular year can be declassified if such stratagems are discovered.

There are minimum, and sometimes maxi-mum, levels of alcohol laid down for each AC and the number of vines per hectare are also regulated. All AC wines must now be sub-mitted to a tasting panel for acceptance be-fore they can be sold, which is perhaps the ultimate test for a wine's suitability to be AC.

There are further quality grades in France over and above AC and sometimes separate from it. The classification systems of Bur-gundy, and Bordeaux and the *Grand Cru* system of Alsace, give more precise quality indications, based on individual fields or even patches of fields. These are dealt with more fully in the relevant regional sections later in the book.

Below: *Azé in Mâconnais. Although the regulations can be quite elastic, in general the higher the classification of a vineyard, the less it should produce.*

*M*ost *vignerons* are not large land-owners. Many have just a few hectares of vines, which they look after themselves, drafting in other family members to help when needed. Drive through any French wine region and you will see them out in all weathers, and in all hours of daylight, bending over their vines. Many have learned how to prune and train vines and treat pests from their fathers, although it is more and more likely that their sons, if they are seriously interested in the subject, will go to a viticultural college.

When the harvest comes the grapes are picked by hand by the whole family. (Mechanical harvesters are for larger landowners who can afford the investment). And then, perhaps, they are sold. Some large wine producing companies have long-standing contracts with growers to buy their grapes year after year: the company makes the wine as it wants, and the grower gets paid quickly for the crop.

If the grower has no such commitment, he may have joined the local *cave coopérative*. If you visit one of these, you may well pass rows and rows of stainless steel tanks, hydraulic presses and up-to-the-minute bottling lines. Or you may step into a rather careless world of second-rate equipment and an unfastidious attitude to cleanliness. Standards vary tremendously, but the wines of a good *coopérative* are often better than the grower could make himself at home.

The biggest co-ops – those with large numbers of members, who make a point actually of marketing their wine – have of course the greatest incentive and the great opportunity to aim for high standards. But large or small, the co-op will make wine from the growers' grapes, and look after it until it is safely bottled.

The grower can, at this stage, buy some of it back. The price he pays for it will not be high and he will want to have something to drink himself throughout the year. He may also be able to sell some of it to passing trade, although the quantity that growers can buy back from the co-operative is limited.

The wine sold by the co-op may have a brand name, or several brand names: it is perfectly common in France for the same blend to be bottled under more than one brand name. Some brand names, for instance, may be kept for the exclusive use of a supermarket chain; co-operatives are good sources for supermarkets because large quantities of wine are readily available.

The grower may, of course, have his own winemaking equipment. The growth in the numbers of mobile bottling lines that travel (by van or lorry) to different producers makes

Below: *Mobile bottling lines like this have made it much easier for the small grower to bottle and sell his own wine.*

life easier for such *vignerons*, and may even encourage others to install winemaking equipment if they know they can get their wine bottled easily and efficiently. Once the year's crop is in bottle, the grower has to sit back and wait for people to be attracted by the *Vente Directe* ("Direct Sale") sign outside his house. If his winemaking operation is somewhat larger, he may have his wine on sale in local or nationwide shops; he may even entertain foreign importers.

He has yet another option, however, which is to sell wine before it is bottled to a merchant house. This may well be a large company with an internationally-known name, who will mature the wine and blend it into one of its standard products, be it AC wine or *vin de table*. Or the growers might, particularly in Bordeaux, find a buyer for the wine via a *négociant* or broker. A broker essentially puts buyer in touch with seller (and takes a percentage for himself, naturally) and his services are useful if, for example, the potential buyer is an importer with neither the time nor the inclination to track down and visit every cellar in the region. *Négociants* are important features of the French wine industry, which, as we have seen, is a multi-layered structure that exists to ensure that the wines of France find their appointed destination; in the glasses of appreciative consumers throughout the world.

Above: *Harvesting at Château Margaux in the Haut-Médoc; this property stands on the top rung of France's wine hierarchy.*

Below: *The co-operative fulfils a vital role in the wine industry; here Merlot grapes are delivered in St-Emilion.*

Certain information is mandatory on all E.E.C. wine labels: the name of the wine, for example, and the name and address of the producer/bottler. The region of production must also be stated, unless it is a plain *vin de table*, in which case it may *not* be stated, but then the alcohol content, and the volume of wine in the bottle must be indicated. Sometimes the vintage (if there is one) will be shown on the neck label but not the main label, but it is not obligatory to state the vintage at all.

Much more information can be given if the producer so wishes. If a Bordeaux *château* is classified, it will generally advertise the fact, and if a wine is made from a single grape variety it will often say so (unless it is, for example, Burgundy, which must be made from a single variety).

Mis en bouteille au château, mis en bouteille au domaine, both mean the wine was bottled at the estate where it was produced. *Mis en bouteille par . . .* followed by the name of a *négociant* does not mean that the grower was not involved – many *négociants* own vineyards. *Mis en bouteille à la propriété* is less specific than "*au château*" or "*au domaine*" and implies that the content is unlikely to be a single estate wine. *Mis en bouteille dans la region de production* also probably means a *négociant*. *Mis en bouteille dans nos caves* simply indicates that the company whose name is on the label did the bottling.

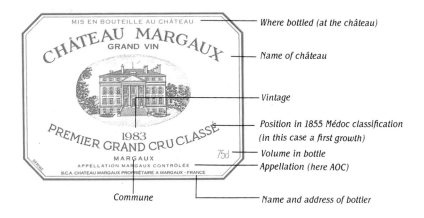

Where bottled (at the château)

Name of château

Vintage

Position in 1855 Médoc classification (in this case a first growth)

Volume in bottle

Appellation (here AOC)

Commune

Name and address of bottler

Where bottled

Vintage

Name of wine (in this case the "second wine" of Château Margaux)

Volume in bottle

Appellation (here AOC)

Commune

Name and address of bottler

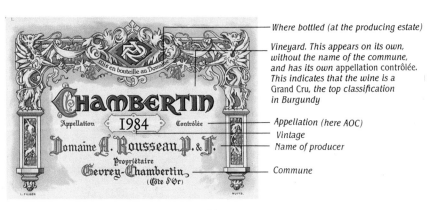

Where bottled (at the producing estate)

Vineyard. This appears on its own, without the name of the commune, and has its own appellation contrôlée. This indicates that the wine is a Grand Cru, the top classification in Burgundy

Appellation (here AOC)

Vintage

Name of producer

Commune

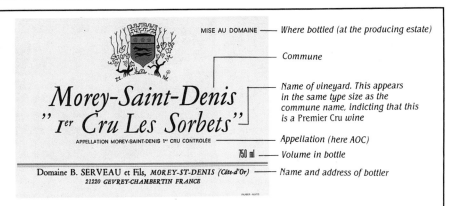

MISE AU DOMAINE —— *Where bottled (at the producing estate)*

—— *Commune*

Morey-Saint-Denis —— *Name of vineyard. This appears in the same type size as the commune name, indicting that this is a Premier Cru wine*

"1ᵉʳ Cru Les Sorbets"

APPELLATION MOREY-SAINT-DENIS 1ᵉʳ CRU CONTROLÉE —— *Appellation (here AOC)*

750 ml —— *Volume in bottle*

Domaine B. SERVEAU et Fils, *MOREY-ST-DENIS (Côte-d'Or)* —— *Name and address of bottler*
21220 *GEVREY-CHAMBERTIN FRANCE*

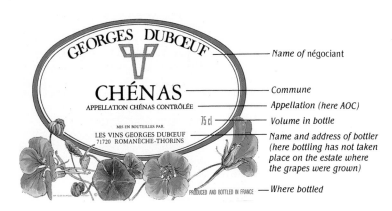

GEORGES DUBŒUF —— *Name of négociant*

CHÉNAS —— *Commune*

APPELLATION CHÉNAS CONTRÔLÉE —— *Appellation (here AOC)*

MIS EN BOUTEILLES PAR. 75 cl —— *Volume in bottle*

LES VINS GEORGES DUBŒUF —— *Name and address of bottler (here bottling has not taken place on the estate where the grapes were grown)*
71720 ROMANÈCHE-THORINS

PRODUCED AND BOTTLED IN FRANCE —— *Where bottled*

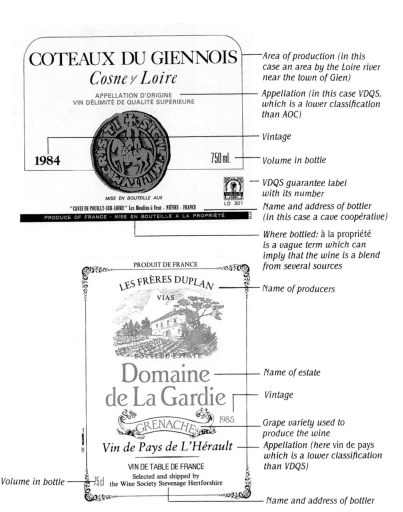

COTEAUX DU GIENNOIS —— *Area of production (in this case an area by the Loire river near the town of Gien)*

Cosne y Loire

APPELLATION D'ORIGINE —— *Appellation (in this case VDQS, which is a lower classification than AOC)*
VIN DÉLIMITÉ DE QUALITÉ SUPÉRIEURE

—— *Vintage*

1984 750 ml. —— *Volume in bottle*

—— *VDQS guarantee label with its number*

MISE EN BOUTEILLE AUX —— *Name and address of bottler (in this case a cave coopérative)*
"CAVES DE POUILLY-SUR-LOIRE" Les Moulins à Vent - NIÈVRE - FRANCE   LD 301

PRODUCE OF FRANCE - MISE EN BOUTEILLE A LA PROPRIÉTÉ

—— *Where bottled: à la propriété is a vague term which can imply that the wine is a blend from several sources*

PRODUIT DE FRANCE

LES FRÈRES DUPLAN —— *Name of producers*
VIAS

BOTTLED ESTATE

Domaine —— *Name of estate*
de La Gardie

1985 —— *Vintage*

GRENACHE —— *Grape variety used to produce the wine*

Vin de Pays de L'Hérault —— *Appellation (here vin de pays which is a lower classification than VDQS)*

VIN DE TABLE DE FRANCE

Volume in bottle —— 75 cl Selected and shipped by
the Wine Society Stevenage Hertforshire

—— *Name and address of bottler*

P art of the fun of going to France is bringing back some wine. If it can be loaded into your car then transport is no problem, and all there is to think about is the reaction of the customs officers back home. Obviously, if you live outside Europe and have to return home by sea or air, the problems of shipment are more severe. Either way, if you plan to buy wine abroad, it is worth checking with Customs & Excise before you leave to find out what exactly is your allowance, and what papers, if any, you will need. You should have no problem in obtaining invoices and the like from growers in France; they themselves ought to know what is necessary.

But anyone planning to buy in France should also analyse their reasons for doing so. First of all, it is fun; and second, it is probably cheaper; but it does not necessarily mean that you will get better wine than you could find in your native country, or even a better selection from which to choose. Where buying in France can enable you to buy wines you might not otherwise encounter is in the lesser-known country regions. You are unlikely to find much of a selection of Madiran, for example, in your local wine merchants; in such an instance, it can be interesting not simply to buy one case from a grower's cellar, but to go to a supermarket while you are in the region and buy wine from a selection of growers. It is the best way to get an overall picture of the wine, and it provides some sort of safeguard against poor individual bottles.

Some years ago wine was generally only available from wine merchants and hardly anywhere else, except restaurants. And wine normally meant just burgundy, bordeaux, champagne and non-French wines like hock, port and sherry. Such specialist wine merchants still exist and often flourish, although these days they may be owned by a big brewing or distilling group. Their lists have changed too. The clarets and burgundies are still there, and they are, or should be, among the best sources for these classic wines. Their

lists are comprehensive, and generally include vintages stretching back 20 or 25 years, but at a price. You will not find cut-price, pile-it-high bottles here because that is not their *raison d'être*. If merchants have to store expensive wines for many years they have to make large enough profits to finance

Above: *The shape of the bottle can often help you to identify the region in which a wine was produced. Shown here are typical shapes from the major regions. Whites and rosés are included where they* predominate. (1) Burgundy, (2) Loire, (3) Bordeaux, (4) vin de table, (5) Champagne, (6) Côtes du Rhône, (7) Alsace, (8 and 9) Provence, (10) Languedoc-Roussillon, (11) Jura.

the capital investment. That is only fair. In exchange they offer first-class advice, and services like storage and delivery.

Included in the specialist wine merchant sector are the companies who concentrate not only on the traditional fine wine areas, but on regions for which they themselves have particular fondness. Often they have led the market to such regions and made a name for themselves at the same time.

So buying fine wine, is, or can be, comparatively easy. Provided that you are prepared to pay the high prices that fine French wines cost, and you are not hunting for bargains, all you have to do is walk into a fine wine merchant and ask for advice. The good thing is that wine merchants are generally scrupulous traders, and pleading ignorance should not land you with a bad buy, nor an overpriced wine you would be ashamed to serve. With one or two exceptions, wine merchants are a helpful lot, keen to share their own enjoyment of the subject. You can even go in, tell them what you are having for dinner in a few hours' time, and ask for a suitable bottle. It would be hard to find a serious wine merchant who would not enjoy a challenge of that nature.

But of course most people do not always

Above: Discovering the local wines in shops such as this one in La Ferté sous Jouarre, Seine et Marne, is one of the pleasures of travelling in France.

want to buy fine wine. Often it is more a question of dashing into the nearest shop on the way back from work to pick up something reasonably priced and, one hopes, reasonably palatable. This is the sort of occasion when a little more knowledge can prove extremely valuable.

You do not have to have details of the weather in each commune of Bordeaux over the last ten years at your fingertips, though an awareness of which were the good and which the poor years would certainly help. What is also important is a rough idea of which wines are liable to need further ageing, and which can be drunk off the shelf. All rules of thumb tend to be rather dogmatic but basically you should remember that the bigger and more tannic the wine, the more ageing it will need. Equally, lighter reds should not be drunk too old, although finding old and tired vintages on the shelf is a problem more commonly encountered with white wines than with red.

Some purist wine lovers are inclined to throw up their hands in horror at the idea of wine as an investment. Wine is for drinking, they say. It is not a commodity. No, indeed, not. But certain wines are not for drinking until ten, or perhaps 20 years after they are made, and somebody has to look after them during that period, when the money put into making and buying them will have nothing to show for it, not even drinking pleasure. Yet the wines, at the end of that ten or 20 years, should be worth more (even taking inflation into account) than they were when bought, simply because they will at last be at their peak, and because there will be fewer cases still available, since many will already have been drunk by other customers.

There has always been investment in wine, though perhaps it has not always been called by such an unequivocally commercial name. Until the collapse of the Bordeaux market in the 1970s and the high inflation that accompanied it, it had long been an assumption on the part of serious wine drinkers that a good cellar would fund itself. You bought an initial amount of fine wine when you started your cellar. As it became drinkable you sold, say, half. The price it fetched paid for the purchase of younger wine, which in turn was cellared until half was sold to pay for new wines. What was not sold was drunk. It was a practical system that financed the development of many a good palate.

It still goes on, but these days there are more variables to consider. The opening prices of the top Bordeaux châteaux are awaited with anxiety each year, since buying *en primeur* (before the wines are bottled) is the main way into the investment market. These prices may in turn be affected by the franc/pound or the franc/dollar exchange rate: the US is a major market for *en primeur* claret, and the state of that market may affect Bordelais decisions on the level of the opening prices.

It is largely Bordeaux that we are talking about here. Red burgundy has never been an investment wine, partly because of the variability of quality to be found there. A few top estates, notably the Domaine de la Romanée Conti at Vosne-Romanée in the Côte d'Or, can be exceptions, as may be, in the future, a few top red Rhônes, but most French red wines laid down for investment purposes are better quality clarets.

Below: *Young wine maturing in oak in the chai at Château Montrose. Claret from classed growth châteaux such as this is often bought* en primeur *(before it is bottled) as a form of investment.*

Above: *Labelling the bottles at Château Peyrabon, a* cru bourgeois *property in the Haut-Médoc. Such wines frequently offer excellent value for money, but are less attractive as investments.*

Below: *Sampling Georges Duboeuf's 1985 vintage in Burgundy. The popularity of Beaujolais Nouveau worldwide is an example of sophisticated marketing.*

For investment, too, you should select top wines from the best vintages. Lesser châteaux and finds from off-vintages are excellent for drinking, but they do not increase significantly in value. Steven Spurrier, who runs the Académie du Vin wine school in Paris, has made a study of the market and discovered that it is not, however, always the first growths of the Médoc that come up trumps as investments. He particularly recommends Châteaux La Mission-Haut-Brion (Graves), Palmer (3rd growth, Margaux) and Pétrus (Pomerol), followed by the St-Julien properties of Ducru-Beaucaillou, Beychevelle and Léoville-Las-Cases.

Most good wine merchants have offers every spring of *en primeur* clarets. It is worth shopping around, because prices – and the availability of individual wines – do vary. Having paid for the wines, you do not receive them until one and a half or two years later, when they are bottled and shipped. The merchant may well be able to cellar them for you, if you do not have suitable cellar space yourself. Naturally, you will have to pay him for such a service.

When the time comes to sell, you may wish to sell privately to a merchant, perhaps even the one you bought the wines from in the first place. But the usual way of disposing of fairly small privately owned parcels of wine is at auction. Christie's and Sotheby's are the main outlets in London, with International Wine Auctions holding several sales a year. In addition, Christie's hold wine sales in Chicago, Geneva and Amsterdam; Sotheby's auction wine in Geneva, Johannisberg and Tokyo.

*T*here are nearly as many "rules" associated with the serving of red wine as there are concerned with what to eat with it. Some of them can be, and are, argued over at length; some are common sense; and some are just misunderstood. "Red wine should be served at room temperature", for example. What is room temperature? And why should young Beaujolais not be chilled, if it tastes better like that? The truth is that what suits one wine does not necessarily suit another, and dogmatic, all-embracing rules are hardly more useful than no rules at all.

The first question is decanting. Wherever you keep your wine, be it in the cupboard under the stairs, in the wardrobe, or in a proper cellar, all that is important is that the storage area should be dark, at a reasonably even and low temperature, and as free as possible from vibration. The bottles should also be kept lying on their sides. If the wine has thrown a sediment you will need to decant it before serving, and it is a good idea to stand the bottle upright for 24 hours or so before opening it to make decanting easier.

The other reasons for decanting are to aerate the wine and thus help the flavour to open out, and because a decanter of red wine on the table looks so good. On the question of aeration, opinions differ strongly. Some

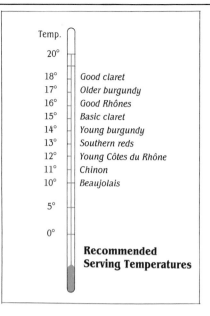

Temp.	
20°	
18°	Good claret
17°	Older burgundy
16°	Good Rhônes
15°	Basic claret
14°	Young burgundy
13°	Southern reds
12°	Young Côtes du Rhône
11°	Chinon
10°	Beaujolais
5°	
0°	

Recommended Serving Temperatures

hold that a young wine should be allowed to breathe for several hours before being drunk; a mature wine for an hour or two; a very old wine not at all. Others, notably the eminent oenologist, Professor Emile Peynaud of Bordeaux, are against decanting to aerate a wine at all, saying that it affords no benefit to the flavour. Most people find that wines change in the decanter, and a young claret, for example, can open up considerably in an hour or so. Burgundy, though, seldom needs decanting, unless it has thrown a sediment. Otherwise the aeration it receives in the glass should be sufficient.

Glasses are a simpler matter – and the simpler the glass the better. Fancy cutting or, worse, coloured glass, detracts from the

Below: *This photograph gives just a small indication of the range of glassware and accessories available to the wine drinker. Collecting them is a pleasure, but it is worth remembering that all you really need to start serving and enjoying wine are simply a suitable bottle, a corkscrew, and a glass.*

Above: *Basic shapes (left to right) - the Paris goblet, Bordeaux bottle, Burgundy bottle, and tulip glass. Thin, clear glasses are to be recommended so that you may better appreciate and enjoy the colour and bouquet of the wine.*

enough to accommodate a normal amount served this way.

When it comes to the order of serving several different reds, commonsense prevails. Young wines before old is fairer to both wines than the reverse, as is lighter wine before heavier. If in doubt, try tasting a light, fresh Beaujolais after a big, meaty St-Joseph: the Beaujolais cannot compete with the Rhône.

The Beaujolais should also be served cooler than the Rhône. Most light reds and most reds from the Midi are best slightly chilled, and in hot weather an ice bucket (containing water as well as ice) may be the best and quickest way of getting the wine to the right temperature. If a wine is too warm, the alcohol evaporates rapidly and the bouquet becomes soupy and unbalanced. This can happen to burgundy at a lower temperature than would affect bordeaux, and it is important to remember too that if the room is warm the wine will continue to rise in temperature in the glass, in which case it can afford to be a little too cool when it is first poured.

The glasses, needless to say, should be absolutely clean and free from smells of either detergents, dishcloths or musty cupboards. The slightest whiff can spoil a wine.

colour of the wine, and the wrong shape can spoil your enjoyment of the bouquet. The ideal is a thin tulip-shaped clear glass with a stem tall enough to grasp comfortably. A glass that narrows at the top concentrates the smell of the wine, whereas one that flares out dissipates it. Nor should the glass be too small. Ideally you should fill a wineglass only half full at the most, so it should be big

Below: *One of the more intriguing wine accessories is the decanting cradle. Turning the handle causes the cradle to tip gently and the wine to pour smoothly. A candle placed behind the bottle's neck shows when the sediment has collected. However, opinions over the need to decant remain divided.*

*T*he number of wines that will go well with food is at least as big as the number of ways that food can be prepared. Add a sauce, and you have yet another factor which will affect the choice of wine. These suggestions that follow are therefore simply suggestions: do not treat them as immutable and exhaustive precepts.

Cheese and red wine is not always the satisfactory combination it is often made out to be – at least, not strongly flavoured cheese. Roquefort and Munster, for example, go far better with certain white wines than they do with red. And cold meats, be they game, beef, lamb or whatever, give the impression of being less strongly flavoured than when they are hot, so need less full-bodied wines. There is also the question of vintage. Some Bordeaux vintages – 1961, or 1975 – produced very big wines, others –

Above: *Beaujolais will generally accompany most food well providing it does not have to compete with particularly strong or spicy flavours.*

Right: *The ingredients of a perfect* al fresco *picnic – French bread, cheese, fruit and red wine. Mild cheeses such as these are fine; stronger ones tend to overwhelm the flavour of the wine.*

1980 – made much lighter ones. So to describe a dish as going well with Bordeaux does not necessarily narrow the field a great deal. But Beaujolais, providing it has not been made by the *macération carbonique* method, will go with most food. *Macération carbonique* wines tend to be too sweet (though not sugary) to match easily.

What to Drink With Your Food

Avocado
Light red: Beaujolais, Loire, Coteaux Champenois, Alsace Pinot Noir.

Barbequed food
Big southern reds: Fitou, Bandol.

Beef
If roast, any fine red. If stewed or casseroled, Rhône: Côtes du Rhône, Gigondas, Hermitage, Côte Rotie; claret: Pomerol, big Médoc, St-Emilion; Cahors; Madiran; Fitou.

Cheese
Mild cheeses go best: very strongly flavoured ones mask the wine. Brie: try claret. Camembert: big Médoc; Bandol. Cheese soufflé: good burgundy or bordeaux. English cheese: big Rhône: Châteauneuf-du-Pape. Dolcelatte: young Beaujolais *cru*.

Poultry
Young red: Brouilly, lesser burgundy, or any fine old red, depending on the occasion.

Chocolate
A Grenache *vin doux naturel*. Some French critics recommend Médoc.

Coq au Vin
Red burgundy, as good as possible.

Duck
Rhône, especially Châteauneuf-du-Pape; burgundy; St-Emilion; Pomerol.

Fish
There is currently rather a fashion for red wine with fish, both in the drinking and the cooking, especially in France. Go by the sauce: if this is very strongly flavoured, then maybe try a Côtes du Rhône, or claret. Or try a fresh young bordeaux, or Loire. Beaujolais is particularly successful with salmon.

Game
The best red in the cellar.

Ham
Young burgundy: Savigny; Corton; Beaujolais *cru*.

Hamburger
Southern red: Fitou, Minervois, Corbières, Bandol, or just a simple *vin de pays*.

Hare
Vigorous claret; burgundy, especially Côte de Nuits; Rhône.

Kidneys
If veal, a young red; if more strongly flavoured; claret, especially St-Emilion, Pomerol; Rhône.

Lamb
If roast, fine claret; if stewed or casseroled: *cru bourgeois* claret; southern Rhône; Fitou; Minervois; Corbières; Bandol; Madiran; Cahors.

Liver
If liver pâté, Loire red: Chinon; otherwise Beaujolais Villages or *cru*: young claret. Chicken liver pâté: Beaujolais, Gamay de Touraine, light Côtes de Provence.

Pasta
This depends on the sauce, but try Corbières; Fitou; Minervois; Cahors, Madiran; southern *vin de pays*; southern Côtes du Rhône.

Pâté
Light burgundy: Mercurey; Beaujolais *cru*.

Pork
Good red. Avoid strongly flavoured sauces.

Rillettes
Burgundy.

Sausages
Fairly young claret; Cabernet-based Côtes de Provence; Languedoc-Roussillon red or other big red.

Steak and kidney pie/pudding
Good claret.

Steak
Any fine red wine. Check the sauce or other accompaniment: if very strongly flavoured, choose a big Rhône. It steak tartare: Beaujolais or light burgundy.

Veal
Mature red, especially claret.

Venison
Rhône, or a weighty claret.

Snails
Light burgundy, or Beaujolais *cru*.

Rabbit
Young Médoc, or Bourg, Fronsac.

Salad
Beaujolais nouveau, provided there is little vinegar in the dressing.

Strawberries
Young *vin doux naturel*.

A
ll vintage charts should be used with care, since no generalisation can give an accurate picture of every wine made in a given year. Some properties will make disappointing wine in an otherwise excellent year, and vice versa. And do not always shun off-vintages; go for good producers and you can find some good buys.

Bordeaux: Médoc and Graves

1986 A huge crop, uneven in quality; best in Haut-Médoc, so choose carefully.

1985 A hot summer produced very good to excellent wines, with good fruit and balance.

1984 The best clarets were from Cabernet Sauvignon-dominated Médoc and Graves; The Merlot was affected by *coulure* and some wines lack roundness. Will mature fairly early.

1983 Very even and very good quality, especially in Margaux. The wines have high tannin with fruit to balance. They were slightly overshadowed by the hype surrounding the 1982.

1982 Highly acclaimed at the time, and deservedly so: the wines have huge fruit, and enough tannin to enable them to last. Probably the best vintage since 1961.

1981 Better in the Médoc and Graves than on the other side of the river. Fine, well-balanced but not as consistent as the following vintage, nor as rich. Early-maturing.

1980 Light wines that can be drunk now and in the next few years.

1979 A large crop and a late harvest produced medium-weight, average quality wines which are nevertheless turning out to be very attractive. Good drinking now and into the mid-1990s.

1978 A long, warm autumn produced classic wines, especially on the left bank. Lesser wines are drinking now, the top wines need keeping, but all will be ready before their equivalents from 1975.

1977 A disappointing vintage: cold weather produced light wines that need drinking now. The better ones are from the Médoc and Graves.

1976 The hot summer produced wines with high sugar but slightly low acidity: they would probably have been better had it not rained at the harvest. The wines are nevertheless generally good, and early maturing – most are now ready to drink.

1975 A fine, very tannic vintage. All but the *petits châteaux* need long keeping. The top wines are taking so long to come round that some critics have wondered if their fruit will last long enough.

1974 Light wines, a definite off-vintage. With careful selection, some attractive wines can be found, but will not keep.

1973 Better than the previous year, but not one to keep.

1972 Simply the worst vintage of the decade. Drink now, if at all.

1971 Less consistent here than on the right bank, but some fine wines, although less rich than in 1970. Drink now.

1970 Very good wines, especially in the Médoc, with plenty of fruit. All can be drunk now, though the top wines may yet benefit from a little further ageing. Other good years: 1966, 1962, 1961, 1959, 1955, 1953, 1952, 1950.

St-Emilion and Pomerol

1986 Plentiful, but not up to the '85s in quality; lighter, for earlier drinking.

1985 Plenty of Merlot, after 1984's failure. Very good wines, very even quality and long keepers.

1984 This was the year when *coulure* almost totally destroyed the Merlot crop, so little was made (and less declared under the château labels) in St-Emilion and Pomerol.

1983 Some prefer this vintage to the 1982. Very ripe wines, though some irregularity.

1982 A great vingate that needs keeping. Particularly good in Pomerol.

1981 A vintage for drinking early – many wines are coming round already. Good, well-balanced wines, though not great.

1980 Problems with the Merlot meant that the other side of the river produced the better wines. Drinking now.

1979 A large crop and a late harvest. Very good in St-Emilion and Pomerol.

1978 The Merlot did not do as well as the Cabernet this year, so Pomerol and St-Emilion are more variable in quality. But these are good wines, drinking well now and for the next few years.

1977 Poor wines from a problematic vintage.

1976 Good to excellent wines from a hot summer slightly spoilt by harvest-time rain. Drink now until the mid-1990s.

1975 Good to excellent wines, very concentrated and rich, and coming round faster than the left bank wines. Many beginning to drink now, though they will keep well.

1974 Light, and diluted by rain at vintage time.

1973 Drinking now: not a vintage to keep. A large crop, and rain at harvest time.

1972 Slightly better than on the left bank, but not much.

1971 The most successful wines of the vintage were on the right bank. Drink now, in most cases.

1970 Big, ripe wines, which can be kept, though many can be drunk now. Other good years: 1967, 1966, 1964, 1961, 1959, 1953, 1952.

Burgundy

1986 Somewhat light, not very tannic.

1985 Lovely rich wines that will mature relatively early and make delicious drinking in the 1990s. Excellent in Beaujolais: the *cru* wines will keep.

1984 Cool weather produced wines that lack richness but which may prove attractive in time. In Beaujolais, concentrate on the *crus*.

1983 Selection is important here: high sugar levels were widespread but there was also a fair amount of rot. The successful wines are tannic and have very good fruit and body. Very good Beaujolais, the *crus* now drinking.

1982 Those growers who selected carefully and kept yields down made concentrated wines, the rest made light coloured wines that will need drinking early. Beaujolais need drinking now.

1981 Rain during the vintage produced uneven wines that need drinking.

1980 The Côte de Nuits made the most successful wines, mostly drinking now. The less good wines lacked fruit and colour.

1979 A vintage that has matured fast. The Côtes de Beaune had the best wines, with good ripe fruit. Drink now.

1978 The best wines are coming round now, and are concentrated, and fruity with plenty of elegance and richness. The quantity was small and the harvest late.

1977 More successful in the Côte de Beaune than in the Côte de Nuits, but all need drinking now. High acidity and insufficient fruit in many wines.

1976 Very high tannin (sometimes too high) in the hot summer but the wines that have enough fruit to stand up to the tannin are concentrated and rich and beginning to drink now.

1975 Rain and rot. Best avoided.

1974 Lean, hard wines, past their prime.

1973 Light, attractive wines that should have been drunk by now.

1972 Firm, good wines that will not improve further, so drink up.

1971 Very good, concentrated wines, mostly now mature.

1970 Good wines that need drinking up.

Other good years: 1969, 1966, 1964, 1962, 1961.

*T*he charts on this page give some general details of recent vintages in the Rhône and the Loire. Reds from the Loire are much lighter than their southern Rhône counterparts and should be drunk comparatively young. For that reason, only the vintages from 1980-1986 are discussed.

Lesser-Known Alternatives

The French AC laws are designed to protect the individual character of each region, but nevertheless there are plenty of regions whose wines resemble the classics without necessarily being copies. Listed here are some lesser-known, and usually cheaper, alternatives to some of the most famous French red wines. A Cabernet-based wine from Provence, for example, can be a very acceptable alternative to a Bordeaux, or a Gamay de Touraine from the Loire an alternative to a Beaujolais.

Burgundy: Light styles are the only real French alternative: Sancerre; Menetou-Salon; Coteaux du Loir; Alsace; Coteaux Champenois; Savoie and Jura; some *cru* Beaujolais (made from Gamay, but with a Burgundian air when mature) such as Morgon and Moulin à Vent.

Beaujolais: Gamay de Touraine; Gamay de l'Ardèche; Côte Roannaise VDQS; some *macération carbonique* reds from Provence.

Bordeaux (light, no wood ageing): Chinon; Bourgeuil; Côtes de Duras; Bergerac.

Bordeaux (rich, oak aged): Cabernet-based Coteaux d'Aix-en-Provence; Château Vignelaure; Cabernet-based wines from Coteaux des Baux-de-Provence and Côtes de Provence; Val Joanis from Côtes de Luberon VDQS.

Above: *The Côtes de Castillon near Bordeaux is a source of good, affordable wine that it is worth looking out for as an alternative to Médoc claret.*

Northern Rhône

1986 Lighter than the '85s, and probably earlier-maturing.

1985 Very fine quality, very concentrated wines with deep colour. Prices rose quickly, and seem likely to go on rising.

1984 Fairly light wines from a cool, wet year. Will mature relatively early.

1983 Tannic, concentrated wines of very good overall quality that need keeping.

1982 A very good vintage, though perhaps not quite up to the heights of 1983. Ageing is needed.

1981 Many wines suffered from rot, but even the more successful wines are overshadowed by subsequent vintages.

1980 Elegant rather than powerful wines of good quality, most beginning to come round now. The Côte Rôties were particularly good and some may need further ageing.

1979 Good, fruity wines, particularly in Hermitage. They are not quite as good as the 1978s, and can be drunk earlier.

1978 Superb wines of great balance and depth. The best will see this century out.

1977 The wines have matured more successfully than was predicted after the vintage, but this is still not a good year.

1976 In some wines the tannin was overdone, but the best ones have fruit and balance. The Côtes Rôties were particularly good, and most are drinking now.

1975 Not very successful vintage with a lot of rot.

1974 A poor vintage in most areas of France, including the Rhône.

1973 The first of three poor years, an unusual run of bad luck in the Rhône.

1972 Good wines which now need drinking. Hermitage was especially good.

1971 Good, but need drinking now: not one of the very long-keeping vintages.

1970 Côte Rôtie made especially good wines, as did Hermitage. A fine vintage generally, which can be drunk now but which will keep.

Southern Rhône

1986 Good, but perhaps a little light.
1985 A very hot vintage produced wines with deep colour, but some lack acidity. Châteauneuf-du-Pape had a particularly good year.
1984 Well-balanced wines, more successful than in the north, even though the Grenache produced less than usual.
1983 The Grenache suffered from *coulure*, making the wines harder and more tannic than usual, and slower maturing. One to watch.
1982 Somewhat unbalanced wines, with high alcohol levels without the structure and tannin to compete. Fast-maturing.

1981 Good wines with nice balance and good fruit, but not a great vintage.
1980 Good sound wines, drinking now.
1979 Elegant rather than concentrated, drinking now but the best will keep.
1978 The best vintage of the decade, with concentration, fruit and balance. The best wines still need keeping.
1977 Light, and drinking now.
1976 Big, alcoholic wines, drinking now.
1975 There were problems with rot, and in any case the wines should be drunk now. Southern Rhônes of earlier vintages are unlikely still to be good.

Loire: Anjou-Touraine

1986 Light wines for early drinking.
1985 Quite concentrated, elegant wines of very good quality.
1984 Light, for early drinking.
1983 Some wines will keep; a very concentrated year, with plenty of tannin.

1982 A large harvest of deep-coloured wines, now at their peak.
1981 Good fruit and colour; the wines are drinking now.
1980 Quite high acidity, insufficient fruit.

BORDEAUX

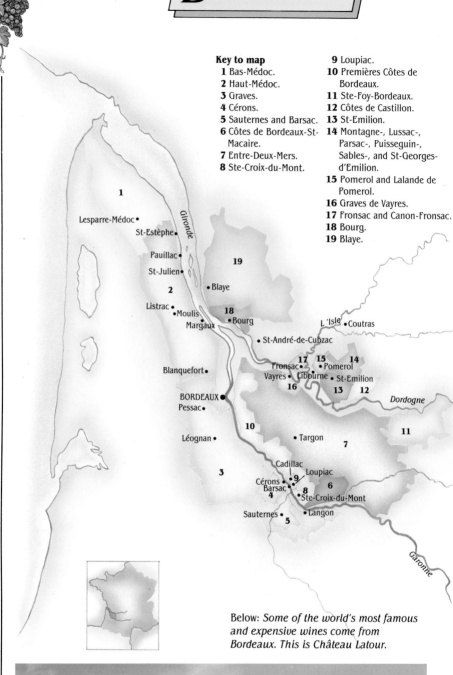

Key to map
1 Bas-Médoc.
2 Haut-Médoc.
3 Graves.
4 Cérons.
5 Sauternes and Barsac.
6 Côtes de Bordeaux-St-Macaire.
7 Entre-Deux-Mers.
8 Ste-Croix-du-Mont.
9 Loupiac.
10 Premières Côtes de Bordeaux.
11 Ste-Foy-Bordeaux.
12 Côtes de Castillon.
13 St-Emilion.
14 Montagne-, Lussac-, Parsac-, Puisseguin-, Sables-, and St-Georges-d'Emilion.
15 Pomerol and Lalande de Pomerol.
16 Graves de Vayres.
17 Fronsac and Canon-Fronsac.
18 Bourg.
19 Blaye.

Below: *Some of the world's most famous and expensive wines come from Bordeaux. This is Château Latour.*

*W*hy should red Bordeaux be called claret? It is an English name; it is not used by the French; and there is no obvious connection between the place name of Bordeaux, and the word claret. It is, in fact, an English adaptation of a French word, *"clairet"*, a name, derived from the French *"clair"* meaning clear or light, which indicated the style of the wine: red Bordeaux was lighter and more elegant than much of the red wine traditionally shipped. Bordeaux has always been export minded, and historically a lot of the exports have been to Britain.

The reasons for this are simple. In 1152 Eleanor of Aquitaine married Henry Plantaganet, later Henry II of England, and with that marriage the links between Bordeaux and England began. 300 or so years later they ended when the English lost control of Bordeaux forever, but in the meantime a market had been established, and a "special relationship" built up, and neither show any sign of waning. Bordeaux is still regarded worldwide as a benchmark by which other red wines, including those made from similar grapes in other countries, are judged.

It is not just the English who have close connections with Bordeaux. The Irish and Scots have been and are just as important. Indeed, if you look at the names of châteaux and *négociants* in the last two or three centuries, you will find more than a sprinkling of names from those countries among them: Hugh Barton, for example, bought part of Château Léoville and part of Château Langoa after the Napoleonic wars, and both estates still bear his name. Hugh Barton was a trader before he bought land, and so was typical of many foreigners who settled in Bordeaux and established themselves in the wine trade as *négociants*, estate owners, or both.

The rise of the *négociants* (a *négociant* being a merchant who buys young wine from the grower, and matures it in his own cellars until it is ready to bottle or to ship) can be traced largely to the 18th century. Today, their role in the Bordeaux trade may not be as all-embracing as in the past, but it is still significant, and very necessary. Basically, they act as a marketplace, buying wine from the growers and selling it to the next link in the chain, usually a wine merchant either in France or abroad. In good years a *négociant* will have buyers hammering on the doors demanding quantities of wine he may not easily be able to supply; conversely, in bad years he may find himself stuck with wines that find no ready market.

Some *négociants* own châteaux themselves, whose wines they handle on an exclusive basis; others deal with a larger number of growers, and share their wines with other *négociants*. Neither group, however, can really be held responsible for the huge increases in the price of top clarets that the market has had to bear in the last few years.

1982 was a fine year, and the crop was a large one. So up went the prices, based on the predictable "vintage of the century" hype which unfortunately never seems to fail to have an effect on demand. 1983 produced another good crop, even bigger than that of 1982, and so prices should logically have fallen, or at least stayed the same. Not a bit of it. The proprietors put them up again, by another 20 to 30 per cent. The wines affected by this were the top ones, the classed growths; basic Bordeaux rouge still struggles to make ends meet. In 1984 these top estates, finding the market would stand the sort of prices they were asking, did it again – when the crop was not only smaller, but the wines were of distinctly inferior quality. In 1985, the gods decreed another good year, and a big crop. An understandably nervous wine trade exerted all the persuasion it could on the château owners, and the result was that on the whole they did not put their prices up significantly. But the dollar and pound both took a tumble, and the result, as far as the overseas buyer of young claret was concerned, was that prices soared yet again.

As for the 1986s, at the time of writing, although the picture is not complete, it seems that commonsense has prevailed, which is no bad thing. The Bordeaux market crashed in the early 1970s (although the precise conditions were different), and nobody wants to see that happen again.

ACs and their Red Wine Production (1986 vintage in hectolitres)
Médoc (220,956)
Haut-Médoc (184,504)
St-Julien (41,851)
Pauillac (59,402)
Margaux (63,452)
St-Estèphe (71,102)
Moulis (24,751)
Listrac (30,601)
Graves (91,352)
St-Emilion (511,692)
Pomerol (43,201)
Lalande de Pomerol (51,301)
Néac (n/a)
Fronsac (67,501)
Bourg (216,456)
Blaye (179,105)
Premières Côtes de Bordeaux (110,703)
Côtes de Castillon (18,781)

Permitted Grape Varieties
Cabernet Franc
Cabernet Sauvignon
Carmenère
Malbec
Merlot
Petit Verdot

Bordeaux is huge by wine producing standards; over 3 million hectolitres of AC wine are produced each year, making it the largest fine wine region on earth. Its landscape can be grand or engagingly unassuming. In some parts of the Médoc, imposing 18th or 19th century châteaux dot the countryside so closely that they are within shouting distance of one another, and one can stand in a vineyard and have half a dozen famous châteaux all within view. Elsewhere vines alternate with pasture, cattle and arable crops, and a wine that bears the name of château so-and-so may come from a building that has a greater resemblance to a farmhouse than a mansion.

The variations in Bordeaux extend further than the landscape. Burgundy relies on just one vine, the Pinot Noir, for its fine red wine; Bordeaux boasts three major varieties, with a further three lesser ones thrown in for good measure. The proportion in which they are planted depends partly on the style of wine the grower wants to make, but also on the soil in each particular spot, and this can vary hectare by hectare. The climate, too, plays its part: more rain falls in the southern part of Bordeaux, the area devoted largely to white wines.

Overall, the climate in Bordeaux is crucial. The region is actually on the same latitude as the baking hot vineyards of the Rhône, but there the similarities end. Bordeaux has the sea and the rivers to moderate extremes of temperature, and the forests of the Landes to moderate the sea breezes. So successfully is the heat moderated, in fact, that the opposite can be a problem and wet springs can lead to the onset of diseases like *coulure* and *millerandage*. Frost, however, is not a major factor. It takes temperatures of at least −20°C to kill a vine, so more northerly regions like Champagne are much more vulnerable than southerly areas like Bordeaux.

The classic grape variety, and the one probably thought of more than any other in connection with claret, is Cabernet Sauvignon. It is a late-ripening, low-yielding vine; its grapes are small and thick-skinned, and produce wines that are tannic and rich in colour. Cabernet Sauvignon is also resistant to *coulure* and rot. It likes gravel soil best, and gravel abounds in the best vineyards of the Médoc. The vine is less happy on clay, so in the colder clay soil of Pomerol it is replaced by Merlot, a higher yielding vine but one which is more susceptible to *coulure* and rot. The wines have good acidity but less tannin than their Cabernet Sauvignon counterparts, and tend to mature rather earlier. They also have plenty of colour, slightly higher alcohol levels than Cabernet Sauvignon, and an appealing plummy flavour.

Cabernet Franc is similar to Cabernet Sauvignon, but less fine: it has plenty of perfume, however, and a grassy taste.

Above: *Cabernet Sauvignon grapes, the classic Médoc variety, are small, thick-skinned, and rich in colour.*

The lesser grape varieties are Petit Verdot, Malbec and Carmenère. Petit Verdot is a late ripener which is not planted in great quantity. However, it is high in alcohol and acidity and can add concentration to a wine that might otherwise be somewhat soft. Malbec was never very widely planted in the past, and it is seldom replanted nowadays, except in Bourg and Blaye. Its advantages are that it ripens early, and produces high yields of wine with good colour and soft fruit. However, it is even more subject to *coulure* than is Merlot, and the wines are not very distinguished. Carmenère is the final variety, but it is very rarely found now in Bordeaux.

Right: *Cabernet Franc is the lesser of the two Cabernets, but its perfume and grassy taste do enhance the blend.*

Left: *Picking at nearly all the finest châteaux is by hand. These are casual workers at Château Mouton Rothschild.*

Above: *Just-picked Merlot grapes at Château Palmer. The wine made from these will have a rich, plummy flavour.*

*T*he words "classed growth" have a fine ring to them. The words "*premier grand cru classé*" sound even finer. Yet one of Bordeaux's (and the world's) finest red wines can lay claim to neither term. It is not because Château Pétrus is inferior in quality to say, Château Lafite; it is just in the wrong place when it comes to classifications.

The classification of 1855, which has given rise to so much subsequent controversy, and which one might be forgiven for thinking applied to the whole of Bordeaux, in fact applies only to the Médoc. St-Emilion has its own classification, and so does the Graves; Pomerol, however, has none, which is why Château Pétrus has no fancy wording to put on its label.

Why make such a classification in the first place? And why be so selective about which areas to classify? For centuries, merchants and brokers have made classifications, partly for business purposes and no doubt partly for amusement. Mostly they concentrated on the Médoc, which were generally the most widely shipped wines from the port of Bordeaux. These classifications were often based on the prevailing market price for each wine, and were by no means all identical. But the 1855 classification, established by a commission of *courtiers* for a presentation of wines at the World Exhibition of Paris, was made official, and thus inflexible. The only change to be made to it since 1855 was in 1973, when Château Mouton-Rothschild was elevated to first growth status.

A new Médoc listing would certainly be very different. Some châteaux are producing better wine, some worse, and others are still producing good wines, but from entirely different vineyards. This is because a major fault

Bordeaux Second Labels

Second label	First label
Amiral de Beychevelle	Ch Beychevelle, *St-Julien*
Ch Artigue-Arnaud	Ch Grand-Puy-Ducasse, *Pauillac*
Ch Bahans-Haut-Brion	Ch Haut Brion, *Graves*
Ch Barthez	Ch Malleret, *Le Pian*
Ch Baudry	Ch Desmirail, *Margaux*
Ch Beau-Mazaret	Ch Grand-Mayne, *St-Emilion*
Ch Bellegarde	Ch Siran, *Labarde-Margaux*
Ch Bellerose	Ch Pedesclaux, *Pauillac*
Ch Bellevue-Laffont	Ch Fourcas-Dupré, *Listrac*
Dom Boisgrand	Ch Ségur, *Médoc*
Bouquet de Monbousquet	Ch Monbousquet, *St-Emilion*
Ch Cantereau	Ch Rouget, *Pomerol*
Ch Cassevert	Ch Grand-Mayne, *St-Emilion*
Ch Chambert-Marbuzet	Ch Marbuzet, *St-Estèphe*
Ch de Clairefont	Ch Prieuré-Lichine, *Margaux*
Ch du Clos Renon	Ch Millet, *Graves*
Connétable-Talbot	Ch Talbot, *St-Julien*
Ch Conquilles	Ch de France, *Graves*
La Cour Pavillon	Ch Loudenne, *St-Yzans-de-Médoc*
La Croix	Ch Ducru-Beaucaillou, *St-Julien*
Dom de Curé-Bourse	Ch Durfort-Vivens, *Margaux*
Ch Demereaulemont	Ch Montabert, *St-Emilion*
Enclos de Moncabon	Ch Croizet-Bages, *Pauillac*
Dom de l'Estremade	Ch Rabaud-Promis, *Sauternes*
Ch Fonpetite	Ch Phélan-Ségur, *St-Estèphe*
Ch Fonseche	Ch Lamothe-Cissac, *Cissac*
Dom de Fontarney	Ch Brane-Cantenac, *Cantenac-Margaux*
Les Forts de Latour	Ch Latour, *Pauillac*
Ch Galais-Belluvue	Ch Potensac, *Médoc*
Ch la Gombaude	Ch Lascombes, *Margaux*
Ch Grand-Canyon	Ch Colombier-Monpelou, *Pauillac*
Ch Grand-Duroc-Milon	Ch Pédesclaux, *Pauillac*
Ch de Grangeneuve	Ch Figeac, *St-Emilion*
Les Gravilles	Ch Coufran, *Haut-Médoc*
Haute-Bages-Averous	Ch Lynch-Bages, *Pauillac*
Haut-Prieuré	Ch Prieuré-Lichine, *Margaux*
Ch des Hormes	Ch Liversan, *St-Sauveur*
Jean-Blanc	Ch Sigalas-Rabaud, *Sauternes*
Ch Labarde	Ch Dauzac, *Labarde-Margaux*
Clos Labère	Ch Rieussec, *Bommes*
Ch Labory-de-Tayac	Ch Tayac, *Margaux*
Ch la Labut	Ch Caronne-Ste-Gemme, *Haut-Médoc*
Ch Lamarzelle-Figeac	Ch Grand-Barrail-Lamarzelle-Figeac, *St-Emilion*
Ch Lartigue de Brochon	Ch Sociando-Mallet, *St-Seurin*
Ch Lemoyne-Nexon	Ch Malleret, *Le Pian*

of the 1855 classification was that it classified the name of the wine, not the soil nor the existing vineyard. So a château can buy an adjacent vineyard, add it to the estate, and the wine made from it is entitled to the château's classification, even if before the sale it had been entitled to nothing better than AC Médoc.

There are also a fair number of châteaux which were ignored in 1855 which are now making remarkably good wines, and which would have to be included in any revision. But if those are the faults, there are also virtues: it is remarkable that so many wines which were the best of their kind in 1855, still remain so well over 100 years later.

To maintain the quality of a fine wine, and to maintain its reputation and thus its price, it is necessary to be ruthlessly selective. Any vat of wine that does not come up to scratch cannot go into the blend, even though this means that the quantity of wine that is sold under the name of the château is reduced. Quality, at this level, is everything. There will always be some wine that the cellarmaster does not consider fit for the *grand vin*, and it may be unsuitable for a number of reasons: the vines may be too young to be making absolutely top quality wine. Or the weather may have hit one part of the vineyard worse than another. Such wine may be sold to a *négociant* for blending, or bottled by the château under its "second" label. The winemaker for a second wine is the same, the estate is the same, the appellation is the same: only the name and the price are different. So, if you cannot afford Château Margaux, some of the same style and quality can be had from a bottle of Pavillon Rouge de Château Margaux, for a much lower price.

Bordeaux Second Labels

Second label	First label
Ch de Lognac	Ch Ferrande, *Graves*
Ch MacCarthy-Moula	Ch Haut-Marbuzet, *St-Estèphe*
Ch Magnan-la-Gaffelière	Clos la Madeleine, *St-Emilion*
Ch Malmaison	Ch Clarke, *Listrac*
Ch Marbuzet	Ch Cos d'Estournel, *St-Estèphe*
Clos du Margins	Ch Léoville-Las-Cases, *St-Julien*
Dom du Martiny	Ch Cissac, *Cissac*
Côtes Mauvezin-Badette	Ch Haut-Sarpe, *St-Emilion*
Ch Mayne d'Artignan	Ch Cap de Mourlin, *St-Emilion*
Clos du Monastere	Ch de Doms, *Médoc*
Moulin d'Arvigny	Ch Beaumont, *Cussac*
Moulin de Calon	Ch Calon-Ségur, *St-Estèphe*
Moulin des Carruades	Ch Lafite-Rothschild, *Pauillac*
Ch Moulin de Duhart	Ch Duhart-Milon-Rothschild, *Pauillac*
Ch Moulin-Riche	Ch Léoville-Poyferré, *St-Julien*
Ch Moulin de St-Vincent	Ch Moulin-à-Vent, *Moulis*
Ch des Moulinets	Ch Liversan, *St-Sauveur*
La Parde de Haut Bailly	Ch Haut-Bailly, *Graves*
Pavillon Rouge	Ch Margaux, *Margaux*
Ch Perroy	Ch Sigalas-Rabaud, *Sauternes*
Ch Peymartin	Ch Gloria, *St-Julien*
Ch Peyrelebade	Ch Clarke, *Listrac*
Ch Plantey-de-la-Croix	Ch Verdignan, *St-Seurin*
Le Prieur de Meyney	Ch Meyney, *St-Estèphe*
Ch Le Priourat	Ch La Commanderie, *St-Estèphe*
Réserve de la Comtesse	Ch Pichon-Longueville-Lalande, *Pauillac*
Ch Romefort	Ch La Cardonne, *Blaignan*
Ch La Roque	Ch La Tour de By, *Begadan*
Ch de Roquefort	Ch Gaffelière, *St-Emilion*
Ch La Rose de Faurie	Ch Cap de Mourlin, *St-Emilion*
Ch La Rose Goromey	Ch Livran, *St-Germain*
Ch La Rose Maréchal	Ch Verdignan, *St-Seurin*
Cru St Estèphe-la-Croix	Ch Le Crock, *St-Estèphe*
Dom du St-Gemme	Ch Lanessan, *Cussac*
Dom-de-Ste-Helene	Ch de Malle, *Fargues*
Ch St-Jacques	Ch Siran, *Labarde-Margaux*
Cru St-Marc	Ch La Tour Blanche, *Bommes*
Ch St-Roch	Ch Andron-Blanquet, *St-Estèphe*
La Salle de Pez	Ch de Pez, *St-Estèphe*
La Salle de Poujeaux	Ch Poujeaux, *Moulis*
Sarget de Gruaud-Larose	Ch Gruaud-Larose, *St-Julien*
Ch de Segur	Ch Broustet, *Médoc*
Ch des Templiers	Ch Larmande, *St-Emilion*
Clos Toulifaut	Ch Taillefer, *Pomerol*
Ch La Tour d'Aspic	Ch Haut-Batailley, *Pauillac*
Clos de la Tournelle	Ch Soutard, *St-Emilion*

Classified Wines of the Médoc

The 1855 Classification of the Médoc

First Growths/Premiers Crus:
Ch Lafite-Rothschild, *Pauillac*
Ch Latour, *Pauillac*
Ch Margaux, *Margaux*
Ch Haut-Brion, *Graves*
Ch Mouton-Rothschild, *Pauillac*
    (upgraded to first growth status in 1973)

Second Growths/Deuxièmes Crus:
Ch Rausan-Ségla, *Margaux*
Ch Rauzan-Gassies, *Margaux*
Ch Léoville-Las-Cases, *St-Julien*
Ch Léoville-Poyferré, *St-Julien*
Ch Léoville-Barton, *St-Julien*
Ch Durfort-Vivens, *Margaux*
Ch Lascombes, *Margaux*
Ch Gruaud-Larose, *St-Julien*
Ch Brane-Cantenac, *Cantenac-Margaux*
Ch Pichon-Longueville-Baron, *Pauillac*
Ch Pichon-Lalande, *Pauillac*
Ch Ducru-Beaucaillou, *St-Julien*
Ch Cos d'Estournel, *St-Estèphe*
Ch Montrose, *St-Estèphe*

Third Growths/Troisièmes Crus:
Ch Giscours, *Labarde-Margaux*
Ch Kirwan, *Cantenac-Margaux*
Ch d'Issan, *Cantenac-Margaux*
Ch Lagrange, *St-Julien*
Ch Langoa-Barton, *St-Julien*
Ch Malescot-St-Exupéry, *Margaux*
Ch Cantenac-Brown, *Cantenac-Margaux*
Ch Palmer, *Cantenac-Margaux*
Ch la Lagune, *Ludon-Haut Médoc*
Ch Desmirail, *Margaux*
Ch Calon-Ségur, *St-Estèphe*
Ch Ferrière, *Margaux*
Ch Marquis d'Alesme-Becker, *Margaux*
Ch Boyd-Cantenac, *Cantenac-Margaux*

Fourth Growths/Quatrièmes Crus:
Ch St-Pierre, *St-Julien*
Ch Branaire-Ducru, *St-Julien*
Ch Talbot, *St-Julien*
Ch Duhart-Milon-Rothschild, *Pauillac*
Ch Pouget, *Cantenac-Margaux*
Ch la Tour-Carnet, *St-Laurent-Haut-Médoc*

Classified Wines of the Médoc

The 1978 Classification of the Crus Bourgeois of the Médoc and Haut-Médoc

A previous listing had been made in 1932, after which a syndicate was formed. The Syndicate in 1978 produced this latest list, but naturally included only its members. There are therefore a number of châteaux which would be considered of bourgeois quality which do not appear in this classification.

EEC regulations mean that the term "Cru Bourgeois" is used for all, so far as the label goes; however, in 1978 the Syndicate made distinctions between Cru Bourgeois, Cru Grand Bourgeois and Cru Grand Bourgeois Exceptionnel. The last has the strictest rules: a Cru Bourgeois need only be a property of 7ha or more making wine at the château, and wine that is good enough to convince the Syndicate of its worthiness to be a Cru Bourgeois. To be a Cru Grand Bourgeois, the wine must in addition be matured in cask. And to be a Cru Grand Bourgeois Exceptionnel the property must be in one of the Haut-Médoc communes, and the wine must be bottled at the property.

A number of properties have joined the Syndicate since 1978, but EEC rules do not allow them to be classified at the moment.

Grand Bourgeois
Ch Agassac, *Ludon (Exceptionnel)*
Ch Andron-Blanquet, *St-Estèphe (Exceptionnel)*
Ch Beaumont, *Cussac*
Ch Beausite, *St-Estèphe (Exceptionnel)*
Ch Bel-Orme, *St-Seurin-de-Cadourne*
Ch Brillette, *Moulis*
Ch Capbern, *St-Estèphe (Exceptionnel)*
Ch La Cardonne, *Blaignan*
Ch Caronne-Ste-Gemme, *St-Laurent (Exceptionnel)*

Ch Chasse-Spleen, *Moulis (Exceptionnel)*
Ch Cissac, *Cissac (Exceptionnel)*
Ch Citran, *Avensan (Exceptionnel)*
Ch Colombier-Monpelou, *Pauillac*
Ch Coufran, *St-Seurin-de-Cadourne*
Ch Coutelin-Merville, *St-Estèphe*
Ch Le Crock, *St-Estèphe (Exceptionnel)*
Ch Duplessis-Hauchecorne, *Moulis*
Ch Dutruch-Grand-Poujeau, *Moulis (Exceptionnel)*
Ch Fontesteau, *St-Sauveur*
Ch Fourcas Dupré, *Listrac (Exceptionnel)*
Ch Fourcas Hosten, *Listrac (Exceptionnel)*
Ch La Fleur Milon, *Pauillac*
Ch Du Glana, *St-Julien (Exceptionnel)*
Ch Greysac, *Bégadan*
Ch Hanteillan, *Cissac*
Ch Haut-Marbuzet, *St-Estèphe (Exceptionnel)*
Ch Lafon, *Listrac*
Ch Lamarque, *Lamarque*
Ch Lamothe, *Cissac*
Ch Laujac, *Bégadan*
Ch Liversan, *St-Sauveur*
Ch Loudenne, *St-Yzans*
Ch MacCarthy, *St-Estèphe*
Ch Malleret, *Le Pian*
Ch Marbuzet, *St-Estèphe (Exceptionnel)*
Ch Meyney, *St-Estèphe (Exceptionnel)*
Ch Morin, *St-Estèphe*
Ch Moulin à Vent, *Moulis*
Ch Le Meynieu, *Vertheuil*
Ch Martinenes, *Margaux*
Ch Les Ormes Sorbet, *Couquèques*
Ch Les Ormes de Pez, *St-Estèphe*
Ch Patache d'Aux, *Bégadan*
Ch Paveil de Luze, *Soussans*
Ch Peyrabon, *St-Sauveur*

Ch Lafon-Rochet, *St-Estèphe*
Ch Beychevelle, *St-Julien*
Ch Prieuré-Lichine, *Cantenac-Margaux*
Ch Marquis-de-Terme, *Margaux*

Fifth Growths/Cinqièmes Crus:
Ch Pontet-Canet, *Pauillac*
Ch Batailley, *Pauillac*
Ch Grand-Puy-Lacoste, *Pauillac*
Ch Grand-Puy-Ducasse, *Pauillac*
Ch Haut-Batailley, *Pauillac*
Ch Lynch-Bages, *Pauillac*
Ch Lynch-Moussas, *Pauillac*
Ch Dauzac, *Labarde-Margaux*
Ch Mouton-Baronne-Philippe, *Pauillac*
  (formerly Mouton d'Armailhacq)
Ch du Tertre, *Arsac-Margaux*
Ch Haut-Bages-Libéral, *Pauillac*
Ch Pédesclaux, *Pauillac*
Ch Belgrave, *St-Laurent-Haut Médoc*
Ch de Camensac, *St Laurent-Haut Médoc*
Ch Cos-Labory, *St Estèphe*
Ch Clerc-Milon-Rothschild, *Pauillac*
Ch Croizet-Bages, *Pauillac*
Ch Cantemerle, *Macau-Haut Médoc*
The 1960 classificiation proposed (but never implemented) by INAO was of three groups instead of the five of the 1855 listing.

Above: *The grandeur of the driveway to Château Margaux seems entirely appropriate to what is one of only four premier cru properties in the Médoc.*

Ch Phélan-Ségur, *St-Estèphe (Exceptionnel)*
Ch Pontoise-Cabarrus, *St-Seurin-de-Cadourne*
Ch Potensac, *Potensac*
Ch Poujeaux, *Moulis (Exceptionnel)*
Ch La Rose Trintaudon, *St-Laurent*
Ch Reysson, *Vertheuil*
Ch Ségur, *Parempuyre*
Ch Sigognac, *St-Yzans*
Ch Sociando-Mallet, *St-Seurin-de-Cadourne*
Ch du Taillan, *Le Taillan*
Ch La Tour de By, *Bégadan*
Ch La Tour du Haut Moulin, *Cussac*
Ch Tronquoy Lalande, *St-Estèphe*
Ch Verdignan, *St-Seurin-de-Cadourne*

Bourgeois
Ch Aney, *Cussac*
Ch Balac, *St-Laurent-de-Médoc*
Ch Bellerive, *Valeyrac*
Ch Bellerose, *Pauillac*
Ch La Becade, *Listrac*
Ch Bonneau-Livran, *St-Seurin-de-Cadourne*
Ch Le Boscq, *St-Christoly*
Ch Le Breuil, *Cissac*
Ch La Bridane, *St-Julien*
Ch De By, *Bégadan*
Ch Castéra, *St-Germain-d'Esteuil*
Ch Chambert-Marbuzet, *St-Estèphe*
Ch Cap Léon Veyrin, *Listrac*
Ch Carcanieux, *Queyrac*
Ch La Clare, *Bégadan*
Ch La Closerie, *Moulis*
Ch Duplessis-Fabre, *Moulis*
Ch Fonréaud, *Listrac*
Ch Fonpiqueyre, *St-Sauveur*
Ch Fort Vauban, *Cussac*
Ch La France, *Blaignan*
Ch Gallais Bellevue, *Potensac*
Ch Grand Duroc Milon, *Pauillac*
Ch Grand Moulin, *St-Seurin-de-Cadourne*
Ch Haut-Bages Monpelou, *Pauillac*
Ch Haut-Canteloup, *Couquèques*

Ch Haut-Garin, *Bégadan*
Ch Haut-Padarnac, *Pauillac*
Ch Houbanon, *Prignac*
Ch Hourtin-Ducasse, *St-Sauveur*
Ch de Labat, *St-Laurent*
Ch Lamothe Bergeron, *Cussac*
Ch Landon, *Bégadan*
Crû Lassalle, *Potensac*
Ch Lartigue de Brochon, *St-Seurin-de-Cadourne*
Ch Le Landat, *Cissac*
Ch Lestage, *Listrac*
Ch MacCarthy-Moula, *St-Estèphe*
Ch Monthil, *Bégadan*
Ch Moulin Rouge, *Cussac*
Ch Panigon, *Civrac*
Ch Pibran, *Pauillac*
Ch Plantey de la Croix, *St-Seurin-de-Cadourne*
Ch Pontet, *Blaignan*
Ch Ramage la Batisse, *St-Sauveur*
Ch La Roque de By, *Bégadan*
Ch de la Rose Maréchale, *St-Seurin-de-Cadourne*
Ch Saint-Bonnet, *St-Christoly*
Ch Saransot, *Listrac*
Ch Soudars, *Avensan*
Ch Tayac, *Soussans*
Ch La Tour Blanche, *St-Christoly*
Ch La Tour du Mirail, *Cissac*
Ch La Tour Haut-Caussan, *Blaignan*
Ch La Tour Saint-Bonnet, *St-Christoly*
Ch La Tour Saint-Joseph, *Cissac*
Ch des Tourelles, *Blaignan*
Ch Vieux Robin, *Bégadan*

Vineyards currently being reconstituted
Ch Les Bertins, *Valeyrac*
Ch Clarke, *Listrac*
Ch Larivière, *Blaignan*
Ch Lavalière, *St-Christoly*
Ch Romefort, *Cussac*
Ch Vernous, *Lesparre*

Grand Cru Classified Wines of St-Emilion

Premiers Grands Crus Classés

Ch Ausone
Ch Cheval-Blanc

Ch Beauséjour Duffau-Lagarrosse	Ch Clos Fourtet	Ch Magdelaine
Ch Belair	Ch Figeac	Ch Pavie
Ch Canon	Ch La Gaffelière	Ch Trottevieille

Grands Crus Classés

Ch L'Angélus	Ch Curé-Bon la Madeleine	Ch Moulin-du-Cadet
Ch L'Arrosée	Ch Dassault	Ch L'Oratoire
Ch Balestard la Tonnelle	La Dominique	Ch Pavie-Decesse
Ch Beau-Séjour-Bécot	Ch Faurie de Souchard	Ch Pavie-Macquin
Ch Bellevue	Ch Fonplégade	Ch Pavillon-Cadet
Ch Bergat	Ch Fonroque	Ch Petit-Faurie-de-
Ch Berliquet	Ch Franc-Mayne	Soutard
Ch Cadet-Piola	Ch Grand-Barrail-	Ch Le Prieuré
Ch Canon-la-Gaffelière	Lamarzelle-Figeac	Ch Ripeau
Ch Cap de Mourlin	Ch Grand-Corbin-	Ch Sansonnet
Ch Le Chatelet	Despagne	Ch St-Georges-Côte-Pavie
Ch Chauvin	Ch Grand-Corbin	Ch La Serre
Ch Clos des Jacobins	Ch Grand-Mayne	Ch Soutard
Ch Clos la Madeleine	Ch Grand-Pontet	Ch Tertre-Daugay
Ch Clos de l'Oratoire	Ch Guadet-St-Julien	Ch La Tour-du-Pin-Figeac
Ch Clos St Martin	Ch Haut-Corbin	(Giraud-Bélivier)
Ch La Clotte	Ch Haut-Sarpe	Ch La Tour-du-Pin Figeac
Ch La Clusière	Ch Jean-Faure	(Moueix)
Ch Corbin	Ch Lamarzelle	Ch La Tour-Figeac
Ch Corbin-Michotte	Ch Laniote	Ch Trimoulet
Ch Côte Baleau	Ch Larcis-Ducasse	Ch Trois-Moulins
Ch Coutet	Ch Larmande	Ch Troplong-Mondot
Ch Couvent des	Ch Laroze	Ch Villemaurine
Jacobins	Ch Matras	Ch Yon-Figeac
Ch Croque-Michotte	Ch Mauvezin	

This, so far, has proved the most flexible classification of all. It was originally made in 1954, and recognised four different appellations: St-Emilion Premier Cru Classé at the top, with two "A" châteaux, Ausone and Cheval-Blanc, and ten "B" châteaux. After them came 72 St-Emilion Grand Cru Classé properties, and St-Emilion Grand Cru came below that. This appellation had to be applied for and granted each year, with a tasting being critical: a wine could thus attain this appellation in some years but not necessarily in all years. At the bottom of the pyramid was plain St-Emilion.

In 1986 all was changed. The four categories were reduced to two, St-Emilion Grand Cru, and St Emilion. Premier Grand Cru and Grand Cru Classé, which were appellations in their own right before, are now subdivisions of the top St-Emilion Grand Cru category. The wines are tasted every year, and there are certain rules laid down about the property, too: at least half the wine must be from vines of 12 years old or more, wine must be bottled at the château, the vineyard must not change its boundaries for ten years (when the next revision of the classification is due) and the yield from the vines must be lower than that for basic St-Emilion.

Classified Wines of the Graves

Ch Haut-Brion, *Pessac*	Ch La Mission-Haut-Brion, *Pessac*	Ch Malartic-Lagravière, *Léognan*
Ch Bouscaut, *Cadaujac*	Ch La Tour-Haut-Brion, *Talence*	Ch Olivier, *Léognan*
Ch Carbonnieux, *Léognan*	Ch La Tour-Martillac (Kressmann La Tour), *Martillac*	Ch Pape-Clément, *Pessac*
Domaine de Chevalier, *Léognan*		Ch Smith-Haut-Lafitte, *Martillac*
Ch Fieuzal, *Léognan*		
Ch Haut-Bailly, *Léognan*		

Château Haut-Brion, which is geographically in the Graves, was counted rather as an honorary Médoc in 1855, and appears among the first growths in that classification. Not surprisingly, it is also classified in the Graves listing, which was made in 1953 and in 1959. There are separate classifications for red and for white wines.

The classification was produced by INAO, and the original one was revised in 1959, but has not been changed since. The difference between it and the Médoc classification is that the 13 châteaux which are classified for red wines are listed equally, without any distinction being made between them. However, the marketplace sorts out the great from the very good.

Above: *Spraying the vines on an estate in St-Emilion. The classification of châteaux in this region is complex, the wines being critically tasted annually.*

Below: *Young vines being nurtured at Château Cheval-Blanc. This is one of the two top estates in St-Emilion as is recognised in its classification.*

*I*t has been suggested that the reason why there are no classed growths in the Bas-Médoc (the northern part of the Médoc, nearer the sea; the "Bas" is often dropped) is because in the 19th Century a trip there was more than a day's journey from Bordeaux. Pauillac, Margaux, St-Estèphe and the rest of the classed-growth-containing communes were handy, but for a merchant or a broker to ride so much further was more difficult. So the wines were less famous, thus less expensive, and hence not classified in 1855.

If they had been classified at that time their story would have been very different. Classed growths, as we all know, can charge more for their wine, because they enjoy all the quality advantages conferred by investment in good cellar equipment and wine-making knowledge, on top of whatever advantages geography has given them. And, in turn, their higher prices enable them to invest still more in their *chais*. However, in unfashionable areas the story is very different. Lack of fame equals a low price, which equals a hand-to-mouth existence, and hence no spare money for the sort of investment that would raise the quality of the wine. This is why a lot of the wine made in the Bas-Médoc used to go into merchants' blends rather than bear a château-bottled label.

So for many years the division of the Médoc into Haut and Bas was more extreme than it is now. The Haut-Médoc is the grand end. The classed growths are situated there, and as well as having its own separate appellation, it contains six other appellations: St-Estèphe, Pauillac, St-Julien, Margaux, Listrac and Moulis. The key to quality in the Médoc is gravel, and the deepest and best-drained gravel beds bear the best wines.

The top châteaux are, generally speaking, nearest the river. The wines have the most finesse, while those behind them are fuller-bodied, but less elegant. And those of the

Château Greysac
CRU GRAND BOURGEOIS
MÉDOC
APPELLATION MÉDOC CONTRÔLÉE
DOMAINES CODEM S.A. PROPRIÉTAIRES À BÉGADAN (GIRONDE)
750 ml

Bas-Médoc Wines

Grapes	Cabernet Sauvignon, Cabernet Franc, Merlot, Malbec, Petit Verdot.
Taste	The wines of the Haut-Médoc (dealt with separately) have more finesse than those further north, and the classed growth châteaux produce some of the most remarkable wines in the world. Bas-Médocs tend to be sturdier, full of ripe blackcurrant fruit, often somewhat rustic.
Value	The Bas-Médoc produces a lot of inexpensive, soundly-made clarets that do not hit the headlines, but that are very enjoyable. In other words, they are very good value.
Ageing potential	The finest clarets are dealt with elsewhere, but the *petit châteaux* are drinkable quite soon after the harvest – maybe after as little as three years. But most can stand, and will benefit from, longer ageing.
Recommended châteaux	(Bas Médoc) Loudenne; La Cardonne; Greysac; Patache-d'Aux; Potensac; La Tour de By; Laujac; Les Ormes-Sorbet; Sigognac; Castéra; La Tour St-Bonnet.

Above: *Château La Tour de By. Not all Bas-Médoc estates are this magnificent.*

Below: *New oak* barriques *in which Tour de By wines are aged for some months.*

Bas-Médoc tend to be the least elegant of all – somewhat solid, fruity, rustic reds.

But they are none the worse for that. It would be nice to live on nothing but Pauillac, preferably from a year like 1961, but for most of us price tags have to play a part in our wine buying, and the price tags of some of the Bas-Médoc wines are very attractive indeed.

Lots are being château-bottled now, which is in itself an incentive to improve the quality. There has been quite a lot of replanting, and investment in stainless steel temperature-controlled fermentation equipment; and in some châteaux, investment in new oak barrels, too. But new oak it not the be-all and end-all in the Bas-Médoc that it is in the top areas. Domaines Rothschild, who own a Bourgeois château, La Cardonne, as well as the famous Lafite itself in Pauillac, see the wines of La Cardonne as being inexpensive and good value. The fermentation equipment is modern, replanting of the vineyards has meant a raising of the quality of the wine, but there is not a barrel to be seen, new or old. Wood ageing just is not necessary for the sort of wine they want to produce, and for the price at which they want to sell it. (At Lafite, of course, it is different – 100 per cent new oak every year is the rule.) Some Bas-Médoc châteaux are aiming at a higher market, of course. Château Loudenne is one, Potensac another: if a new classification of the Médoc were made, it would be interesting to see how many new entrants would come from the Bas-Médoc. The best areas are centred on the communes of Bégadan, St-Christoly, St Yzans, St-Germain-d'Esteuil, Ordonnac, Potensac, and Blaignan. Most communes have their own co-operative, and a lot of the region's wines are made this way. By no means everything is château bottled, and the co-operatives provide a good source of wine for the *négociants'* bottlings.

The commune of Margaux is at the southernmost end of the Médoc, the end nearest the city of Bordeaux. Château Margaux is there, too, but there is more to Margaux than its eponymous château, and indeed more than the village of Margaux, too: the communes of Arsac, Labarde, Cantenac and parts of Soussans are included in the appellation. This extension of a commune appellation to neighbouring areas that make a similar style of wine is more common in Germany than in France, but it makes sense where, as in Margaux, the appellation standards have been applied rigorously. Margaux, throughout the appellation, makes good wine. The area of classed growth vineyard is much greater than that of non-classed growth, and many of the best estates are clustered close together round the village of Margaux, with no break between them.

The soil is partly responsible for this concentration. It is high in gravel, with the best vineyards distinguishable to the eye by the amount of gravel in their soil. From any other point of view, the soil itself is poor, but all that gravel means that it drains well, and the wines it produces are among the most silky and supple in Bordeaux.

The top property is Château Margaux, a first growth. It looks the part: immaculately kept, with a pair of stone sphinxes flanking steps up to a gracious neo-classical house. It is owned by the Mentzelopoulos family, mother and daughter, since the death of André Mentzelopoulos in 1980. He had bought the château in 1976, and had immediately set about improving its wines which had suffered from some neglect in the final years of the previous ownership.

After Château Margaux, the only first growth in the appellation, there are a number of second growths; Rausan-Ségla, Rauzan-Gassies, Lascombes, Durfort-Vivens and Brane-Cantenac. But the next real "star" is

Margaux Wines

Grapes	Carbernet Sauvignon, Cabernet Franc, Merlot, Malbec, Petit Verdot.
Taste	Margaux is characterised by its silkiness, not its weight. Often it is quite light, without the body of, say, a Pauillac. They can be among the most seductive clarets around.
Value	It is an expensive appellation, and if you go for the top wines, very expensive indeed. But you get the quality you pay for.
Ageing potential	Most Margaux will need at least ten years to develop (and that is a minimum time; most vintages of good wines will require 15 years or more).
Recommended châteaux	Margaux; Rausan-Ségla; Rauzan-Gassies; Lascombes; Durfort-Vivens; Brane-Cantenac; Palmer; d'Issan; Kirwan; Cantenac-Brown; Boyd-Cantenac; Malescot St-Exupéry; Marquis d'Alesme-Becker; Giscours; Ferrière; Pouget; Prieuré-Lichine; Marquis-de-Terme; Desmirail, du Tertre; Dauzac, Siran; La Tour-de-Mons; Bel-Air-Marquis d'Alègre; d'Angludet; Labégorce-Zédé; Martinens.

Palmer, a third growth. The quality of the wine is better than its third growth status would indicate, and it performs well as auction, too, making it a favourite of investors. Palmer was going through a difficult period when the 1855 classification was made, and this may have affected its position.

Among the other thirds, Malescot St-Exupéry stands out for finesse, and Giscours, too, for its quality. The winemaking varies in its details according to the ideas and beliefs of the winemakers, and according to the precise balance of grape varieties in the vineyard, but generally speaking it is classic Bordeaux, with much picking still being done by hand, the grapes being destalked and crushed, and fermentation (in steel, concrete or wood) at around 28 to 30°C. Sometimes the skins and pips are left on the new wine for a further period to extract more colour and tannin, and then the young wine is transferred into barrels.

The very top châteaux buy new oak _barriques_ for the whole of the new vintage, but new barrels are expensive, and a more common practice is to put half or one-third of the crop into new wood, the rest into barrels that are perhaps one year old. There is also a healthy trade in one-year-old barrels from the top estates – lesser properties buy them, perhaps in the hope that a little _premier cru_ elegance will rub off on their own wine.

Above: _Harvesting Merlot grapes at Château Palmer. This third growth wine is a favourite with investors, as it nearly always does well at auction._

Below: _The first year chai at Château Margaux. This famous property has been extensively renovated and improved by the owners, the Mentzelopoulos family._

The curious thing about St-Julien is how great a proportion of classed-growth vineyard it encompasses in its small area, and how it nevertheless lacks a first growth. However, with châteaux like Léoville-Las-Cases and Ducru-Beaucaillou to fly the flag for St-Julien, it certainly does not lack star names.

It is a small appellation, the smallest of the four main Haut-Médoc commune appellations, and covers only the commune of St-Julien itself. Almost all of the vineyards belong to classed growths, with a few *cru bourgeois*, and what is left over excluding those two categories is very small, and generally makes perfectly respectable wine. Given this small size and high standard, it is not surprising that generic St-Julien is a wine rarely seen nowadays – almost all of it is château-bottled, and precious.

In style the wines are usually placed between Pauillac and Margaux, with roundness and richness combined with some of Margaux's finesse and some of Pauillac's body. They sound like, and are, archetypal claret, and the mere fact of there being no first growth there means little, because in some years St-Julien's top châteaux can produce wines that are the equal of any in the Médoc.

As always in the Médoc, the soil, and particularly its drainage, helps. There is plenty of gravel, although it is less deep than in Pauillac, and there is more clay. The best vineyards, producing wines with the most finesse, are nearest the river; further inland the wines are richer, and fuller.

The best part of one of the best vineyards, Léoville-Las-Cases, is near the river. Léoville-Las-Cases is one of three châteaux in St-Julien which bear the prefix Léoville: the others are Léoville-Barton and Léoville-Poyferré. These three do not share the same name because two of them are grabbing reflected glory, but because all three, before the Revolution, formed a single estate, that

Above: *Château Beychevelle, an elegant property that produces an elegant wine that is distinctly different from many other St-Juliens in style.*

Right: *The gateway of Château Léoville-Las-Cases, one of the Médoc's best-known landmarks. The two other Léovilles were originally part of the same estate.*

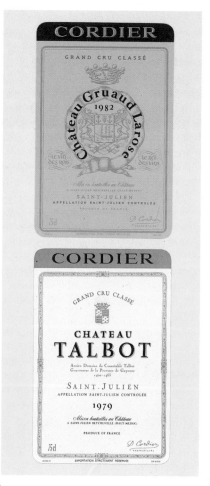

St-Julien Wines

Grapes	Cabernet Sauvignon, Cabernet Franc, Merloc, Malbet, Petit Verdot.
Taste	Between Margaux and Pauillac in style, with some of the characteristics of each, and an extra roundness. But individual wines naturally show different styles: Léoville-Las-Cases and Beychevelle tend to have more finesse than, say, Gruaud-Larose.
Value	Little produced in St-Julien is cheap, but some of the bourgeois growths make good value wine. The top wines are good value, but in a different price league.
Ageing potential	As always, the ability to age depends on the vintage. But a good wine from a good year will need ten years or so to come round, and will improve for much longer.
Recommended châteaux	Léoville-Las-Cases; Léoville-Poyferré; Léoville-Barton; Gruaud-Larose; Ducru-Beaucaillou; Langoa-Barton; Lagrange; Beychevelle; Branaire-Ducru; Talbot; St-Pierre; Gloria; La Bridane; Terrey-Gros-Caillou.

of the Marquis de Las Cases. The present Château Léoville-Las-Cases is the largest portion of that estate, although nowhere on its label does it state the name by which it is known: instead the label states, somewhat idiosyncratically, "Grand Vin de Léoville du Marquis de Las Cases". The gateway that is pictured on the label can be seen from the road; it is one of Bordeaux's most famous landmarks. Of the other two parts of the former estate, Léoville-Barton belongs to the Barton family; of Irish extraction, they have lived in Bordeaux since the 18th century, own the adjacent Château Langoa-Barton, and started the merchant firm of Barton & Guestier.

Still on the subject of origins, the name (and English connections) of Château Talbot have tended to increase its popularity in the UK. The Talbot in question was the Earl of Shrewsbury who was killed in battle in the area in 1453, shortly before the English crown lost Bordeaux altogether, but it is not certain that the property ever belonged to him. Now it belongs to the firm of Cordier, who also own the nearby Château Gruaud-Larose, also in St-Julien. The wines make a good pair, with Gruaud-Larose often having the edge in quality.

St-Julien can boast a long list of other second, third and fourth growth wines, but of those châteaux particularly worth watching, one is not classified at all. Château Gloria is a bourgeois growth, simply because it did not exist in 1855 when the quality classification was drawn up. After World War II, Henri Martin decided to create an estate by buying up various parcels of vineyards, and the Gloria estate now comprises land that at various times has come from Châteaux Gruaud-Larose, Léoville-Poyferré, Duhart-Milon-Rothschild and St-Pierre. Given good viticulture and good vinification, it is hardly surprising that the wine's reputation is equivalent to that of a classed growth.

Pauillac, Margaux and St-Julien are all crammed with classed growths, but not St-Estèphe. There are some, to be sure, and good ones too, but the bulk of St-Estèphe vineyards come under the heading of *crus bourgeois* or *petits châteaux*. Some wines are good, some less exciting, and many have a distinct *goût de terroir* and a robustness that mark them out from the other three main Médoc communes.

St-Estèphes tend to be big, even chunky, wines, without the finesse of Margaux but with, at their best, plenty of richness and an assertive character. The soil counts, of course, and in St-Estèphe the gravel that lies in deep dunes along the river further up the Gironde peters out, there being a higher proportion of clay here. The majority of the classed growth vineyards lie in the south of the commune; Lafon-Rochet, Cos Labory and Cos d'Estournel face Château Lafite-Rothschild (itself in Pauillac) across the vineyards and across the Jalle (or stream) du Breuil, which acts as the boundary between the two communes.

Cos d'Estournel (the "s" of Cos *is* pronounced) is probably the best wine of St-Estèphe, although it is not without competition. The most remarkable building at Cos, and the most famous, is actually the *chai*, a fantastic oriental-style construction topped with pagodas, gloriously out of place among the pepperpot towers and eighteenth and nineteenth century correctness of many of its neighbours.

The wine of Cos d'Estournel often tastes fatter and fruitier than other St-Estèphes, particularly in years when the general style is rather thin. This is perhaps partly because of the high proportion of Merlot in the vineyard. Strict selection of *cuves* for the *grand vin* is practised, as at all top châteaux. Maitre de'Estournel, which sounds as though it should be a second wine of Cos, is not: it is a branded wine with the appellation of Bordeaux, although made by the same company.

Cos d'Estournel's closest rival in St-Estèphe is its fellow second growth, Château Montrose. It has been in existence for a much shorter time, since it was planted only in the early nineteenth century. Woodlands were cleared to make way for vines, but unlike Cos there is no preponderance of Merlot here. The amount of Cabernet Sauvignon in the blend tends to make Montrose tough when young, and slow to mature.

Below: *The first year* chai *at Château Montrose. The wines are high in Cabernet Sauvignon, and are slow to mature.*

The other leading estate is Calon-Ségur, with less star quality than Cos d'Estournel, and more softness than Montrose. The wine is consistent, even if it does not generally beat the others for quality. But is is certainly worthy of its third growth status.

The other classed growths in St-Estèphe are Lafon-Rochet and Cos Labory, but it is worthwhile to look out for a couple of bourgeois growths, Phélan-Ségur and de Pez. Both wines have the sort of weight and rich-

Above: *Cos d'Estournel's mock Oriental architecture makes it one of Bordeaux's most remarkable estates. The quality of the wine is also out of the ordinary.*

ness that indicate that they deserve a higher status than they have: de Pez, especially, would find itself up with the leading lights of the commune were a new Médoc classification to be made.

St-Estèphe Wines

Grapes	Cabernet Sauvignon, Cabernet Franc, Merlot, Malbec, Petit Verdot.
Taste	Always more robust than Margaux, at their best St-Estèphes are round, rich wines. In lesser years they can lack fruit and seem rather harsh, although the best wines have the depth to overcome this.
Value	Cos d'Estournel has led the field in recent years in trying to restrain the annual price rises for top class claret – and it has to be said that they have sometimes been almost alone in so doing. But apart from the top wines, there are plenty of châteaux of *cru bourgeois* status and lower, making good wine.
Ageing potential	They are not wines to drink too young, because they can seem somewhat hard and unyielding in youth. The best wines in a tough vintage will need perhaps 15 years to come round.
Recommended châteaux	Cos d'Estournel (nowadays usually given the prefix "Château); Montrose; Calon-Ségur; Lafon-Rochet; Cos Labory; de Marbuzet; Beau-Site; Haut-Marbuzet; Phélan-Ségur; Meyney; Capbern-Gasqueton; Tronquoy-Lalande; Les Ormes-de-Pez; Le Boscq; Pomys; de Pez; Beau-Site-Haut-Vignoble; Canteloup.

*I*f ever proof were needed that there is more to wine than technology, it would be found in Pauillac. Of the three first growths in the commune, two, Lafite and Mouton Rothschild, are so close that their vineyards almost touch in places. Yet no two first growths are more different in style. Lafite is all elegance and finesse, Mouton is a bigger, fuller wine, firmer and tougher. Both are superb, although Mouton was re-classified as a first growth (from being a second) only compraitively recently – in 1973 in fact, after a long campaign by Baron Philippe de Rothschild, who started to manage the estate in 1923. He has put his stamp on the place in no small way, even down to building his tomb in the grounds (though not in the vineyards). For visitors, as well as a tour round the winery, the château also offers a superb museum of applied arts in which everything has a connection, albeit sometimes a tenuous one, with wine.

Lafite is also Rothschild-owned, but by a different branch of the family. Baron Eric de Rothschild took over the running of Lafite in 1977 and is deeply involved with the estate and with the quality of the wine. A new *chai* has been built to an octagonal design that is unprecedented in the Médoc; another innovation is the stainless steel fermentation vats that, as from the 1987 vintage, will be used alongside the existing large wooden ones.

In spite of the proximity of the two vineyards, the soils are slightly different. Both are basically gravel, but even small variations can make a difference to the wine. The balance of grape varieties, too, is different, with more Cabernet Sauvignon at Mouton, and some (though not a great deal of) Merlot at Lafite.

Below: *The vineyards of Château Mouton Rothschild. The crock of gold at the end of the rainbow was, for Baron Philippe, promotion to* premier cru *status in 1973.*

Lafite and Mouton are both at the northern end of Pauillac, near the boundary with St-Estèphe. The other Pauillac first growth, Latour, is in the south of the commune, and is nearest in style to Mouton. The most famous building at Latour is not the château itself at all, because the 17th century tower that gives the property its name stands a little way apart from the main building. Latour is now largely English-owned, with a majority share being held by interests headed by Viscount Cowdray. Wine merchants Harveys of Bristol have another 25 per cent, and members of the de Beaumont family, who were part-owners until 1963, still retain a small share.

Pauillac Wines

Grapes	Cabernet Sauvignon, Cabernet Franc, Merlot, Malbec, Petit Verdot.
Taste	With such variations in style possible, it is difficult to define exactly what Pauillac tastes like. Lafite has finesse, Mouton body and firmness, yet both have elegance, the power for long life, and a fascinating balance of flavours.
Value	Pauillac is expensive by any standards, and the top wines are millionaire drinks – or more likely, millionaire investments. The second wines of the top châteaux (see page 39) are more affordable, and have something of their class and style.
Ageing potential	These wines are so marvellous when they are old that it seems a crime to drink them too soon. In any case, they are not particularly pleasant when young, and youth can mean, in a good year, ten or 15 years; perhaps even longer.
Recommended châteaux	Latour; Lafite-Rothschild; Mouton Rothschild; Pichon Baron; Pichon Lalande; Duhart-Milon-Rothschild; Pontet-Canet; Grand-Puy-Ducasse; Grand-Puy-Lacoste; Lynch-Bages; Batailley; Haut-Batailley; Lynch-Moussas; Pédesclaux; Croizet-Bages; Mouton-Baronne-Philippe (known before 1975 as Mouton-Baron-Philippe, and before 1956 as Mouton d'Armailhacq); Clerc-Milon; Haut-Bages-Libéral; La Couronne; Haut-Bages-Avérous; Pibran; Haut-Bages-Monpelou.

The Latour vineywards surround another château, the second growth Château Pichon Lalande – or Pichon Longueville, Comtesse de Lalande, to give it its full title. The Comtesse in question was the mistress of a mid-19th century de Beaumont. The present Pichon Lalande estate comprises some three-fifths of what was once a much larger holding: the remainder is now known as Pichon Baron, or, in full, Pichon-Longueville-Baron. The two châteaux are across the road from one another, but about one third of the Pichon Lalande vineyard is in the commune of St-Julien. it is by no means unknown for a château to have vineyards in two appellations (Lafite has some vines in St-Estèphe) but to have such a large proportion is unusual. For a while the two parts had to be bottled separately, with separate appellations, but now the whole estate is accepted as Pauillac.

The list of classed growths in Pauillac is a long one, partly because it is the largest commune appellation in the Médoc. Other recommended châteaux will be found in the accompanying fact box.

Below: *The first year* chai *at Château Latour. The new oak* barriques *do not stay as pristine-looking as this for very long in any château; before long they are stained by the new wine.*

The four best-known communes of the Médoc, Margaux, St-Julien, St-Estèphe and Pauillac, produce the best known wines, but there are two other communes deemed good enough to have their own appellations. Moulis and Listrac are situated inland from the Gironde. The gravel that denotes the finest vineyards elsewhere is more sparsely distributed here. Nevertheless, it is still more concentrated than in the surrounding soil, and while the wines seldom reach the heights of the best Médocs, there are some that would expect to be classified should a new classification be made.

Chasse-Spleen is one such. It is the leading wine in Moulis, and recently, under the ownership of the Merlaut family, a great deal of investment has gone into new equipment and into research into the effects on the wine of maturation in different sorts of oak. Mme Villars took over the management of the estate in 1983, and found the 1982 vintage still in cask, but in old wood: she immediately bought new oak *barriques* for the wine, believing that the quality of the 1982 would prove crucial to the reputation of the château.

Chasse-Spleen is situated on the outskirts of the village of Grand Poujeaux, the name of which has been attached to a number of châteaux in the close vicinity. There are Château Poujeaux-Theil, Gressier-Grand-Poujeaux, Dutruch-Grand-Poujeaux and La Closerie-Grand-Poujeaux; all are close together and most are bourgeois growths.

Listrac is to the north-west of Moulis; its vineyards consequently are further from the river. The wines are quite tough, especially in youth, and may have less fruit than Moulis, but there are many good, round, typically Médoc wines to be found here. The best are Châteaux Fourcas-Hosten and Fourcas-

Above: *Older vintages in storage at Château Peyrabon, an AC Haut-Médoc cru bourgeois property.*

Moulis and Listrac Wines

Grapes	Cabernet Sauvignon, Cabernet Franc, Merlot, Malbec, Petit Verdot.
Taste	Moulis and Listrac lie between Margaux and St-Julien; the wines have greater body and firmness than those of the former, but plenty of fruit as well, especially the wines of Moulis.
Value	There is good value to be found here, partly because of the lack of classified wines. It is a less fashionable area than some, which also helps.
Ageing potential	These wines age well – six to eight years is needed for most, and more for the best.
Recommended châteaux	(Moulis) Chasse-Spleen; Gressier-Grand-Poujeaux; Poujeaux-Theil; Dutruch-Grand-Poujeaux; La Closerie-Grand-Poujeaux; Maucaillou; Moulin-à-Vent. (Listrac) Fourcas-Hosten; Fourcas-Dupré; Lafon; Fonréaud; Lestage; the Listrac co-operative. (Other AC Haut-Médoc wines) La Lagune; La Tour Carnet; Belgrave; Cantemerle; de Camensac; d'Agassac; Caronne-Ste-Gemme; Cissac; Citran; Bel-Orme-Tronquoy-de-Lalande; Lamarque; Larose-Trintaudon; Liversan; Peyrabon.

Dupré, Fourcas being the name of a hamlet just outside Listrac. Château Lafon is another name to look out for, and the local co-operative wine is good.

At the moment there are no classed growths in either commune. However, all the *crus classés* in the Haut-Médoc do not fall neatly into the main areas: Château de Camensac, for example, at St-Laurent, just misses being in the St-Julien appellation, and although a fifth growth, is AC Haut-Médoc instead; Château Cantemerle and La Lagune (fifth and third growths respectively), likewise, are to the south of the Margaux commune boundary and they, too, are AC Haut-Médoc. La Lagune was from 1957 until the early 1960s the property of Georges Brunet, who was responsible for the revival of its fortunes; he then sold the château and moved south to the Coteaux d'Aix-en-Provence, where he now owns the much-respected Château Vignelaure.

These parts of the Haut-Médoc are in fact good hunting grounds for the *crus bourgeois* and *petit château* enthusiast. Gravel appears in the soil intermittently but not extensively, and the variety of soils and of winemaking styles in evidence in this region produces a fascinating range of styles of wine, some big and robust, some light, some round and fruity.

*I*f you stand in the Médoc, and follow the vineyards south-east you will come to the city of Bordeaux. Continue in the same direction, and you will find yourself in the Graves. As its name suggests, the gravel that marks the best areas of the Médoc is found here in abundance, but particularly in the north of the region, near Bordeaux itself. Unfortunately, the city has expanded and areas of land that produced good wine are now submerged under Bordelais suburban houses. Sadly, that always seems to happen when city and vineyard contest the same ground.

Nevertheless, the top vineyards are mostly untouched, and further south, where the soil is sandier, what used to be a somewhat dull source of anonymous blending wine is developing into a region of good-value, flavoursome reds competing in a market that wants more of exactly that.

Much of the Graves is covered with woodland. This is the forest of the Landes, an extensive belt of pine and fir that helps to protect the Gironde vineyards from the excesses of the weather. The trees, in fact, cover more ground in the Graves than the vines do. The vineyards themselves are likely to have a little more Merlot in them than their Médoc equivalents, but the blend of grapes is typically Bordelais, and the wines sometimes resemble those of the Médoc. Generally, though, they have a distinctive *goût de terroir*, a spicy, almost tobacco-like, touch to them, and richness of flavour. The lesser wines tend to have the *goût de terroir* but with less of the richness that characterises the better growths.

There is a classification of Graves wines (see pages 42/3) but, unlike the example of

Below: *Claude Ricard, the manager of the famous Domaine de Chevalier, with his new vintage.*

the Médoc, the châteaux are listed without any differentiation between them in terms of quality. They are also divided by colour, with separate classifications for red and white wines, although there is a degree of overlap since most châteaux in the Graves normally make both types.

Of the 37 communes in the region, a handful stand out on account of the quality of their wine. The best are Talence and Pessac, both merging in the suburbs of Bordeaux with consequent loss of vineyard land, but between them accounting for the two top reds of the region.

Château Haut-Brion in Pessac is of course listed with the first growths of the Médoc, but

it is classified in the Graves as well, and it and its neighbour and rival estate La Mission-Haut-Brion (in Talence) are almost entirely surrounded by the buildings of Bordeaux. The wines of the two properties are entirely different in character, despite their geographical proximity: La Mission is the bigger, more concentrated, wine. For the last few years, though, both châteaux have been under the same ownership, the Dillon family, the American owners of Haut-Brion having bought La Mission in 1984.

Nearby is Château Pape-Clément, a consistently popular wine, and a clutch of Haut-Brion sound-alikes: Les Carmes-Haut-Brion; Laville-Haut-Brion and La Tour-Haut-Brion.

Above: *This aerial view of Domaine de Chevalier shows graphically how vineyards in the Graves are surrounded on all sides by the wide expanses of the forest of the Landes.*

Larrivet-Haut-Brion is further south, in the commune of Léognan. Classed growth châteaux like Haut-Bailly, Domaine de Chevalier, Malartic-Lagravière, Carbonnieux and others are there too; large quantities of reds are produced here. Martillac, to the east of Léognan, also makes good reds. The other main communes are those of Villenave d'Ornon and Cadaujac.

Graves Wines

Grapes	Cabernet Sauvignon, Cabernet Franc, Merlot, Malbec, Petit Verdot.
Taste	Typical Bordeaux, with a distinctive *goût de terroir*, and in the case of the best wines, a rich spiciness. The Merlot content tends to soften the flavour.
Value	The lesser wines are increasingly sought after for their value, and the south of the region is a good source of *petit château* wine, or just generic Graves.
Ageing potential	Graves will last as long, generally speaking, as their Médoc equivalents, but are often ready to drink earlier.
Recommended châteaux	Haut-Brion, Bouscaut; Carbonnieux; Domaine de Chevalier; Fieuzal; Haut-Bailly; La Mission-Haut-Brion; La Tour-Haut-Brion; La Tour-Martillac; Malartic-Lagravière; Olivier; Pape-Clément; Smith-Haut-Lafitte; Laville-Haut-Brion; Les Carmes-Haut-Brion; La Louvière; Le Pape; Pontac-Monplaisir; La Garde; Rahoul.

St-Emilion's remoteness from the city of Bordeaux and the centre of the claret trade has not served it well, historically. Médoc wines found fame and fortune abroad, while St-Emilion stayed relatively unknown in foreign markets until this century. It is still comparitively remote – not to get to, now, but to find one's way around. The estates are small and bear little resemblance to the grander Médoc châteaux, and vines are crammed into every spare corner. It is the prettiest part of Bordeaux and has plenty of Roman remains to testify to its history.

What has changed in St-Emilion is its marketability: the wines are as sought after as any from the Médoc. In their youth they can be more appealing than Médocs, since not only do they mature earlier, but the preponderance of early-ripening Merlot in the vineyards gives an extra degree of alcohol and a softness to the wine, compared with the much sharper-edged Médocs. The Cabernet Sauvignon is grown little here. It does not thrive in the colder soil, and seldom ripens as well as it does on the other side of the river. The main grape is therefore the Merlot, with Cabernet Franc in second place.

This order of preference is pretty uniform throughout St-Emilion, although the soil exhibits considerable variations. The commune of St-Emilion itself is divided into Côtes and Graves, the Côtes being the limestone slopes round the town of St-Emilion, the Graves being the plateau that stretches to Pomerol, and where the soil is basically gravel and sand.

The limestone of the Côtes has been put to more uses, however, than merely growing vines. St-Emilion's origins are Roman, and the cellars cut into the rock beneath the town are still used for storing wine. The rock provides the ideal cool temperature for the wines, although the cellars can also be damp. It is not unusual for a cellar to be right underneath the roots of the vines that filled it.

The best wines of the appellation come from St-Emilion itself. There are seven other communes included within the boundaries: St-Etienne de Lisse; St-Hippolyte; St-Pey d'Armens; Vignonet; St-Christophe des Gardes; St-Laurent des Combes, and St-Sulpice de Faleyrens. The quality of the wines from these communes is pretty well on a par with those of the St-Emilion satellites. These are four nearby communes which have their own appellations which they may hyphenate with that of St-Emilion: thus, Lussac-St-Emilion; Montagne-St-Emilion; St-Georges-St-Emilion, and Puisseguin-St-Emilion.

The wines from St-Emilion itself need the longest ageing, and mature into the most complex, satisfying wines. The others are delicious, certainly, but are not in the same league: they can (and should) be drunk earlier, when they will be fruity, and soft but well-balanced – archetypal St-Emilion, but not as exciting as the best wines.

Of the two wines that are recognised as the peak of St-Emilion, Château Ausone was not

Above: *The pretty town of St-Emilion; it can be seen how vineyards are crammed tightly into every available plot.*

Below right: *The gateway to Château Ausone, one of Bordeaux's "greats" which is in huge public demand.*

so acknowledged until the late nineteenth century. It was well into the present century that Château Cheval-Blanc joined it in that general estimation. The classification of St-Emilion does not discriminate in the same way as that of the Médoc, and while these two châteaux are given a billing above the rest, there is little difference drawn between the majority of good to very good St-Emilions.

St-Emilion Wines

Grapes	Merlot, Cabernet Franc, Cabernet Sauvignon, Malbec, Petit Verdot.
Taste	St-Emilions, being made predominantly from Merlot, are rounder and more generous than Médocs, with less obvious tannin, but still well-balanced. The best wines, in addition, have richness and great breeding.
Value	St-Emilion has, in fairly recent years, risen to the price level of the Médoc. There is little scope now for bargain hunting. But if you forget about seeking rock-bottom prices, there are some good value châteaux to be found.
Ageing potential	These wines mature earlier than Médocs, but that does not mean they do not last. It simply means they have a longer life. They become drinkable between four and nine years before a Médoc of equivalent standing, and their longevity depends on the year and the wine itself: if it has the structure, it will last.
Recommended châteaux	Ausone; Cheval-Blanc; Belair; Canon; Clos Fourtet; Figeac; La Gaffelière; Magdelaine; Pavie; Trottevieille; Balestard la Tonnelle; Canon-La-Gaffelière; Dassault; La Tour-Figeac; Fonplégade; L'Angélus; Curé-Bon la Madeleine; Fonroque; Corbin; Grand-Barrail-Lamarzelle-Figeac.

*P*omerol is a remarkably small and insignificant place to be producing some of the world's greatest red wines. The vineyards begin where the suburbs of Libourne finish, and they continue without a break right across the appellation area. There is no woodland to speak of, no crops of any other kind. Just vines, shoehorned into every available space, taking advantage of the fact that world demand is for Pomerol, Pomerol and yet more Pomerol.

It was not always so. Before the last war Pomerol was regarded as the back of beyond by the haughtier elements of the Médoc trade. It is still the back of beyond, geographically speaking – there is no village of Pomerol, just a scattered series of houses for which the term château can only be a courtesy title. But vinously speaking, sometimes it can seem more like the centre of the red wine world.

The reason lies in a number of quality châteaux situated here of which Château Pétrus is the undisputed star. There is no classification in Pomerol, and opinions vary greatly as to which order the other good châteaux should be placed (if indeed they should be placed in order at all); but there is no argument about the general standard in Pomerol. It is high, and remarkably consistent from property to property. The taste of Pomerol is more difficult to define. It is plummy, and mellow, and soft, without the definition of a Médoc, and with greater depth than St-Emilion; often there is a minerally backbone to the flavour.

The plumminess comes from the Merlot, which is *par excellence* the grape of Pomerol. It ripens early, and thrives on the cold, clay soil in the way that the later-ripening Cabernet Sauvignon never could. Cabernet Sauvignon is therefore seldom seen in Pomerol: the next-most-widely planted variety is

Pomerol Wines

Grapes	Merlot, Cabernet Franc, Cabernet Sauvignon, Malbec, Petit Verdot.
Taste	Pomerol is often described as coming between Médoc and St-Emilion in style, with more softness than the former and more depth than the latter. But its flavour is more endlessly fascinating than such a description implies, with great perfume, richness, and good backbone.
Value	Pomerols are expensive at every level, from the millionaire wines at the top to the still-not-cheap lesser wines. But standards are high.
Ageing potential	The wines are drinkable earlier than Médocs of equivalent standing: they lose their tannin earlier and have in any case a soft mellowness that makes them attractive when young. But they will age every bit as well as a St-Emilion, and perhaps as well as Médocs.
Recommended châteaux	Pétrus; Vieux Château Certan; La Fleur-Pétrus; La Conseillante; l'Evangile; Latour à Pomerol; Trotanoy; Gazin; Certan de May; la Croix; Petit-Village; Beauregard; Lafleur; Nenin; La Pointe; Clos-René; de Sales; Clinet; Certan-Giraud; La Croix-de-Gay; l'Enclos; Lafleur-Gazin; Plince; Lagrange; de Sales; Taillefer.

Above: *Although Pomerol itself is fairly unassuming, its wines, made from grapes like these, are world-renowned.*

the Cabernet Franc, with sometimes some Malbec also being cultivated.

It is this clay soil that helps to make Pomerol so different from Médoc and different, too, from neighbouring St-Emilion. It is tightly-packed, heavy, and with a high iron content, and the gravel topsoil is very thin indeed in the best parts of the appellation. There is most clay in the east, towards the border of St-Emilion; in the west of Pomerol the soil is sandier and the wines less fine.

Pétrus itself is small by Médoc first growth standards. The vineyard extends for only 11ha and production is less than 4,000 cases a year. No wonder, then, that it is generally more expensive than the first growths of the Médoc. The *cépage* is almost entirely Merlot – the vineyard is planted with 95 per cent of that grape – which gives the lie to the sometimes-heard statement that Merlot wines do not age.

The best châteaux in Pomerol stand even more cheek by jowl than they do in Pauillac, partly because they are so small. Pétrus' neighbour, La Fleur-Pétrus, has only 9ha, and is run by the firm of JP Moueix, who also

own and run Pétrus. The confusingly-named Château Lafleur is a mere 4ha in size.

Vieux Château Certan is bigger, with a larger annual production than Pétrus, and is one of the few Pomerol properties to boast a château that really looks the part. Château La Conseillante is also of reasonable size for Pomerol, as is Château l'Evangile. Château Gazin, with around 25ha, is positively huge.

To the north of Pomerol is Lalande de Pomerol, which is a satellite of Pomerol rather in the same way that, for example, Puisseguin-St-Emilion is of St-Emilion. There is also the region of Néac which used to have its own appellation; now producers there are permitted to use that of Lalande de Pomerol instead, and not surprisingly, most do. The wines of both areas are like Pomerol writ small: certainly worth trying, but more careful selection is needed than for the wines of Pomerol itself.

*I*t may seem strange that an area whose wine was widely known abroad long before the now-famous wines of the Médoc should now be trying to convince the world that it can make good wine, but such is the fate of Bourg and Blaye. And while it may not be good news for the wine growers there, it is very good news for wine drinkers, because it means that these reds can be added to the list of wines in classic styles that are available at non-classic prices.

If you cross the Gironde river from the Médoc, the chances are that you will land in Bourg or Blaye. The vineyards run alongside the Gironde, with the best châteaux (as is the case in much of the Médoc) closest to the river. Although Bourg and Blaye are generally grouped together, they make different styles of wine. Bourg generally makes the better reds. Think of the style of the lesser Pomerols and St-Emilions, and you will be near the mark: lots of Merlot give the wines their big, plummy, sometimes rather raisiny, fruit, with Cabernet Sauvignon and Malbec to provide an attractively austere background. There is a fair amount of tannin in these wines, making them worth keeping for at least a few years.

The soil in Bourg is mostly clay over limestone, with some gravel, and while the wines it produces may be like the classics in miniature, the countryside itself looks very different from the great regions. For a start, it is prettier. In the Médoc the landscape is, to be honest, boring: the ground is relatively flat, there are not many trees, and the only features that break the monotony are the châteaux themselves. But here, just over the river, there are more hills, the landscape is more irregular, and it looks much more like rural France ought to look. Most of the reds are AC Côtes de Bourg; an alternative appellation is that of Bourg or Bourgeais, but effectively there is no difference between the two designations.

In Blaye the list of possible appellations is longer. The most basic is that of Blaye or Blayais, which demands 10° of alcohol from the usual Bordelais grape varieties plus the possible addition of Malbec. Most of the red wine produced in the region, however, goes under the appellation of Premières Côtes de Blaye, for which another 0.5° alcohol is required, from Cabernet Sauvingon, Cabernet Franc, Merlot and Malbec only. The AC of Côtes de Blaye is for white wines only.

Blaye, although a much larger area than that of Bourg, has less land planted with vines. It used to be a predominantly white wine area, too, but that is changing: in Bordeaux (in contrast to much of the rest of the world) profits lie in red wines, and more and more growers in Blaye are changing colour to keep up with demand.

The soil in Blaye is much more varied than than in Bourg and while there is nothing wrong with the vines being grown there, the results so far are not up to the standard of the reds from Bourg. They are lighter, often taste slightly ''cooked'', and sometimes a

Bourgeais and Blayais Wines

Grapes	Merlot, Cabernet Sauvignon, Cabernet Franc, Malbec.
Taste	Plenty of rich fruit-cakey taste, but sometimes the fruit can seem a little cooked and raisiny, particularly in Blaye.
Value	Quite good, compared with the prices of wines from more famous Bordeaux regions. But it should be remembered that *petit château* wines from a lot of Bordeaux areas are good value – Bourg and Blaye are not unique in this.
Ageing potential	Blaye wines can be drunk earlier than Bourg, within a few years of the vintage. But they can lack the richness of Bourg.
Recommended châteaux	(Bourg) Brulescaille; de la Grave; Lidourie; du Bousquet; Rousset; Sauman; de Barbe; Coubet; de la Croix-Millorit; Tayac. (Blaye) Haut Sociondo; Segonzac; le Menaudat; Grand Barrail; Loumede; Barbé.

little stalky. However, they are not as unpromising as they might sound from that description, because the winemaking is improving, and there are a number of châteaux making good, easy to drink wines. Because they are lighter than Bourg wines, they generally need less ageing.

Below: *Harvesting underway in vineyards near Blaye. This region used to produce more white wine than red, but this is gradually changing and the reputation of the reds is growing. They are lighter in character than wines from neighbouring Bourg, and can be drunk sooner.*

ronsac has been the coming area of Bordeaux for a number of years now, and yet it still has not really arrived. Mention the wines and Bordeaux enthusiasts are apt to say "Ah, yes. Fronsac. Good wines, aren't they? Pity one doesn't see more of them." And perhaps that is the problem. The wines *are* good, but they are not widely available outside the region – presumably because there is little demand for them. Yet if you took Fronsac out of Bordeaux and put it in, say, the South, such well-made and stylish wines would be acclaimed as bargains.

Indeed, Fronsac wines are well made and they have improved over the years, benefitting from earlier bottling than other parts of Bordeaux and thus great fruit in the mature wine. The grapes used are basically Bordelais varieties, but unusually, the main grape is the Cabernet Franc, which also helps to distinguish the style of the wines from that of neighbouring Pomerol. Some of the Pomerol plumminess is there, tempered with a distinctly Médocian character.

The area itself is hilly and wooded, and lies to the west of Pomerol. To the east, and forming the boundary of the region, is the river Isle, and the vineyards are on high ground, which offers them some protection against frost. There are two appellations. Fronsac and Côtes de Canon-Fronsac, which used to be known as the Côtes de Fronsac. The Côtes de Canon-Fronsac is generally accepted as the better area. It is in the south, bordering the river Dordogne, and it holds the leading growths of both areas. The lesser growths of the Côtes de Canon-Fronsac are, however, not necessarily any better than the better wines of Fronsac itself. The wines of the two appellations are similar in style,

Right and lower right: *Mechanical harvesters are widely used in the lesser regions of Bordeaux, at least where the size of the vineyard justifies the expense. The grapes are dislodged by rotating mechanical "fingers".*

Fronsac and Canon-Fronsac Wines

Grapes	Cabernet Franc, Cabernet Sauvignon, Merlot, Malbec.
Taste	The preponderance of Cabernet Franc in Fronsac gives the wines an appealing grassy edge to their smooth fruit. They are typically Bordeaux, but have their own distinctive character. The wines of the other, lesser regions are often somewhat rustic.
Value	Very good in Fronsac. The only problem at the moment is availability. The other wines are fair value as everyday drinking.
Ageing potential	They are not wines for long keeping, which is just as well: if all Bordeaux needed laying down for years, it would have limited appeal to those of us who want some wine we can drink immediately. So a few years ageing only is the general rule.
Recommended châteaux	Canon de Brem; Junayme; Canon; Vray-Canon-Boyer; Vrai-Canon-Bouché; Gaby; Belloy; Grand Renouil; La Marche; Moulin-Pey-Labrie; Mazeris Bellevue; Mausse; Mazeris; Haut Mazeris; Coustolle; de Carles; La Dauphine; Rouet; Vincent; Tasta; Trois Croix; La Lague; Jeandeman; Bourdieu-la-Valade; Mayne Vieil; des Tonnelles.
What to look for on the label	The best wines are made in the Côtes de Canon-Fronsac, but they are by no means the only good ones.

which makes the division slightly artificial. Fronsac is larger, with nearly 700ha under vine; Côtes de Canon-Fronsac has nearly 300ha.

There are still other regions in Bordeaux which may one day be deemed up-and-coming. Such a description is probably unfair to Côtes de Castillon, which is a cut above such regions as Graves de Vayres and Ste-Foy-Bordeaux both in fame and the quality of its wine. But even so, it has a way to go yet. The Côtes de Castillon umbrella covers two appellations: Bordeaux Côtes de Castillon and Bordeaux Côtes de Castillon Supérieur. The minimum alcohol level for the

latter is 11° and most of the red wine of the district falls into the *supérieur* category.

The grapes are similar to those used in St-Emilion, the region immediately to the west, with Merlot the most widely grown – the others are Cabernet Sauvignon, Cabernet Franc and Malbec. Not surprisingly, in style they resemble the lesser St-Emilions, with plenty of fruit and a certain rustic character.

Just to the north of the Côtes de Castillon are the Côtes de Francs. The wines are similar in style, if a little less tough, and the alcohol level is the same. Nearly all the wine made in the Francs area is red, from Cabernet Sauvignon, Cabernet Franc, Merlot and Malbec, with again a predominance of Merlot.

The appellation of Entre Deux Mers is only applied to the white wines, so those reds made there are only entitled to call themselves plain Bordeaux or Bordeaux Supérieur. In the north of the region, however, is Graves de Vayres, where a concentration on Merlot produces soft, fruity reds. Still in the Entre Deux Mers region, the AC of Ste-Foy-Bordeaux deserves a mention, even though its wines are unlikely to make much of a splash in the market yet. Much of the production is white, but reds are made from the classic Bordelais varieties, and must attain a minimum alcohol level of 10.5°.

The large Premières Côtes de Bordeaux is rather misnamed – it is not as grand as it sounds. Its reds are produced mostly in the north, although there are more reds generally in the region than there were a few years ago. To the north of the northern tip of the Premières Côtes, on the right bank of the Dordogne, is the Cubzaguais. This is a small area without AC, and the wines are called either Bordeaux or Bordeaux Supérieur.

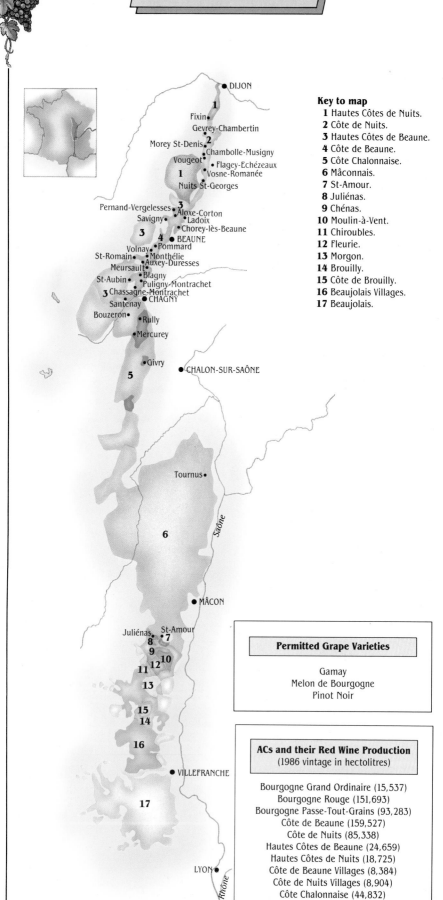

BURGUNDY

Key to map
1 Hautes Côtes de Nuits.
2 Côte de Nuits.
3 Hautes Côtes de Beaune.
4 Côte de Beaune.
5 Côte Chalonnaise.
6 Mâconnais.
7 St-Amour.
8 Juliénas.
9 Chénas.
10 Moulin-à-Vent.
11 Chiroubles.
12 Fleurie.
13 Morgon.
14 Brouilly.
15 Côte de Brouilly.
16 Beaujolais Villages.
17 Beaujolais.

DIJON
1
Fixin
Gevrey-Chambertin
2
Morey St-Denis
Chambolle-Musigny
Vougeot
Flagey-Echézeaux
1
Vosne-Romanée
Nuits St-Georges
Pernand-Vergelesses 3 Aloxe-Corton
Savigny Ladoix
3 Chorey-lès-Beaune
4 BEAUNE
Volnay Pommard
St-Romain Monthélie
Auxey-Duresses
Meursault
St-Aubin Blagny
Puligny-Montrachet
3 Chassagne-Montrachet
Santenay CHAGNY
Bouzeron Rully
Mercurey
Givry
CHALON-SUR-SAÔNE
5
Tournus
6
Saône
MÂCON
Juliénas St-Amour
8 7
9
12 10
11 13
15
14
16
VILLEFRANCHE
17
LYON
Rhône

Permitted Grape Varieties

Gamay
Melon de Bourgogne
Pinot Noir

ACs and their Red Wine Production
(1986 vintage in hectolitres)

Bourgogne Grand Ordinaire (15,537)
Bourgogne Rouge (151,693)
Bourgogne Passe-Tout-Grains (93,283)
Côte de Beaune (159,527)
Côte de Nuits (85,338)
Hautes Côtes de Beaune (24,659)
Hautes Côtes de Nuits (18,725)
Côte de Beaune Villages (8,384)
Côte de Nuits Villages (8,904)
Côte Chalonnaise (44,832)
Mâconnais (67,389)

*B*uying bordeaux is simple. There are regions, and châteaux, and vintages to remember, but as long as you get the name of the château and the year right you should be home and dry. Compared with Bordeaux, Burgundy presents a much more complicated picture.

Not the least offputting factor in Burgundy is price. You can get a reasonable *petit château* claret for little more than you would pay for some branded liebfraumilchs, but not a basic burgundy. And if you are looking for more serious wine, be prepared to pay some pretty serious prices: prices that are sometimes out of all proportion to the quality of the wine. In the last few years growers' prices have risen sharply, and though it is easy to criticise them for greed, it is understandable that they want to get everything they can when they see the sort of crazy prices that the merchants are prepared to pay for the wines their customers want – and the customers, or so it seemed for a while, would pay practically anything that was asked.

There are signs that the price spiral is slowing down, and even if the annual auction at the Hospices de Beaune does sometimes produce headline-hitting figures, they do not always reflect what is going on in the outside world. The Hospices sale takes place each November and is of wine from the Hospices' own vineyards, sold to support the Hospices itself, which is still a working hospital, just as it has been since Nicolas Rolin, Chancellor of the Duke of Burgundy, founded it in 1443. What with its original endowment of vineyards, and those that have been left to it over the years, the Hospices is now among the major vineyard owners in Burgundy. In general, holdings here are not large, and they are immensely split up. This situation stems from the days of the Revolution, and

the breaking up of land owned by the Church, and has been exacerbated by the Napoleonic laws of inheritance, which mean that with every generation the vineyard holdings get more divided.

What it has also meant is that the *négociant* has been – indeed, still is – a very important figure in Burgundy. Houses like Chanson or Louis Latour buy wine from numerous growers, as well as owning vineyards themselves; they take the wine they buy into their own cellars and mature it and bottle it themselves. The results can be excellent, but they can also lack the stamp of individuality that a grower's own wine has. Happily, more and more growers are bottling their own wine. And more and more growers are making good wine.

Tastes in red burgundy fall into two basic types: the heavy and soupy, and the fresh, clean and fruity. The heavy type is something of a hangover from the past days of "doctored" burgundy, when the public taste, and particularly the British taste, called for wines that were richer and bigger than Burgundy could generally produce unaided. So help was enlisted, generally from the south of France, and tannic, tough reds, high in alcohol, were added to the Burgundian blending vats to pep up the colour and the alcohol of the native brew. That sort of blending is illegal nowadays, but chaptalisation is not, and over-chaptalisation can result in some rather thick, heavy wines.

A better way to achieve depth in Burgundy is by restricting the yield from the vines. The principal grape varieties cultivated for red wine are the Pinot Noir and Gamay. Yields have been, and still are, a problem in the area. The Pinot Noir can be coaxed into producing some surprisingly high quantities of grapes if the right (or, from the point of view of quality, the wrong) clones are planted. Furthermore, while the rules governing yields per hectare are in theory strict, in practice they are not always adhered to strictly. And with the Burgundian weather being somewhat unpredictable, there is a great temptation for the more money-conscious and less quality-conscious grower to make hay while the sun shines. One prominent UK Burgundy merchant reckons that Burgundy only gets the weather it needs in one year out of three. This is not really surprising when one thinks of how far north it is: it is in fact, at its northern end, the most northerly fine red wine area in France. Frost can be a hazard in spring, as can localised summer hail storms that can completely wipe out the grapes on a patch of vines.

Left: Vineyards in Burgundy are often small, and get further subdivided with each new generation. The biggest owners are often the négociant *houses.*

G reat burgundy ranks among the finest wine tastes in the world, but, obviously, all burgundy is not great. Bourgogne Grand Ordinaire, for example, is usually more *ordinaire* than it is *grand*, and of the 100 or so appellations to be found in Burgundy, names can be deceptive. Gevrey-Chambertin, for example, is by no means the same thing as Le Chambertin.

The heart of Burgundy is the Côte d'Or. The famous red wine names are all there, and it is some of the most valuable vineyard land in the world. Given its price, it is surprising how ordinary it looks. Just a range of hills, with soil that is basically limestone or marl, with trees on the skyline and well-ordered vines on the slopes. Nothing dramatic, no perilous steepness, no granite boulders overshadowing deep gorges.

To the north, lie the white wine vineyards of Chablis. But to the south of the Côte d'Or are found first of all the Côte Chalonnaise; then the Mâconnais; then the Beaujolais, where the soil is granite-based, there are even more little hamlets tucked cosily into even more hills, and the wines cannot be called burgundy. Carry on South, and after negotiating the road system of Lyon, you will be in the Rhône Valley.

As nearly always happens in France, the more specifically the origin of the wine is given on the label, the higher the quality ought to be. At the lower end lies Bourgogne Grand Ordinaire. So humble is it that it does not even have to be made entirely from Pinot Noir, but can contain some white grapes, namely the Melon de Bourgogne. The latter is grown very little in Burgundy, if indeed it is still grown at all, so the permission is academic. The home of the Melon de Bourgogne these days, in fact, is the Loire where it has taken the name of Muscadet.

Bourgogne Passe-Tout-Grains is a more attractive drink. By law it has to be one-third Pinot Noir to two-thirds Gamay from the Côte d'Or, where it is still grown a little. Like Bourgogne Rouge, it is a regional appellation, and thus on the same sort of level as basic Beaujolais. Usually such wines bear a vintage date.

Above that level, you are into more specific appellations. Wines called Côte de Beaune or Côte de Nuits come from those

Above: *Pinot Noir grapes can make some of the most valuable wines in the world, and some of the most ordinary. Much depends on the* appellation; *in theory, the more specific this is, the higher the quality of the wine should be.*

Monts de la Côte d'Or

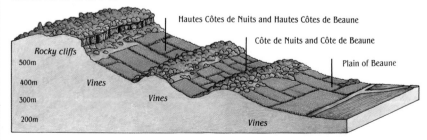

Hautes Côtes de Nuits and Hautes Côtes de Beaune

Côte de Nuits and Côte de Beaune

Rocky cliffs

Plain of Beaune

500m

400m *Vines*

300m *Vines*

200m *Vines*

Above: *This diagram shows the topography of the vineyards in the Côte d'Or. The area is divided into three parts: the plain of Beaune, the Côte de Nuits and* Côte de Beaune, *which make the greatest wines and whose best vineyards face due east, and the Hautes Côtes in the lee of the chalky upland plateau.*

Above: *The Gamay grape is the workhorse of Beaujolais. In Burgundy it may be blended with Pinot Noir to make wine called Bourgogne Passe-Tout-Grains.*

parts of the Côte d'Or, while Hautes Côtes de Beaune or Hautes Côtes de Nuits come from the higher slopes.

Then there are Côte de Beaune Villages, Côte de Nuits Villages and Mâcon Villages, coming from selected villages whose wine is not quite good enough for its own appellation. Village wines that stand alone bear names like Beaune, but if a wine is a *premier cru* it will have a vineyard name attached to the name of the village: Beaune Les Marconnets, for example. And *grands crus*, right at the top of the tree, carry just the name of the vineyard, and dispense with the village altogether: chambertin, for example. But, to confuse the issue, various villages have tagged the name of their most prestigious vineyard on to their own name in order to catch a little reflected glory. The village of Gevrey, therefore, attached the name of the Chambertin vineyard to become Gevrey-Chambertin, Aloxe became Aloxe-Corton, and so on.

Côte de Nuits wines are bigger, richer and more deeply coloured than those of the Côte de Beaune, and the northern end produces the biggest, deepest wines of all. Even so, they are not as big as they used to be. One reason was the application of EEC regulations to the UK in 1973, which prohibited the blending of southern wines with burgundy, and ensured at least that what reached these shores was definitely from where it claimed. The other reason normally given is the removal of most of the stalks during the winemaking process: this both stops the tannin from reaching too chewy a level, and reduces the longevity of the wine. A shorter maceration of five to six days, instead of around a fortnight, also reduces the heaviness of the wine, although it should not affect the colour much, since colour is extracted early on in the fermentation.

The most northerly Côte de Nuits village to have its own appellation is Fixin, but its wines lack the power of those from Gevrey-Chambertin, just a little further along the Côte. Quality, though, is fairly good, so long as the chaptalising sugar has not been tipped too liberally into the vat, which is frequently a problem throughout Burgundy. Brochon is the next village, some of the wines of which are entitled to call themselves Gevrey-Chambertin. The rest must style themselves Côte de Nuits Villages or just plain Bourgogne; there are no *grands crus* in the commune, nor any *premiers crus* except for that part of the La Perrière vineyard which is not in Fixin.

Gevrey-Chambertin itself is a different

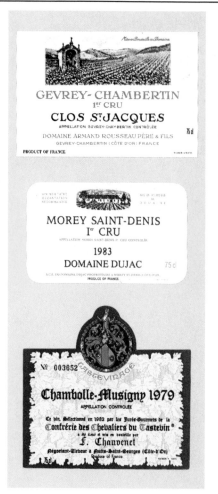

Côte de Nuits Wines: Fixin to Chambolle-Musigny

Grape	Pinot Noir
Taste	The biggest, richest wines of the Côte de Nuits, which means of Burgundy. Gevrey-Chambertin is probably the biggest, with lashings of depth and the elusive perfume that is part farmyard and part flowers, and wholly characteristic of great burgundy.
Value	How can any burgundy be described as good value? Maybe the best wines in the best years are worth their price – but they are practically impossible to afford! There is no getting away from the fact that good burgundy (and bad burgundy too) is expensive.
Ageing potential	Chambertin, the biggest wine, needs maybe 15 years to show its best; Chambolle-Musigny rather less.
Recommended producers	Domaine Pierre Gelin; Domaine de la Perrière; Camus Père et Fils; Domaine Pierre Damoy; Duroche; E Geantet-Pansiot; Naigeon-Chauveau et Fils; Mme Veuve Joseph Beaudot; Domaine Joseph Roty; Thomas-Bassot; Domaine Louis Trapet; Domaine G Tortochot; Domaine Ponsot; Domaine Dujac; Domaine Grivelet; Clergets; Michel, Georges & Veuve; Alain Hudelot-Noëllat; Paul Hudelot et ses Fils; Domaine Comte Georges de Vogüé, Clos de Tart from Mommessin; Domain Marion; Louis Latour; Joseph Drouhin; Roumier.
What to look for on the label	If you are going to lash out on a *grand cru*, then it is worth making sure that you have selected a good grower and a good year. Even a bad year will cost a lot, so it is worth checking carefully.

matter. Go just to the south of the village and it is difficult to move without coming upon a *grand cru* or *premier cru* vineyard. Nearly one-fifth of Gevrey's vineyard area is *grand cru*, in fact, and anyway Gevrey-Chambertin itself is the largest village appellation on the Côte de Nuits.

Much smaller is the commune of Morey St-Denis to the immediate south, which is again packed with *grands crus* and *premiers crus*. Even the plain village wine is good. It used to be said that Morey St-Denis produced the best value village wine of the Côte de Nuits, and that, almost inevitably, made the price rise. There are not so many bargains to be found there today. The soil is limey, and gets stony towards the top of the hill where a little white wine is made.

At Chambolle-Musigny, the marvellous coincidence of the Côte d'Or whereby the best soil occurs on those slopes with the best exposure to the sun is also be be found. Traditionally Chambolle-Musigny is among the more delicate wines of the Côte de Nuits. Nowadays, it can still be, if you pick your grower carefully, but delicacy is only one of the qualities that can be lost by heavy-handed winemaking.

Right: *Clos de Tart is a* grand cru *in Morey St-Denis owned by Mommessin.*

Below: *Fixin, the most northerly village of the Côte de Nuits to have its own appellation, lacks* grand cru *vineyards.*

Grands Crus
Gevrey-Chambertin:
Chambertin
Clos de Bèze
Charmes-Chambertin
Griotte-Chambertin
Chapelle-Chambertin
Latricières-Chambertin
Mazis-Chambertin
Ruchottes-Chambertin
Morey St-Denis:
Bonnes Mares
Clos de Lambrays
Clos St-Denis
Clos de Tart
Clos de la Roche
Chambolle-Musigny:
Musigny
Bonnes Mares

South of Chambolle-Musigny, the Côte de Nuits boasts some of the most famous wine names in the world; and some of the most expensive, too. Wines from the Domaines de la Romanée-Conti can only be topped in price by one or two very top clarets. A famous and expensive name does not, however, guarantee a fine wine. The Clos de Vougeot is a case in point: it dominates the appellation of Vougeot, and is classified as a *grand cru*, but the sheer numbers of people who own vines in that one 50 hectare vineyard means that there simply cannot be any consistency of style or quality. Add to that the basic subdivisions of soil, with the wettest, clay soil with the poorest drainage at the bottom and the much better drained limestone and clay at the top, and it becomes clear that "Clos de Vougeot" is not in itself sufficient guarantee of quality on a label. The château of Clos de Vougeot is the headquarters of the Chevaliers de Tastevin, which has its own labels for wines that have been approved by a tasting panel: otherwise it is chiefly known for its large-scale dinner in the château and its energetic PR activity on behalf of Burgundy wines.

Vosne-Romanée is, if anything, even more famous, and certainly pricier. The Domaine de la Romanée-Conti is among the biggest vineyard owners in Burgundy, and what they do not own, of Romanée-Conti, La Tâche, Richebourg and Romanée-St-Vivant, they manage, either entirely or jointly. Vines of about 40 years of age are the order of the day here; the DRC replanted all its vineyards in 1945 because the pre-phylloxera vines that were then grown were so old and unproductive as to be completely unprofitable.

Vosne-Romanée is not all *grand cru*, of course, and there are plenty of *premiers crus* to be had, with vineyards like Les Suchots and Les Malconsorts producing some fine wines. But with these, as with the *grand cru* and indeed the village wines, it is as well to find a grower's name which you can trust.

Côte de Nuits Wines: Vougeot to Nuits St-Georges

Grape	Pinot Noir.
Taste	Vougeot is a varied in style and quality as its growers and soils, but it is fair to say that it is not one of the biggest burgundies in style. The DRC wines are certainly more robust, and at their best they are marvellously silky, spicy and perfumed. Nuits St-Georges often has more robustness than elegance, with great individuality and complexity.
Value	Burgundy is never a bargain wine, and as ever it is a question of what can be found at affordable prices.
Ageing potential	Many of these wines will need ten or 12 years ageing, although they can be so attractive when young that infanticide can be appealing!
Recommended producers	L'Héritier Guyot; Domaine de la Romanée-Conti; Jean Grivot; Veuve Gaston Grivot; Domaine Henry Lamarche; Jayer Pasquier; Gros Frère et Soeur; Mongeard-Mugneret; Charles Noëllat; Henri & Michel Noëllat; Henry Gouroux; Domaine Marey-Monge; Louis Gouroux; Jean-Claude Boisset; Domaine Henri Gouge; F Chauvenet; J H Faiveley; Geisweiler et Fils; Hospices de Nuits; Labouré-Roi; Charles Vienot; Lupé Cholet et Cie; Domaines Tim Marshall; Moillard-Grivot.
What to look for on the label	The Tastevinage label conferred by the Chevaliers du Tastevin at Clos de Vougeot can be found on wines from all over the Côte d'Or, not just Vougeot.

Left: *Romanée-Conti is a grand cru vineyard in Vosne-Romanée. Until 1945, pre-phylloxera vines were grown here.*

Below left: *Picking the grapes at the Domaine de la Romanée-Conti. This Domaine is one of the most famous vineyard owners in Burgundy.*

Below: *Jean Grivot, one of the most respected vignerons in the area, has major holdings in the Clos de Vougeot.*

To the south of Vosne-Romanée comes one of the most beloved names of the old wine trade – Nuits St-Georges. So popular was the name with customers that the style of the wine, as it came to be known, bore little resemblance to the individual, uncompromising nature of the wine as it really is – or should be. They are big wines, but they should not be soupy in the way they so often were in the past.

Nuits St-Georges is a large appellation, but it has no *grand cru* vineyard. It is also a decent-sized town, fulfilling much the same function for the Côte de Nuits as Beaune does for the Côte de Beaune – a lot of the local merchant houses are based there.

The wines from the southern part of the commune tend to be the more robust, while those from the northern, Vosne-Romanée end are altogether lighter. The appellation also covers the wines from the more southern village of Prémeaux, whose *premier cru* vineyards can produce some fine wines.

Grands Crus

Vougeot: Clos de Vougeot
Vosne Romanée: Grands Echézeaux
Echézeaux
La Tâche
Richebourg
Romanée
Romanée-Conti
Romanée St-Vivant

*T*he Côte de Nuits has built its reputation on its red wines, but in the Côte de Beaune the laurels are more evenly spread between red and white. In fact some of the most stunning wines from this southern half of the Côte d'Or are the whites; the only *grand cru* red vineyards are in Corton. This notwithstanding, some of the red *premiers crus* are very good indeed.

Corton has the most northerly vineyards of the Côte de Beaune, if one excludes those in-between vineyards that do not merit a commune appellation. The Corton hill itself is the centre of all the action, and it has lent its name to the village of Aloxe, which has become Aloxe-Corton. The hill has woods on the summit, while vineyards extend round a good portion of it, with the famous white wine vineyards on the higher slopes and the Pinot Noir growing just below. Anything called after Corton, or any of the Corton vineyards, like Corton-Bressandes, is *grand cru*; Aloxe-Corton, at the foot of the hill, produces *premier cru* or commune wines.

The communes of Pernand-Vergelesses and Ladoix-Serrigny also have vineyards that are inside the appellation boundaries of Corton, but a few wines under the commune appellations of Pernand-Vergelesses and Ladoix-Serrigny are also found.

Being a *grand cru* does not automatically make Corton the best red wine of the Côte de Beaune. This is Burgundy, after all. There would be some pretty strong contenders from Beaune itself, even though there are no *grand cru* vineyards there. And wines that are extremely appealing, if generally not great, come from Savigny-lès-Beaune. The "lès" here means near, and indeed the two towns are not far apart, with Savigny-lès-Beaune in a valley to the north of Beaune itself. The wines exhibit different styles depending on whether they come from the northern slopes near Pernand-Vergelesses, or from the other side of the village, nearer Beaune. The latter tend to produce the fuller wines.

Beaune itself is to the Côte de Beaune what Nuits St-Georges is to the Côte de Nuits – the local centre, the town where the *négociants* and brokers have their offices and cellars, and, incidentally, the place where some very fine wine is made. The wines are generally reliable, which is good since Beaune is the largest appellation in the Côte d'Or in terms of numbers of hectares. Curiously, there are not that many growers here as a lot of the vineyards are owned by merchant houses and quite a few, as elsewhere on the Côte be Beaune, are owned by the Hospices de Beaune. The Hospices continues today to look after the sick and aged, but the original 15th century buildings have been turned into a museum, and are well worth a visit.

Grands Crus

Aloxe-Corton: Le Corton, is the only *grand cru* red on the Côte de Beaune. To its name may be added the names of individual vineyards – Les Renardes, Le Rognet-Corton, Les Vergennes, Les Bressandes, Le Clos du Roi, Les Grèves, Les Perrières, Les Languettes, Les Pougets, Les Maréchaudes, Les Chaumes, Les Meix, Les Combes, La Vigne au Saint. Also Château Corton Grancey from the house of Louis Latour.

Above: *Reine Pedauque are* négociants *based in Aloxe-Corton, a village named after its most famous vineyard.*

Above: *The vineyards on the hill of Corton extend almost all the way round. Pinot Noir is grown on the lower slopes for red wine; further up, nearer the woods, the vineyards produce white wine from the Chardonnay grape.*

Côte de Beaune Wines: Pernand-Vergelesses to Beaune

Grape	Pinot Noir
Taste	Côte de Beaune wines are generally lighter and less tannic than those of the Côte de Nuits, with a more straightforward strawberry Pinot Noir character.
Value	Slightly better than wines from further north. Beaune and the nearby communes are worth a close look, although Corton is pretty highly priced.
Ageing potential	If the big wines of the Côte de Nuits often need ten years or more, the Côte de Beaune wines are for earlier drinking. Corton is the biggest, but six or seven years will suffice for most Cortons, and less for a Beaune.
Recommended producers	Domaine de la Guyonnière, Château Corton Grancey; Tollot-Beaut; Charles Viénot; Michel Voarick; Louis Jadot; Chanson Père et Fils; Domaine Bonneau du Martray; Rapet Père et Fils; Joseph Drouhin; Champy Père et Cie; Prince Florent de Mérode; Henri de Villamont; Hospices de Beaune.
What to look for on the label	Burgundy labels sometimes state whether the wine is a *grand cru* or *premier cru*, but often they say nothing at all on the matter, leaving the uninitiated in the dark. The *grand cru* wines are listed in a separate table.

Pommard is neither a particularly big town, nor a particularly big commune, but its international fame has long outstripped its size. It has for many years been a popular wine abroad, and international popularity, especially when burgundy is concerned, means high prices.

The other danger when demand is high is that quality falls away. It does not always happen, and the top Bordeaux châteaux are examples of how quality can be maintained. But attitudes have been rather different in Burgundy, and in Pommard the growers have had quite an easy time of it, commercially. So if a lot of Pommards are big firm wines, fuller bodied than Beaune and with good colour, but nevertheless somehow a trifle dull, maybe one should not be too surprised.

There are no *grands crus* vineyards in Pommard. There are none for red wines at all on the Côte de Beaune except in Corton, but Pommard does not even have a single vineyard with an exceptionally high reputation. Several are good, especially the *premier cru* of Les Rugiens, but none are outstanding enough to warrant the surprisingly high reputation of Pommard.

If Pommard is big wine, the neighbouring commune of Volnay makes what is probably the lightest, most delicate red on the Côte de Beaune. It is silky and elegant rather than tough and brawny, and none the worse for that: it is often compared in style to the white wine of Meursault a little to its south. The two communes actually do share a vineyard, called Les Santenots. This vineyard lies within the boundaries of Meursault, but red wine from there can be called Volnay.

There are, as ever, differences in style in Volnay. Near the town itself is a strip of very chalky subsoil which tends to produce light

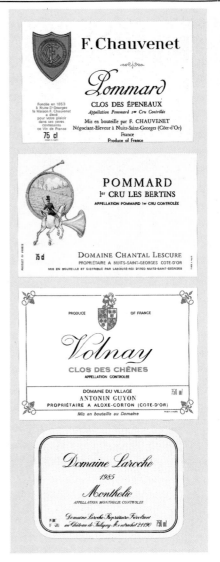

Côte de Beaune Wines: Pommard to Monthélie

Grape	Pinot Noir.
Taste	Pommard is the biggest, toughest wine of the three, maturing to a savoury ripeness. Volnay and Monthélie are lighter and more elegant.
Value	Monthélie is probably the best value, and, conversely, the hardest to find. Volnay and Pommard have famous names, which pushes their price up.
Ageing potential	Pommard is of course the longest lasting. The best *premiers crus* will need five to eight years to mature, the commune wines less, and a top Volnay needs less time than a top Pommard – it can be over the top when the Pommard is at its peak.
Recommended producers	Domaine Parent; Robert Ampeau; Domaine de la Pousse d'Or; François de Montille; Bouchard Père et Fils; Domaine des Comtes Lafon; Domaine A Ropiteau-Mignon.
What to look for on the label	There are no *grands crus*, but *premiers crus* like Les Rugiens, Les Epenots and Les Arvelets are good in Pommard, and Les Chevrets, Clos de la Bousse d'Or, Les Champans and Les Caillerets in Volnay.

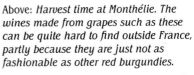

Below: *Volnay makes light, silky red wine that is some of the most delicate on the Côte d'Or. There are some fine growers and fine vineyards, but none of the latter are classified as* grand cru.

Above: *Harvest time at Monthélie. The wines made from grapes such as these can be quite hard to find outside France, partly because they are just not as fashionable as other red burgundies.*

wines. Further down the slope is soil that is less chalky but which contains more iron, and the wines tend to be more complex: most of the best growths are here. Further down again the soil becomes less well drained, and the wines lack the quality of those higher up.

Monthélie is a smaller town than either Pommard or Volnay, and its wines are nothing like as well known. Indeed, it can be quite difficult trying to locate a bottle of it at all, outside France. Monthélie does not produce an awful lot of wine, but most of it is red, and because it is not fashionable, prices for the commune are not astronomical. In style the wines most resemble Volnay, although they are not as good. In the last century the price of Monthélie was in fact linked to that of Volnay, the former being three quarters of the latter; it is not so very different now.

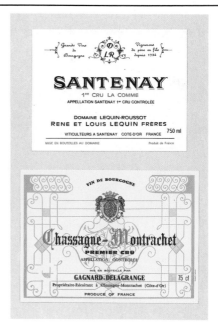

Just to the south of Monthélie lies Auxey-Duresses. The wines are scarcely better known than those of Monthélie, and are sometimes blended into a more anonymous Côte de Beaune Villages. There are several *premier cru* vineyards of which the most famous, les Duresses, lent its name to the village in 1924: the village was previously known as Auxey-le-Grand. The wines are firm, even hard, when young, but are certainly worth looking out for.

To the east, Meursault, one of the Côte d'Or's largest appellations, produces one of the world's most famous white wines. What little red it produces is of nowhere near the standard of the white, and most of it is not sold under the name of Meursault. Pinot Noir from the Santenots vineyard goes under the name of neighbouring Volnay, and the wine in the hamlet of Blagny adopts the latter name. Red Meursault itself is made in tiny quantities.

The next commune to the south, Puligny-Montrachet, also makes only minute quantities of red wine, but Chassagne-Montrachet, best known for its whites, actually produces rather more reds. They are of a high standard, but not as good as the whites. There are no red equivalents of the white *grands crus*, and the quality of the *premiers crus* is more uneven than that of the white *premiers crus*. There is a touch of softness to the reds, but apart from that the wines can seem more typical of the Côte de Nuits than of the Côte de Beaune. One reason – probably the main reason – is the soil. The limestone that gives the Côte de Nuits wines their character surfaces again both here and in Santenay, giving the wines that significant extra bit of power.

Before coming to Santenay itself, it is worth having a look at two small villages just off the main part of the Côte: St-Romain and St-Aubin. St-Romain's nearest town is Auxey-Duresses, and it is more of a hamlet than a village, with only a few hectares of vines. Slightly more than half of these are red, and most of the wine is marketed by Roland Thévenin, a grower and merchant who also sells wines from other parts of Burgundy. The wines are attractive, though they cannot really be classed as great.

St-Aubin is next door to Chassagne-Montrachet, and is more wine-oriented than is St-Romain. The village also includes the

---

Below: *Château Philippe in Santenay. Vines here are often trained using the Cordon de Royat rather that the Guyot employed in the rest of the Côte.*

hamlet of Gamay, from which the Beaujolais grape took its name: when the Seigneur de May returned home from the Crusades clutching sprigs of Gamay (which had until then been unknown in Burgundy), Gamay was where he settled. It was only some while after this that the total unsuitability of Gamay to the Côte d'Or was understood, and it was banned in favour of Pinot Noir.

Santenay is the most southerly village appellation on the Côte de Beaune, and thus on the whole of the Côte d'Or. The streak of limestone that reappears here and in Chassagne-Montrachet gives the wines of Santenay some of the character of a burgundy from the Côte de Nuits, and the wines need plenty of time in the bottle to open out.

As much depth as possible is coaxed from

Above: *Clos St-Jean in Chassagne-Montrachet. This village is better known for its white wines, although it actually produces more red – 8,800hl in 1986, as opposed to 7,750hl of white.*

the vines by the method of pruning here and in Chassagne: while the rest of the Côte generally uses the Guyot method, the Cordon de Royat is practised in Santenay and Chassagne. The essential difference between the two systems is that the Guyot system allows for the replacement of the main branch every year, and the Cordon de Royat method provides for the replacement of the young shoots. The vines are thus made to work harder, but are less susceptible to frost.

Côte de Beaune Wines: Auxey-Duresses to Santenay

Grape	Pinot Noir.
Taste	These southern Côte de Beaune wines can be among the least appealing when young, and do not always develop as successfully as, say, a Volnay. But there are some good Pinot-tasting wines to be had.
Value	Good value is best found in Auxey-Duresses, St-Aubin and St-Romain; not, frankly, in the famous wines unless you are extremely rich.
Ageing potential	Chassagne and Santenay need several years to develop in bottle, while lesser wines age proportionately faster. But none should be drunk too young.
Recommended producers	Roland Thévenin; Hubert Lamy; de Marcilly; Domaine du Duc de Magenta; Château de la Maltroye; André Ramonet; Prosper Maufoux; Leroy.
What to look for on the label	With no *grands crus*, and few *premiers crus* of any fame, the best bet is to concentrate on good village wines.

*T*he Côte Chalonnaise can also be called the Chalonnais, or the Region de Mercurey, and the latter name gives an indication of priorities in the region. Mercurey is the largest appellation, accounting for over half the wine produced, and it is also, not surprisingly, the best known.

The Chalonnais is at the lower end of Burgundy. It starts with Chagny, to the south of the Côte de Beaune, and has four appellations of its own: Mercurey, Rully, Givry and Montagny. The last is for white wine only, but the others, when they make red wine, produce a sort of Côte d'Or in miniature: less depth, less weight, less quality. In theory, less expensive too, but recent years have changed things a bit there.

Mercurey, being the biggest of the ACs, is the area on which the large companies have turned their attention. A number of grower/merchants own chunks of vineyard here. However, the vineyard area is more fragmented than on the Côte d'Or, with vineyards interspersed with other crops. Ninety per cent of the vines are Pinot Noir, and grapes can come from two neighbouring communes (St-Martin-sous-Montaigu and Bourgneuf-Val-d'Or) as well as from Mercurey itself, and the resulting wine will still bear the Mercurey name. There are five *premier cru* vineyards, though until comparatively recently it was rare to see a Mercurey at all, never mind a *premier cru* wine: the majority of the produce was blended by the merchants into a Côte de Beaune.

Givry's wines, too, generally suffered this fate until recent years. A bigger threat nowadays is the urban expansion of nearby Chalon-sur-Saône, which pushes up land prices, although not for vine growing. However, the bigger growers in the commune seem determined to stay.

The third red wine appellation, Rully, produces nearly as much white wine as it does red, and what is more, the white is rather better. Nevertheless the red, though somewhat light, is an attractive buy if Côte d'Or prices are borne in mind, and the appellation is an expanding one, with more vineyards being planted. There are a fair number of *premier cru* vineyards already, but none with enough of a reputation to bring fame to the commune.

Methods of winemaking all over the Chalonnais tend to be traditional. Fermentation is often in cement vats; there is less anxiety for a short fermentation than there is further north and there may, too, be less anxiety to chaptalise. Winemaking in the Chalonnais is by no means confined to the four appellation areas, but other vineyards produce basic *bourgogne* when they produce appellation wine. There is no general AC designation for the Chalonnais itself.

Above: *Not a welcome to another planet, but the most important appellation in the Côte Chalonnaise. Its wines are less stylish versions of Côte d'Or reds.*

Right: *In the cellars at Château d'Etroyes in Mercurey. This property is owned by the well-known* négociant *house of François Protheau et Fils.*

Côte Chalonnaise Wines

Grapes	Pinot Noir and Gamay.
Taste	Like a Côte d'Or burgundy but less so. The wines are lighter and certainly do not have the class of the better Côte d'Or communes, but there is plenty of Pinot Noir strawberry fruit there.
Value	Not such good value as they used to be, and when prices start to rise they have a tendency to keep going.
Ageing potential	Two or three years are generally enough for these wines to start to show their style. Until then they can seem rather hard, even mean.
Recommended producers	J-F Delorme; J Faiveley; Bouchard Aîné; Antonin Rodet; Baron Thenard; Michel Voarick; F Protheau.
What to look for on the label	Some wines from Mercurey may bear ''Chante Flûte'' labels conferred (after tasting) by the local *confrérie*. Otherwise there are some single vineyard wines, but in Rully and Givry these are unlikely to be very much better than the commune wines.

Above: *Grape pickers hard at work during harvest time at Rully. This appellation has yet to establish a firm reputation for itself, although it boasts several* premier cru *vineyards. In the past it was better known for sparkling wines, but nowadays that has changed, and the production of red is expanding.*

The Mâconnais is in-between country in more ways than one. Geographically, it lies between the Chalonnais and Beaujolais, a juxtaposition that is reflected in the style of the wine also. The region consists of chains of hills to the south of the Chalonnais, but these hills are quite unlike those of the Côte d'Or. For a start, they are less devoted to wine. There are plenty of vineyards, of course, but wine is not the only important agricultural endeavour here. The rearing of animals, and harvesting of other crops, must also have their share of the farmer's time, and his time is short, since most of the plots are smallholdings, run by one family and handed down (in the usual divided manner) to the next generation. The small size of the vineyard holdings has encouraged the growth of co-operative cellars. There are about 15 of them now, accounting for a large part of the region's wine output.

The quality of wine in the Mâconnais generally is pretty good. The Pinot Noir is not up to Côte d'Or standards and the Gamay seldom reaches the levels of the better Beaujolais, although a decent red Mâcon is often superior to the average Beaujolais Nouveau. Red grapes, grown mostly in the north of the region, cover just under half the vineyard area, and most of the red grapes are Gamay; Pinot Noir forms only a small proportion. With so much Gamay, it is not surprising that some of the winemaking techniques that make much of the Beaujolais crop so instantly attractive, have been exported to the Mâconnais. These days, a touch of *macération carbonique* (see pages 84-85) softens the edge of some of the earthier Mâcons.

The climate in the Mâconnais is such that the grapes can be picked as much as a week before the harvest starts in the Côte d'Or, and earlier, too, than it begins in the Chalonnais. July and August are hot, which brings the vines on well and speeds the ripening of the grapes. But the climate is by no means ideal: the year can 'get off to a late start, with spring frosts a constant threat after a February that can be bitter. It is the uncertainty of the climate here that is the main problem, and that makes the microclimate of each vineyard very important indeed.

The basic appellation is Mâcon Rouge. Beyond that the classification becomes more complicated, although many of the appellations apply to white wines only and are thus beyond the scope of this book. If the red wine manages 1° alcohol above the basic 9° that is required for the Mâcon Rouge appellation, it can call itself Mâcon Supérieur. Surprisingly, it is not a distinction that is used very often, although 9° alcohol is not a very demanding level to achieve. In addition, there are 43 villages whose white wines are entitled to the Mâcon Villages appellation. And a further step up the quality ladder are the wines which attach the name of an individual commune to that of Mâcon — Mâcon-Mancey, for example. Such wines can be white or red, but in practice only a few are red.

Below left: *The village of Berzé le Chatel in the Mâconnais. Microclimate is crucial in this part of Burgundy where the winters can be very severe.*

Above: *Pinot Noir grapes. These are in the minority in the Mâconnais, with most of the red crop from this region being composed of Gamay.*

Mâconnais Wines

Grapes	Pinot Noir and Gamay.
Taste	Mâconnais Pinot Noir most resembles Côte d'Or burgundy, but in miniature, without the elegance or depth. There is a distinctive earthiness, perhaps a touch of astringency, too, about both the Pinot Noir and the Gamay.
Value	Quite good, for a wine that is within the Burgundian orbit, which is not to say that there are not better value country wines to be found in France, nor better value Beaujolais.
Ageing potential	Again, think in terms of mini-burgundy and mini-beaujolais. Most reds are best within two or three years of the vintage.
Recommended producers	The co-operative of Lugny St Genoux-de-Scisse; Guffens-Heynen; the co-operative at Chardonnay; the co-operative at Buxy; Château de Byonne; Georges Duboeuf.
What to look for on the label	The name of a good *négociant* is a reassuring sign here, since most growers are too small to market their own wine.

Roughly half the Gamay vines in France grow in Beaujolais. The others are grown predominantly in the Loire and Savoie, and they produce wine that is attractive, pretty reliable, and reminds the drinker of Beaujolais. That may seem an obvious statement, but Gamay, left to itself, produces wine that is really rather dull. It used, after all, to be widely planted on the Côte d'Or until it was banned because of its total inferiority in that area to the Pinot Noir. The Gamay grape and the Beaujolais region have proved such a remarkably successful combination partly because of the soil in Beaujolais, which is granite-based and thus completely different from that of Burgundy proper, and partly because of carbonic maceration – *macération carbonique.*

Carbonic maceration is a winemaking technique designed to extract all the fruit and all the aroma from the grapes, but virtually none of the tannin. It produces a wine that is immediately appealing, even to people who do not terribly like the taste of other wines, and its clean, fresh taste is such that it slips down easily in large quantities. And it has made possible one of the greatest wine marketing success stories ever, that of Beaujolais Nouveau.

Having thus won its commercial spurs, the technique is spreading. Variations on it are used not just in the Loire, but also in places where Gamay is unfamiliar: the Rhône, and Provence. Wherever it is used, it imparts its characteristic plummy, sappy, boiled-sweet taste and smell to the wine, which is why in some of those regions it is used with care, in combination with other methods, for perhaps half or less of a particular wine.

What the process consists of is fermentation within each unbroken grape (California growers call it whole berry fermentation). Normally grapes for red wine are crushed and partially or wholly destalked as soon as they arrive at the winery. If carbonic maceration is the order of the day, the grapes are brought to the winery with great care being taken that they should not be damaged or broken. Plastic tubs are best for this, the ideal size being those that hold no more than 60kg (132lb) of grapes. From these, the grapes are transferred directly to the fermentation vats, and again size is important. Sixty-hectolitre vats are the biggest that some perfectionists advocate using, although most large companies use bigger vats.

The weight of the grapes alone presses a certain amount of juice out of those grapes

---

Below: *The soil in Beaujolais is granite-based, unlike that of the Côte d'Or, and this difference makes it an ideal region for growing the Gamay grape from which Beaujolais is made.*

Above: *It is always crucial to keep the temperature of the fermenting must at the correct level. One method is to pump it through cooling apparatus and then back to the vat, as is being done here.*

Above: *The fruits of labour: hand picking is exhausting work, and the workers require appropriate sustenance!*

at the bottom of the vat, and this juice begins to ferment. As it ferments it produces carbon dioxide which rises to surround the grapes above, and fermentation then starts to take place inside each unbroken grape. A fermentation temperature of 25 to 28°C will give maximum perfume to the wine.

In its classic form, the technique involves pumping bottled carbon dioxide into the vat to blanket the grapes immediately the vat is filled, after which the maceration would last ten days or so. In Beaujolais it is more usual to have a maceration of five or six days, and to pump the liquid from the bottom of the vat over the grapes. Sulphur dioxide is used to prevent oxidation, and sugar is added to increase the alcohol level – typically this is done every year, not just in those years where the grapes need it. This is apt to happen in most French regions, as well as in other countries where it is permitted: chaptalisation is such an easy option.

After the maceration is complete, the juice is drained off and the grapes are pressed in the normal way. Carbonic maceration produces wine that can be drunk immediately, which is why it is so perfect for Beaujolais Nouveau, which finds itself in the shops only a couple of months after the vintage.

Not all Beaujolais is Nouveau, in spite of the impression that could be gained from the annual late-November hype. In fact, roughly half the annual Beaujolais crop goes into Nouveau. It means some fast work at the wineries: fermentation must not take too long, and the wine must be clarified and stabilised in time to get it bottled, shipped, and into the shops by Nouveau day. This used to be 15 November, as regular as clockwork, but now it has been changed to the third Thursday in November to give everyone a bit longer to get organised.

Most of the Nouveau comes from the vineyards in the south of the region, and accounts for the lion's share of their crop. This is basic Beaujolais country, the area where the wine is mostly straight AC Beaujolais, or, when the wine has one more degree of alcohol, Beaujolais Supérieur. However, north of the town of Villefranche the wine becomes more serious. The countryside is archetypally storybook: the hills are steep but rounded and wooded, the roads are narrow and winding, the streams gush, and the houses are red-roofed.

Some of the more serious Beaujolais is to be found under the appellation Beaujolais Villages. This comes from 39 villages in the region north of Villefranche. Beaujolais Nouveau Villages can be found, too, and it should be a cut above the straight Nouveau. But the cream of Beaujolais is found in the nine *crus*. These are St-Amour, Juliénas, Chénas, Moulin-à-Vent, Fleurie, Chiroubles, Morgon, Brouilly and Côte de Brouilly. The villages are situated in the north of Beaujolais, where the

Above: *A typically picturesque Beaujolais landscape. The best wines of Beaujolais come from the region to the north of Villefranche. This is the area where the nine* crus *are situated.*

Beaujolais Wines

Grape	Gamay.
Taste	All Beaujolais, coming from the Gamay grape, has a single basic taste: a supple plummy freshness, very clean, and very refreshing. With age, some of the bigger *crus* acquire a taste akin to that of burgundy.
Value	Beaujolais Nouveau is sold at some pretty cut-throat prices, so it has to be good value – providing the quality is not cut-throat, too. Fleurie is fashionable, so expensive – lesser-known *crus* can be better value.
Ageing potential	Nouveau can often last far longer than is generally realised – try it the following spring. And keep the bigger *crus*, like Côte de Brouilly, a big Morgon, or (especially) a Moulin-à-Vent, for three years or more.
Recommended producers	Henri de Villamont; Louis Jadot; Thorin; Chanut Frères; Georges Duboeuf; Louis Latour; Loron; Château de Juliénas; Louis Jête; Château de Moulin-à-Vent; Mommessin; Caveau de Fleurie; Pasquier-Desvignes; Jean Descombes; Jean Ruet; Depagneux; Ferraud; Sapin; Sarrou.
What to look for on the label	Single vineyard *cru* wines are worth looking out for, otherwise the name of the *négociant* is the best guide to quality. At Nouveau time, don't always be tempted to buy the cheapest, unless there is a reliable name on it.

Above: *Gathering Gamay grapes. Roughly half each year's crop (1,346,000hl of red were made in total in 1986) becomes Beaujolais Nouveau to be shipped to the customer as soon as it is ready.*

soil is different – more schistous, granitic and clayey than in the south, where marl and chalk predominate. The grape is the same, the Gamay Noir à Jus Blanc, to give it its full title, and the method of pruning the vines is the same. Gobelet is the usual technique here, although Guyot is sometimes used for basic Beaujolais.

The most northerly of the nine *crus* is St-Amour. Not seen in the shops as much as some, it is nevertheless a reliable wine and best drunk fairly young. Its neighbour Juliénas can be quite weighty, and worthy of ageing; often it is a bigger wine than St-Amour although the latter stands up well to some bottle age.

Chénas is probably the least well known of the nine. Its sales suffer accordingly, although they should not, because it is good, quite big, Beaujolais. South of Chénas lies Moulin-à-Vent, widely regarded as the best of the lot: solid wines, needing age, and acquiring with it a smell and taste more than slightly reminiscent of burgundy.

Just south of Moulin-à-Vent comes Fleurie, one of the lightest, but most fashionable, *crus*. It is plummy and chocolatey, and very attractive when young. It is not, however, as light as Chiroubles, which is the *cru* to drink before all the others.

Morgon can be quite big and tough, needing time in bottle to acquire the Burgundian tones of maturity, but some of the wines follow fashion and are made to be lighter. Brouilly is the largest appellation, producing one of the lightest growths, but Côte de Brouilly, coming from hillier vineyards, produces fuller wines.

RHÔNE

Key to map
1 Côte-Rôtie.
2 St-Joseph.
3 Hermitage.
4 Crozes-Hermitage.
5 Cornas.
6 Côtes du Rhône.
7 Châtillon-en-Diois.
8 Côtes du Vivarais.
9 Coteaux du Tricastin.
10 Gigondas.
11 Châteauneuf-du-Pape.
12 Lirac.
13 Tavel.
14 Côtes du Ventoux.
15 Côtes du Lubéron.

*I*f the finest reds of the north come from Bordeaux and Burgundy, it is the Rhône that puts the south through its paces. On the map the two look close together, with the smallest of gaps between the southern tip of Burgundy and the north of the Rhône vineyards: in geography, in climate, and above all in the style of the wine, they prove themselves to be a world apart.

Not that the Rhône can really be thought of as one area. The north-south divide is inescapable: the wines taste different; the countryside looks different. In the north, the river cuts its way through steep granite slopes on which the vineyards are angled to catch the sun: in the south it meanders flatly through hot, dry plains which, south of Avignon, abruptly become Provençal rather than Rhône.

The difference between north and south is crucial to understanding the wines of the Rhône. Those of the south are southern wines in every aspect: the climate is Mediterranean, and the grape varieties are those which reappear in Provence. In the north, all is changed. It is a staging post, if you like,

Above: *Picking the grapes in the vineyards of the Côtes du Rhône.*

between the restraint and elegance of the north and the broad generosity of the south, with good helpings of both. The wines are big, and tough, and tannic, often almost black in early youth, but mellowing over the years into elaborate nuances of flavour.

Lyon is actually further north than Bordeaux, but it is far inland, miles from any moderating sea breezes, and it feels like the south. The wines in the northern chunk of the Rhône vineyards are predominantly red, and they are, with a few notable exceptions from the south, the finest of the Rhône wines. The only red grape here is the Syrah, a heat-loving variety which yields pretty well, provided the weather during flowering is good enough to prevent *coulure*, to which it can be susceptible. The danger is less great now than it was because a lot of work was done on clonal selection in the 1970s, to produce more resistant vines. These tougher versions are, however, likely to produce higher yields of fruit which thus lack the concentration of flavour and colour produced by the older kind of vines.

Principal Grape Varieties
Carignan
Cinsault
Counoise (also known as Aubun)
Grenache Noir
Mourvèdre
Muscardin
Picpoul Noir
Syrah
Terret Noir
Vaccarèse
Viognier (white)

In the south, the single red variety is replaced by a complete menu of grapes, on which the Syrah appears but does not dominate. That role is often handed over to the Grenache, an altogether more typically southern vine that flourishes in a sun-baked landscape. It came originally from Spain, where it is widely grown in Rioja, Navarra and Catalonia. It produces wines that are high in alcohol and low in tannin, and are prone to oxidise: not, therefore, wines for a very long life. Châteauneuf-du-Pape, the most famous wine of the southern Rhône (indeed perhaps of the whole region), is based on Grenache and therefore will not last as long as the Syrahs of the north.

It is in the south of the Rhône that the term "red wine", which in the north means anything the red side of black, can extend to wines that really are little more than rosé as well. The range of colour here is enormous, and the shade of a wine depends on whether the blend relies on deeply-coloured grapes like Mourvèdre or Syrah, and how heavily the vines were pruned: with the Grenache, the larger the yield, and the less demanding the terrain, the lighter the wine. In fact the choices open to the winemaker in the southern Rhône are wider than perhaps anywhere else in France. Numerous grape varieties are open to him, and he can pick and choose among them as he pleases — for many ACs there is no set requirement.

ACs and their Red Wine Production (1986 vintage in hectolitres)
Châteauneuf-du-Pape (106,578)
Cornas (2,858)
Côte Rôtie (3,803)
Côtes du Rhône (1,954,554)
Côtes du Rhône-Villages (216,961)
Crozes-Hermitage (41,161)
Gigondas (37,622)
Hermitage (3,166)
Lirac (19,522)
Rasteau vdn (153)
St-Joseph (16,005)
Coteaux du Tricastin (86,026)
Côtes du Ventoux (254,182)
Châtillon-en-Diois (1,914)

*T*he most northerly Rhône appellation, Côte Rôtie, produces one of the most distinctive red wines in France, and one that at its best can stand alongside the finest from almost any region in the country. What makes Côte Rôtie different from other Rhônes is the 20 per cent of a temperamental, low-yielding white grape, the Viognier, that may be included in the blend of grapes. The Viognier produces only about 17hl/ha, but wine made from its grapes has a remarkable flowery-spicy character, full of body and finesse, and when it is added to the tough, tannic, blackcurranty Syrah it has the effect both of softening it, and adding a touch of floweriness. Without any Viognier added, Côte Rôtie can seem very green when young. Not that it is really a wine to drink young: it always needs several years to come round: usually about five, sometimes as many as ten or 15 may be needed.

The vines are grown beside the river, on slopes that are as steep as any in France, and the terraces have hardly changed since Roman times. The walls supporting the terraces are generally built without any cement, and so need regular attention: in addition, the granite-based soil is so rocky that planting new vines is pretty hard work. The Syrah vines are trained by the Guyot method along wires, and the slopes give them the best possible exposure to the sun. What is not such good news for Côte Rôtie are the newer plantings on the plateau at the top of the slopes. The soil is different, the exposure to the sun is different, the vines are planted further apart in order to allow for mechanical working of the vineyards, and the wines, so far at least, just do not have the concentration or depth of colour that is associated with good Côte Rôtie.

Of the traditional plantings, the best areas are the twin hillsides of the Côte Brune and the Côte Blonde. They make a good pair: dif-

ferent yet complementary, and the wines are often blended. The Côte Brune has clay soil, producing wines that are initially tough and chewy, but long-lasting; those coming from the limestone soil of the Côte Blonde have a touch of delicacy but a shorter life-span.

Inevitably, some Côte Rôtie is now being vinified so as to produce a light, fruity wine for drinking after only three or four years' ageing. The top growers, however, have not so far gone down this path. For them the rule is still a deep colour, no destalking of the grapes, and a long fermentation of up to 14 days, often in wooden vats.

Côte Rôtie is not, on the whole, one of the most high-tech appellations in France. There are a lot of old wooden barrels in evidence, some new ones, but not much stainless steel at all. It makes sense: ageing wine in wood does soften it more rapidly than leaving it in concrete or stainless steel, and providing hygiene is strict there is little reason for change. Chapoutier, one of the biggest (and best) Rhône companies, indeed make a virtue of being somewhat old-fashioned, and boast they tread the majority of their Syrah wines (including Côte Rôtie) by foot.

Below: *The Syrah is the main grape used in Côte Rôtie, but to it can be added up to 20 per cent Viognier, a low-yielding but intensely perfumed white variety.*

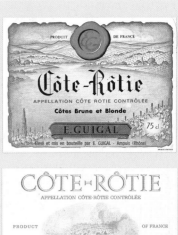

Left: *The characteristically terraced vineyards of the Côte Rôtie, the two slopes of which, the Côte Brune and the Côte Blonde, produce different styles of wine. The clay soil of the Côte Brune makes wines that are longer lasting.*

Côte Rôtie Wines

Grapes	Syrah and Viognier
Taste	Huge, chewy, blackcurrant tasting wines, with a softening edge of floweriness if Viognier has been added. With long ageing (up to ten years) they develop wonderful tarry complexities.
Value	Good. They are expensive, but the best ones are worth more.
Ageing potential	A wine from a good year and a good grower will need at least five, probably ten, years. Lesser years need less, and some wines are being made to be drunk within three or four years.
Recommended producers	E Guigal; Georges & Robert Jasmin; Guy Bernard; Emile Champet; M Chapoutier; Delas Frères; L de Vallouit; Alfred Gerin; Joseph Jamet; Vidal Fleury; George Vernay; Albert Dervieux; Chol et Fils; Les Jumelles from Paul Jaboulet Aîné.
What to look for on the label	If the wine is a blend of the Côte Blonde and the Côte Brune, it may well name both. Some growers produce individual vineyard wines, like Guigal's La Mouline and La Landonne: such are generally a grower's best.

The wines of Hermitage and of neighbouring Crozes-Hermitage come from regions that are close geographically, the names are similar enough to cause confusion, and the wines are similar too, but only up to a point. What, then, are the similarities and the differences?

The grape is the Syrah. Tough, rich, bursting with flavour, it soaks up the sun and the heat on the high Hermitage hill. Over at Crozes-Hermitage the slopes are gentler, and there is even some flat ground planted with vines, which makes Crozes-Hermitage one of the few communes in the northern Rhône where you can see vineyards being worked mechanically. Hermitage itself is too steep: here, it is necessary to grow the vines on terraces, as at Côte Rôtie, with all the manual labour that implies. The vines are trained by the Gobelet method, with the branches tied to wooden stakes. They have often been planted rather haphazardly over the years, with white Marsanne vines growing in among the rows of Syrah. Perhaps this, as much as the effect on the wine, explains why up to 15 per cent white grapes can be added to the fermentation vat for red Hermitage. This is also allowed in Crozes-Hermitage, although the white grapes there are usually both Marsanne and Roussanne. When used in this way, the white grapes have a softening effect on the wine.

Granite soil is the key to Hermitage, and to a lesser extent to Crozes-Hermitage also. The granite of the Hermitage hill serves to hold the heat during the day and to reflect it back on to the maturing grapes at night. Some of

Below: *Hermitage hill and the chapel from which it takes its name. The soil is granite, which retains the heat and produces tough and complex wines.*

Above: *A highly traditional way of submerging the* château *photographed at the house of Chapoutier. More commonly, a wooden* pichet *is used to do this.*

Tain is also the local centre for Hermitage.

Despite the similarities between the two wines, just noted, they nevertheless manage to be completely distinct. And if that implies that one is better, then yes, that is pretty fair. Hermitage is the bigger wine. It is huge and mouthfilling, tannic and rather unripe in flavour when young, just like many long-lived reds. Twenty years on, it is a different story. That is the time the best wines will take for all the promise of their deep-coloured, rather green-tasting youth to develop, and even a lesser wine from a lesser year will need five years or so. Then the full depth of flavour emerges, with all its complexities of blackcurrants and raspberries.

Crozes-Hermitage also has the ripe blackcurrant fruit of the Syrah when mature, but it is not so massive, and it matures more quickly – in roughly half the time, usually.

In both appellations, the style of the wine comes from the style of the vinification which is utterly traditional. The crushed grapes are fermented in open wooden vats, and if the temperature of fermentation seems to be getting too high, the *vigneron* takes a wooden implement called a *pichet*, and uses it to submerge the floating *château* of stalks and skins, so that the overall temperature will drop. In Hermitage the fermentation lasts at least two weeks (slightly less in Crozes-Hermitage), and then the new wine is run off into wooden barrels, to spend at least 12 months there. These can be small *pièces* of 225 litres, large *foudres* of 3,000 litres, or any size in between. Over in Crozes-Hermitage, the wood ageing is generally shorter, often of six months' duration upwards, simply because this suits the lighter style of the wine.

the best slopes at Crozes-Hermitage are also on granite – those of Gervans, for example, which produce a big wine, slow to develop. Other Crozes-Hermitage vineyards make lighter more delicate styles, and it is common in Crozes-Hermitage for all the wines of a grower's vineyards to be blended together to achieve just the right balance of characteristics. Crozes-Hermitage can come from any of 11 villages loosely grouped around the town of Tain. They are: Crozes-Hermitage itself (the wine used to be known as just "Crozes"); Serves; Gervans; Larnage: Evôme; Chanos-Curson; Mercurol; Pont-de-l'Isère; Beaumont-Moteaux and La Roche-de-Glun.

Hermitage and Crozes-Hermitage Wines

Grapes	Syrah, Marsanne and Roussanne
Taste	When properly aged, the wines have great depth and fruit to balance the tannin, and flavours of blackcurrant, raspberries and smoke.
Value	Hermitage tends to be more expensive than Crozes-Hermitage, and be better known. But both are good value for their quality.
Ageing potential	They not only benefit from ageing, they positively need it. Hermitage needs from five to 20 years to mature fully, depending on the quality of the wine and the vintage; Crozes-Hermitage roughly half that.
Recommended producers	(Hermitage) Jean-Louis Chave; Paul Jaboulet Aîné; M Chapoutier; Delas Frères; L de Vallouit; Jules Fayolle et ses Fils; Jean-Louis Grippat; Sorrel: the co-op at Tain. (Crozes-Hermitage) Paul Jaboulet Aîné (Domaine de Thalabert); Jean-Louis Pradelle; the co-op at Tain; Chapoutier et Cie; Bernard Chave; Collogne; Delas Frères; L de Vallouit; Raymond Roure; Jules Fayolle et ses Fils; Desmeure Père et Fils
What to look for on the label	Individual vineyard names, like Paul Jaboulet Aîné's La Chapelle at Hermitage.

St-Joseph and Cornas make an interesting yet contrasting pair. St-Joseph is the lightest red of the northern Rhône, while Cornas is the biggest. St-Joseph is an expanding appellation (although whether it is expanding in the right way for the future quality of the wine is another matter); Cornas is limited by the availability of land and the steepness of the slopes. What they do have in common are the Syrah grape, traditional winemaking methods, and response to market forces.

To say that St-Joseph is the lightest of the northern Rhônes does not mean that it is a light wine in absolute terms. Its colour can be almost black, its style uncompromising if it is compared with as light a wine as, say, Beaujolais. Nevertheless, it lacks the depth and solidity of Hermitage, compensating for lack of weight with greater fruitiness. Ten per cent of the volume can be made up with white grapes, which are Roussanne and Marsanne since the classier Viognier is not grown here. This is a comparatively new regulation, introduced in 1980, possibly more for expediency than for the sake of the wine.

But it is not the white grapes that make St-Joseph a relatively light wine. Partly the soil contributes to this, since it is not as granitic as at Hermitage, but contains clay and sand

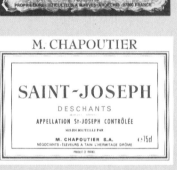

St-Joseph and Cornas Wines

Grapes	Syrah, Roussanne and Marsanne.
Taste	St-Joseph can be dark in colour but is nevertheless comparatively light and fruity. Cornas is the more massive of the two, softening with age though not developing the complexity of a Hermitage.
Value	Good, especially so because less known than some Rhône appellations.
Ageing potential	St-Joseph is usually best drunk within ten years; some of the lighter wines are at their best before the end of four or five years. Cornas needs longer, seven or eight years usually, and has a lifespan of up to 20 years.
Recommended producers	(St-Joseph) Pierre & Gustave Coursodon; Jean-Louis Grippat; Jean-Louis Chave; Jean Marsanne; Raymond Trollat; M Chapoutier; Delas Frères; L de Vallouit; Georges Vernay; Paul Jaboulet Aîné. (Cornas) Auguste Clape; Guy de Barjac; Marcel Juge; Delas Frères; Alain Voge; Marc Maurice; Louis Gilles; Robert Michel; Noel Verset.
What to look for on the label	There are few individual vineyard wines, so look for the name of the grower.

as well. In addition, the excellent exposure to the sun enjoyed by vines on the Hermitage hill is not to be found in St-Joseph. Furthermore, the new plantings have generally been made on the plain. New plantings are allowed because of the increased area given to the appellation in the 1970s, and production has increased dramatically. These newer vines have so far produced wines that are lighter than traditional St-Joseph, the best of which

Below: *Growers in St-Joseph may add the white Roussanne and Marsanne grapes to the classic red Syrah if they so wish.*

Below: *Châteaubourg in the appellation of St-Joseph. Wines from here are lighter in style than others from the northern Rhone; the soil partly accounts for this, but St-Joseph also lacks the excellent exposure to the sun enjoyed by its geographical neighbours.*

still comes from the long-standing quality centre of the appellation, the villages of Tournon, Mauves and St-Jean-de-Muzols. These maintain vineyards planted on slopes, which are, however, more expensive and obviously more difficult to work.

A similar experiment was tried at Cornas a few years ago, and vineyards were planted on some flat ground. Here, though, the growers made the wine, matured it, tasted it – and went back to the old plantings. Even the hard labour of tending these terraced vineyards was preferable, apparently, to the quality of wine produced by the plain.

If St-Joseph lacks really good exposure to the sun, Cornas has it in full measure. It is to the south of the (much larger) appellation of St-Joseph, also on the west bank of the river, but is sheltered from the driving Mistral wind, which is a major factor in keeping temperatures down in these parts. The soil at Cornas is different, too. There is clay and sand as well as granite, just as at St-Joseph, but the sand tends to be towards the southern end of the appellation where the lightest Cornas comes from, and there is a fair bit of limestone as well.

Whatever the dominant reason – and it is probably the microclimate – the wines of Cornas are massive. Seven to eight years' bottle ageing is not too much for them, and more is needed for more powerful vintages – 15, perhaps even 20 years. So, almost inevitably, some growers are making lighter wines for more immediate consumption. This is usually achieved by reducing the length of the fermentation, and then giving the wine less time in oak before bottling. Two years used to be the rule, now up to 18 months is common.

As demand for the wines increases, so does pressure on the growers to release them earlier. Cornas may not be one of the Rhône buzz words like Hermitage or Châteauneuf-du-Pape, but demand is steady. Expansion to increase production, however, is both difficult and unlikely in this region: work in such vineyards is harder, and financially less rewarding, than work in nearby Valence.

At Gigondas, we reach the southern Rhône. Instead of being strung out along the river banks like beads on a necklace, the wine communes here are more scattered, and often not even that close to the Rhône: Gigondas' nearest river is in fact the Ouvèze, a tributary which runs south-west to join the Rhône just north of Avignon. The southern terrain introduces more gentle slopes, with none of the steep terracing of the northern communes. Gobelet or Royat training is normally used for the vines, which also are different here: the Syrah's northern monopoly here gives way to a base of Gre-nache, which can form up to 65 per cent of the blend, plus Clairette, Cinsault, Mour-vèdre, and Syrah, with the last three forming at least 25 per cent.

Gigondas is one of the Rhône's success stories. Until 1953 it was just another rather anonymous Côtes du Rhône-producing com-mune, with no particular claim to fame, except that its wines were considered some-what better than run-of-the-mill Côtes du Rhône. They were not good enough to be made AC, though, and so the idea of giving them some other identity was born. Along with Gigondas, Cairanne, Chusclun and Lau-dun were given the right to call their wines Côtes du Rhône followed by the name of the village, and the new title proved a stimulus as well as a reward. The quality of the wine con-tinued to improve, the *vignerons* upgraded their vines, and in 1971 Gigondas became AC – so far the only one of the original four villages to do so.

It has quickly built up a following, too, because the wines are generally consistent. They are big, black, wines, with lots of fruit and lots of alcohol; too much alcohol can in fact be their disadvantage. The Grenache grape does tend to produce pretty heady wines, but since a Gigondas is generally a blend from vineyards all over the appellation, it is possible to mix in some less ripe grapes (if there are any!) to keep the strength down to below the 14° it can easily attain.

Gigondas is not essentially an elegant wine. It is very ripe, much broader in taste than the northern Rhônes, and with a black-berryish, slightly spicy earthiness – real *goût-de-terroir*. It is tremendously appeal-ing, but while the reds from further south, in Provence, are often best chilled and drunk in the summer, Gigondas is very much a winter wine, needing good strongly-flavoured food to accompany it.

Another of its attractions is that it is not a *vin de garde* (a wine that needs keeping) in the way that, say, Hermitage is. Grenache matures more quickly than Syrah, and a Gigondas is probably ready to drink after about five years. After eight years or so it will need drinking up before it starts to fade.

It is curious that the Grenache grape should do so well here, because normally it likes a much harsher environment – the stony ground of Provence, for example. The soil in Gigondas is basically clay on the higher slopes, which is quite rich, but

elsewhere there is stonier soil, and near the river Ouvèze, a lot of sand. Winemaking is traditional in style: a lot of wooden vats and barrels, some cement vats, but not much stainless steel to be seen. Some winemakers put all the different grape varieties into the fermenting vat together, while others prefer to ferment them separately and blend later on; either way, fermentation lasts from one to two weeks. Once that, and the malo-lactic, fermentation are both complete, the wine goes into cask to start is maturation, and in the past it used always to stay there for two years. Some growers still make their wines like that, and if the vintage is a tough one and can stand it it is a satisfactory method. But

Gigondas Wines

Grapes	Grenache, Clairette, Cinsault, Mouvèdre and Syrah.
Taste	Big, generous wines tasting of blackcurrants and blackberries, with a lot of *goût-de-terroir*.
Value	Pretty good. Less precipitous vineyards mean lower labour costs and often higher yields.
Ageing potential	The Grenache content makes it a wine to drink, not keep. It is good after about five years, less good after about eight.
Recommended producers	Roger Meffre; Gabriel Meffre; Les Fils de Les Pallières; Domaine de Longue-Toque; Château de Montmirail; Domaine de Raspail-Ay; Pascal (Domaine de Grand Montmirail); Pierre Amadieu; Domaine du Terme; Henri de Barruol; Domaine de la Tuilière; Château-St-André; Paul Jaboulet Aîné.
What to look for on the label	If you want individuality, choose a wine from a small grower. But the big concerns generally produce reliable wines, even if they lack a little excitement.

there are other winemakers who place a high value on aroma and finesse, and at such establishments the wine seldom stays in wood for longer than a year. As is so often the case, one method is not necessarily better than another. It is a question partly of the preferred style, and partly of the potential of the raw materials, the grapes.

Quite a lot of Gigondas is produced in bulk. Small *vignerons* exist, of course, but there are also large scale operations like Meffre whose vineyards, often on the plains that stretch, dotted with vines, to the horizon, are designed to be worked mechanically, and whose wines are shipped in bulk, as well as in bottle. Some of these companies' best wines can be very good, but inevitably the lesser ones tend to lack the individual touch.

Below: *The vine-bearing slopes of Gigondas at the foot of the Dentelles de Montmirail are much gentler than those of the northern Rhône. The soil on the hills is basically clay.*

*I*t was at this village near Avignon that Clément built his château when he became Pope in 1309 – hence the name. It was intended as a summer retreat, and Clément's successor at Avignon also proved fond of it. But after 1410 the papacy was based solely in Rome, and Châteauneuf's brief fame expired. In the 19th Century, however, the wine acquired a notoriety of a sort because it was used as a booster wine for Burgundy, to be added to the vats when the Burgundian summer had failed to produce wines of sufficient colour or alcohol to satisfy its customers.

However, this should not imply that the winemakers did not care what was sold under the commune name. Châteauneuf-du-Pape was the first place in France to lay down strict rules for the production and nature of its wines. These laws were passed in 1923, and later became incorporated into the *Appellation Contrôlée* laws. They included a delimitation of the area according to the soil, with only the poorest soil being allowed to grow vines. The practical test was that if only lavender and thyme could grow there, it was permissible to plant vines. The permitted vine varieties (13 of them in all) were listed, along with the pruning and training methods to be used. The resulting grapes have to be sorted before fermentation, with at least five per cent being rejected (and usually used to make *rapé*, a thin-tasting wine that livens up the working day in the vineyards). Pink Châteauneuf-du-Pape was banned in the same original laws. A tasting panel was also established, which had to taste all wines before they could be sold under the commune name. This was revolutionary in France in

1923, and still is in some parts of the vinous world. Finally, a minimum alcoholic content of 12.5° was established, the highest in France. It is not difficult for the wines to exceed this minimum with room to spare, if the alcoholic Grenache is grown in quantity: 13° or 14° for Châteauneuf-du-Pape is not unusual.

The amount of Grenache in the blend is generally lower than it used to be, although Chapoutier use around 80 per cent for theirs. Of the 13 permitted varieties, eight are red, and apart from Grenache, consist of Syrah, Mourvèdre, Muscardin, Vaccarèse, Cinsault, Terret Noir and Counoise. The white varieties are Clairette, Bourboulenc, Picpoul, Picardin and Roussanne, and one or two other white grapes like Grenache Blanc and Terret Blanc, also appear in the vineyards.

The Syrah, in particular, has increased in popularity down here, presumably because it provides rich flavours and good colour; Mourvèdre does that too, but can be a little hard, and Cinsault on its own tends to lack colour. But whether or not Châteauneuf winemakers use all eight varieties for their blend, they will defend the inclusion of whatever they do use on the grounds that each gives its own particular quality to the wine.

The result of having so many possible permutations is that it is very difficult to say exactly what Châteauneuf-du-Pape tastes like, especially with at least 1,000 Châteauneufs on the market. Some winemakers are also using *macération carbonique* for a part of their crop which, if it is not overdone, can give the wine more fresh fruit aroma and flavour without making it all taste like Beau-

Châteauneuf-du-Pape Wines

Grapes	Grenache dominates, but there are 13 permitted varieties, 8 red and 5 white (see text).
Taste	It is hard to say what is typical, but a lovely southern raspberry and blackcurrant fruitiness is often present, with considerable tannin. *Macération carbonique* is often used to "lift" the fruit.
Value	A famous name, so there are not too many bargains to be had. But the quality is good to very good.
Ageing potential	The wines should be drunk between 4/5 and 12 years old, depending on the vintage. They need some time for the tannin to smooth out, but with the exception of a few estates are not long keepers.
Recommended producers	Château Fortia; Château de Beaucastel; Château Rayas; Domaine Chante-Cigale; Domaine du Vieux Télégraphe; Domaine de Beaurenard; Domaine de la Nerte; Clos du Mont-Olivet; Les Cailloux; Domaine de Mont-Redon; Domaine de Nalys; Chante-Perdrix, Les Clefs d'Or; Domaine de la Bernardine from Chapoutier, especially the Grande Cuvée; Domaine du Grand Tinel; Domaine de la Solitude; Le Bosquet des Papes.
What to look for on the label	Look at the bottle, not just the label: a fair proportion of the wine is sold in bulk, but growers who bottle themselves are entitled to use a bottle embossed with the papal coat of arms, plus the words "Châteauneuf-du-Pape Contrôlée".

Above: *The unmistakeable soil of Châteauneuf-du-Pape. The stones absorb heat during the day, and radiate it at night, helping the grapes to ripen.*

jolais. Mostly, Châteauneuf-du-Pape is deep in colour, and high in both tannin and fruit flavours. Its staying power, though, does not resemble that of the Syrah-based wines of the northern Rhône: it needs perhaps four or five years to mature, but will seldom keep entirely happily after about 12 unless it is a very big, concentrated wine. What is likely to happen then is that the fruit fades, particularly if the Grenache is involved in large quantities, and you are left with tannin, which is far less appealing on the palate.

If one part of Châteauneuf's fame lies in its varied blend of grapes, another must stem from its soil. There are no steep terraces here, and the vineyards are covered with large pebbles and stones. They do not make planting vines very easy, especially since all but the Syrah are generally Gobelet-pruned, necessitating one hole for the vine and another for its accompanying stake, but the advantage is that the stones hold the heat. Having absorbed sunshine throughout the day, they reflect it back on to the vines at night, which works wonders for the maturation of the grapes. The north and north-west of the appellation are the stoniest areas, with a preponderance of gravel in the south, and some sand and clay in the east and north-east. Single vineyard wines are not the norm here, however; instead wines from different sites are blended together to create the style of wine that each individual winemaker desires. As so many grape varieties are involved, the blending of Châteauneuf-du-Pape is a tremendous art.

*L*irac is, one might say, the red version of Tavel – what Tavel might produce if it discarded rosé and opted for more colour. The two communes are certainly close together, on the other (westerly) side of the Rhône from the other major red appellations like Gigondas and Châteauneuf-du-Pape. Moreover, Lirac used to be a predominantly rosé appellation, until the growers took a closer look at the market and decided that what most people want is red wine; this is what they predominantly make now.

It is, though, a light red, not in the normal Rhône blockbuster mould. Lirac is a wine for the summer, for drinking slightly chilled, and for drinking young. It will cope with fairly strongly-flavoured food, and there are some wines made to be more robust, but its attraction lies in its lightness and fruitiness.

The grapes are typical of the south. Grenache forms the basis of plantings, but there is plenty of Syrah, Clairette and Mourvèdre also. The white Ugni Blanc is also planted, along with Bourboulenc, Calitor, Picpoul, Maccabéo and Carignan, the last-named, however, being grown less and less. It may not form more than ten per cent of the production of a vineyard.

The freshness of the wine is something that the winemakers like to accentuate, so there is a certain amount of macerating the grapes under carbonic gas at the more progressive domaines. Otherwise growers tend to destalk the grapes and crush them before fermentation, which lasts up to eight days or so. Wood ageing is a rarity. All this helps Lirac keep its attractively uncomplicated style.

The soil is not greatly different from that of Châteauneuf-du-Pape. There are areas where it is just as stony, with the soil otherwise sandy, and here, as in the more famous appellation, the stones perform the function of soaking up the southern heat during the day and radiating it out again at night, thus giving the grapes a helping hand in their maturation. Vines have been grown here since Roman days (such a history is commonplace in the Rhône) but quite a lot of Lirac is of pretty recent cultivation and is now based on four villages: Lirac itself, Roquemaure, nearer the Rhône; St-Laurent-des-Arbres and St-Genies-de-Comolas. It has been AC since 1945.

Its greatest recent expansion came in the 1960s, when some *pieds noirs* from newly-independent Algeria arrived and took up vinegrowing, as they did in so many parts of southern France. Land that was forest and scrub – the sort of scrub that extends for miles in the Midi – was cleared and planted with vines, and the results have been successful. The plateau near Roquemaure was also largely cleared and planted at this time (apart from this one area, most of the vineyards are on slopes).

One reason why there was so much land available for clearance (it could not happen, for example, in the Médoc) was that in the latter part of the 19th Century phylloxera had dealt such a blow to the vineyards that other

crops had tended to be grown thereafter. Phylloxera was devastating everywhere, of course, but Lirac did not enjoy the reputation that would enable it to charge high prices for its wines, and thus make replanting worthwhile. After the First World War, too, there was a general move away from employment in the vineyards.

Phylloxera was particularly bad news for Lirac because many growers claim that the first outbreak in France occurred here. The story (possibly apocryphal) is that an innovative grower at the Château de Clary brought over some native American vines to see how they would fare in his vineyards. Such vines

are not only immune to the phylloxera louse; they also have it with them as a constant companion. Inevitably, the phylloxera spread to the French vines and the rest, as they say, is history. Wine, incidentally, is still made at Château de Clary.

Above: *Lirac. Apart from this village, wines from three other villages are entitled to the Lirac appellation: they are Roquemaure, St-Laurent-des-Arbres, and St-Genies-de-Comolas. Lirac wines are light and fruity.*

Lirac Wines

Grapes	Principally Grenache, Syrah, Clairette and Mourvèdre. (Also Ugni Blanc, Bourboulenc, Calitor, Picpoul, Maccabéo and Carignan).
Taste	The reds are light, without the massive alcohol of, say, Châteauneuf-du-Pape, and with lots of appealing plummy fruit. They can be very good lightly chilled.
Value	Good, because the wines are not too well known – yet.
Ageing potential	Really best drunk young. Some more robust wines are made, however, which will keep six or seven years.
Recommended producers	Domaine du Château St-Roch; Château de Ségriès; Domaine de Castel Oualou; Château de Clary; Philippe Testut; Domaine du Devoy; Domaine de la Tour de Lirac; Domaine de Sablon; Cave Coopérative de Roquemaure; Domaine Méjan; La Fermade; Gabriel Rondil et Fils; Domaine Rousseau.

The basic appellation wine of the Rhône is Côtes du Rhône; below this level lie *vin de pays* and *vin de table*. Sometimes, tasting some of the wine that appears under the Côtes du Rhône label on the shop shelves, one is tempted to question which is the better value. Nevertheless, it is Côtes du Rhône that has the AC. It comes from a large area – the whole lower Rhône valley, in fact – and accounts for roughly 80 per cent of all AC wine made south of Vienne and north of Avignon. Given that, one should not expect too much of it. A lot of it is sold in bulk and most is produced by local *caves coopératives*; it has no pretensions to greater glory.

The next step up is Côtes du Rhône-Villages: the wine from a series of villages in the Côtes du Rhône, all of which are considered to make wine above the basic appellation level, but not quite far enough above to justify having their own appellation. The Villages system in the Rhône was started in 1953, when four villages were so promoted, and allowed to sell their wine as Côtes du Rhône, followed by the village name – Côtes du Rhône Chusclan, for example. Those first four were, apart from Chusclan, Laudun, Cairanne and Gigondas. The last-named has since acquired its own individual AC, and the remaining three have been joined by Vacqueyras, and then Vinsobres. A total of 17 villages now come into the appellation, which was given its final form in 1967 (see table). Two of the names on the Villages list have other connotations: Beaumes de Venise is more famous abroad for its *vin doux naturel* made from the Muscat grape, and Rasteau, too, makes a vdn, this time from Grenache. Most of it is vinified as white wine, although there is a little red made.

The differences between Côtes du Rhône and Côtes du Rhône-Villages start in the vineyard. For Côtes du Rhône, the only restrictions on vine varieties are that they must not be hybrid, and that Carignan must not form more than 30 per cent of the vineyard.

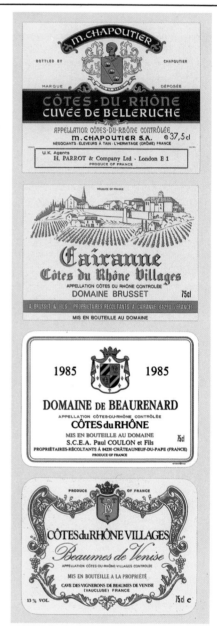

The Côtes du Rhône Villages

There are currently 17 villages in the Côtes du Rhône region which are entitled to use their name and the appellation *Côtes du Rhône-Villages*:

Beaumes de Venise
Cairanne
Chusclan
Laudun
Rasteau
Roaix
Rochegude
Rousset-les-Vignes
Sablet
St-Gervais
St-Maurice-sur-Eygues
St-Pantaléon-les-Vignes
Séguret
Vacqueyras
Valréas
Vinsobres
Visan

Below: *Regulations governing grape yields are stricter for Côtes du Rhône-Villages than plain Côtes du Rhône.*

Côtes du Rhône Wines

Grapes	Grenache, Syrah, Mourvèdre, Cinsault and Carignan.
Taste	The most attractive have a soft, earthy taste of raspberries, very typical of the south, and not too much tannin.
Value	The better ones are good value, and reliable. But the tendency is to make wine to a price, which can result in a lowering of quality.
Ageing potential	Best drunk young, within three or four years.
Recommended producers	Domaine des Travers; L'Oratoire St-Martin; Domaine Rousseau, Cave des Quatre Chemins, Domaine Pélaquié, Château Redortier; Domaine des Richards; Château l'Estagnol; Jacques Sabatior; Joseph Pinet.
What to look for on the label	A lot of the wines are sold in bulk, and are generally sound, but unexciting. Wines from a good *négociant* can be better, but the most interesting probably come from individual domaines, so look for the grower's name.

If a grower has vineyards in the appropriate commune and aspires to make Villages wine (because vineyards in, say, Cairanne, can also make basic Côtes du Rhône, if those are the rules the grower wants to stick to), he has to have no more than 65 per cent Grenache in his vineyard, and at least 25 per cent of Syrah, Mourvèdre and Cinsault, either individually or in any combination. Both appellations, then, are flexible, and the grower has a lot of room for experiment. He can even make single varietal wines, if he wants to.

For Villages wine, the maximum yield is 3,500 litres per hectare, and for Côtes du Rhône, 5,000l/ha. The Villages figure can be raised in particularly abundant years, but even so, there is a problem. If the vineyard over-produces, as many do, the wine that cannot be sold as AC Côtes du Rhône-Villages must be demoted to *vin de pays*. So it can be financially to the grower's advantage to aim for a higher yield, and sell the whole lot as AC Côtes du Rhône – at least he is getting an AC price for all of it.

The soil and winemaking vary not so much according to the AC as according to the individual village or grower: the land can be clay, or limestone, or sand, or gravel, or endless combinations of these. It is Mistral country – the wind whips across the gentle slopes and flat plains, and it can be surprisingly bleak in the winter. The wines in general are not intended to be kept for long periods, although a grower with a high proportion of Syrah and some wooden vats can overturn that theory.

To the north east of the sprawling Côtes du Rhône lies the VDQS area called Côtes du Vivarais, which grows the same grape varieties plus Gamay. Nearly all the wine is red, and provides a slightly lighter alternative to the AC wine. On the other side of the Rhône there is the area of Haut-Comtat. Hardly anything is sold under this name these days, as most of the wine is from the villages of Rousset and St-Pantaléon-les-Vignes, and can be sold as Côtes du Rhône-Villages.

Below: *Séguret is one of the 17 villages that are entitled to use their own names with the Côtes du Rhône-Villages AC.*

In the annals of the Rhône, 1974 was a good year. It was then that the Côtes du Ventoux, Coteaux du Tricastin and Chatillon-en-Diois all became appellation contrôlée, whereas previously they had been VDQS.

First of all, how do they fit into the Rhône? Well, they are really slightly peripheral areas, not slotting into the Rhône hierarchy. The Côtes du Ventoux is a huge, sprawling region to the east and south-east of the Côtes du Rhône; the Coteaux du Tricastin is more compact, and adjoins the Côtes du Rhône to the north-west. The least known of the three, Chatillon-en-Diois, is situated about half way down the Rhône vineyards, out to the east a little way, and is actually on the Drôme river. Chatillon-en-Diois comes in all three colours and is made largely by the Cave Coopérative de Die – the same co-operative that is responsible for much of the production of Clairette de Die. The latter is quite popular, reliable fizz; the red tends to get fewer accolades. The grapes used are quite respectable, 75 per cent minimum of Gamay, and 25 per cent maximum of Syrah and Pinot Noir, but the wines are not deep in either colour or flavour, and they tend to lack distinction.

The Côtes du Ventoux is more typical Rhône in both grapes and character. The blend of grapes used is much the same as that of the Côtes du Rhône: Grenache, Carignan, Mourvèdre, Syrah and Cinsault, but the wines are lighter. The reds are sometimes hardly darker than rosés, and they are delicious when drunk young and cool, when all their lively fruit comes through. The wine-making is partly responsible for the wines' style, with a short (48-hour) fermentation followed by a brief period in the vat, and then bottling and sale. And sale should be quickly followed by drinking because Côtes du Ventoux are not wines to keep. The area is quite hilly, and the vineyards are higher up than

Above: *These vines will produce Rasteau which can either be a Côtes du Rhône-Villages red, or a sweet fortified* vin doux naturel. *Red Rasteau vdn is made from Grenache grapes.*

their Côtes du Rhône neighbours, which might account for some of the difference in style. The soil also counts – here it varies between gravel, clay, chalk and sand.

In the Coteaux du Tricastin the soil is much stonier – in places, indeed, it is as stony as that of Châteauneuf-du-Pape. And just as the stones hold the heat and help the ripening of the grapes there, so they do in the Coteaux du Tricastin, which in turn means that the wine is bigger than that of the Côtes

Above: *A proud* vigneron *from the Côtes du Ventoux. Wines from this region tend to be light for early drinking.*

tion lasting from four to six days, the grapes having been crushed and destalked beforehand. Bottling takes place some months after the fermentation, and the blend (50 to 60 per cent Grenache, around 15 per cent Cinsault, about 20 per cent Syrah, Mourvèdre and Carignan) was intended, when it was first specified under the AC rules, to resemble that of Châteauneuf-du-Pape. It was possible to lay down a permitted blend with such ease when the region became AC because its promotion coincided with a great expansion in the vineyard area. It had been a fast-growing region before 1974, and with promotion to AC, ground was planted that had not borne vines since the days of phylloxera, making it possible to plan the area's future with great care and deliberation.

There is one more AC wine in the Rhône to consider and, by way of contrast, it is high in alcohol, deep in colour, and sweet. It is a *vin doux naturel*, made from the Grenache grape, from Rasteau. Rasteau is also one of the 17 villages that figure in the Côtes du Rhône-Villages AC, but this vdn is another matter. Rasteau vdn is a specialised taste, acquiring with age a madeira-like flavour to which the term "rancio" is applied. Rancio Rasteau is prized locally, but not so much abroad. Most of it is vinified as a white wine; the colour tends to be rather murky and unattractive when it is vinified as a red, although some is made.

du Ventoux, and more resembles Côtes du Rhône in style. The colour is deeper, the flavour is bigger, with lots of fruit. However, there is still not a lot of tannin and the wines are not really keepers.

The winemaking is based on a fermenta-

Côtes du Ventoux, Rasteau and Coteaux du Tricastin Wines

Grapes	Grenache, Carignan, Mourvèdre, Syrah and Cinsault.
Taste	Côtes du Ventoux has lots of fresh, raspberry-type fruit; Coteaux du Tricastin is somewhat bigger, with a broad, southern earthiness to it. But neither can compete in terms of alcohol or sheer mouth-fillingness with Rasteau, which has the toffeeish taste of Grenache plus, when older, a flavour which resembles the tang of Madeira.
Value	Good. The table wines are not expensive, and make reliable drinking. Rasteau is not cheap, on the other hand, and is an acquired taste.
Ageing potential	Drink the table wines young; most are best drunk before they are two or three years old. To ensure a consistent style, Rasteau vdn is mostly a blend of different years; aficionados say it needs four or five years in cask before bottling.
Recommended producers	(Rasteau) The Cave des Vignerons make a red; most others stick to white. (Côtes du Ventoux) Domaine de Tenon; Château du Vieux-Lazaret; Domaine Ste-Croix; most Caves Coopératives; Domaine des Anges; Domaine St Sauveur; La Vieille Ferme. (Coteaux du Tricastin) Domaine de Grangeneuve; Domaine de la Tour d'Elyssas; Cave Coopérative Le Cellier des Templiers; Berthet-Rayne, Père et Fils; Paul Berthet; Les Cellier des Dauphins; Domaine du Vieux Micocoulier; Domaine des Lônes. (Chatillon-en-Diois) Cave Coopérative de Die.
What to look for on the label	Côtes du Ventoux and Coteaux du Tricastin are widely sold in bulk, so there is likely to be a *négociant*'s name on the bottle. Most are perfectly reliable, but a grower's wine would be worth trying for interest.

The Loire is white wine country. Muscadet, Saumur, Sancerre, Pouilly – these are familiar names; Chinon, Bourgueil, or Sancerre Rouge are comparatively neglected. This only goes to show how illogical wine fashions are, because the reds have got fresh young fruit, not too much alcohol, and they taste good. They are not that cheap, but then nor are the whites these days, and price does not seem to hold *them* back.

In order to come to terms with the diversity of red wines produced in this region, it helps to divide the vineyards into four separate areas, just as we do for the whites. These are Muscadet, Anjou-Saumur, Touraine, and Sancerre. The Muscadet region is near the sea. There is little red here, except for the VDQS region of Coteaux d'Ancenis on the right (or northern) bank of the river. The grapes are Gamay and Cabernet Franc and the prevailing atmosphere of this Atlantic coast end of the river is maritime, with the sea's influence moderating climatic extremes, which helps to explain why the wines are light.

Moving inland, we come to Anjou-Saumur. This is a red wine area on a much bigger scale – still not outdoing the white in quantity, but producing some good quality wines. Saumur and Saumur-Champigny are the stars, par-

ticularly the latter. Both are made from Cabernet Franc and Cabernet Sauvignon with some Pineau d'Aunis. There are other reds worth considering also: Anjou can produce red as well as pink or white, and there is Gamay d'Anjou, and a VDQS or two to take note of. The climate, as one goes up river, changes, becoming less maritime and gradually more continental in character, and the soil changes, too. There is a lot of clay in the Muscadet region, and chalky-clay in Anjou-Saumur and Touraine. Having said this, one should be wary of generalizing about such large winegrowing areas when it comes to soil, because it does of course vary tremendously; and climate can be greatly influenced by a microclimate.

In Touraine, the red wines to look out for are Bourgueil and Chinon, both AC and often remarkably good, and St-Nicolas-de-Bourgueil, which is similar to Bourgueil. Touraine AC can be red (and almost anything else), as can Touraine-Amboise and Touraine-Mesland, and numerous VDQS areas also produce red wine in this region.

The next stop is much further inland, at Sancerre. The official name for this region is Central Vineyards, because that is just where they are – in the middle of France. The climate is continental, geographically Sancerre

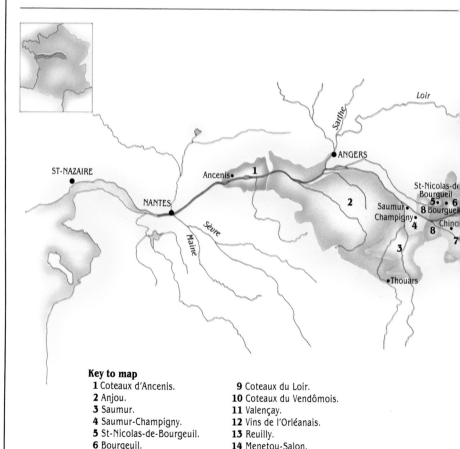

Key to map

1 Coteaux d'Ancenis.
2 Anjou.
3 Saumur.
4 Saumur-Champigny.
5 St-Nicolas-de-Bourgueil.
6 Bourgueil.
7 Chinon.
8 Touraine.

9 Coteaux du Loir.
10 Coteaux du Vendômois.
11 Valençay.
12 Vins de l'Orléanais.
13 Reuilly.
14 Menetou-Salon.
15 Sancerre.
16 Coteaux du Giennois.

Above: *Réné Marchais with his range of wines from Quincy in the eastern Loire.*

is nearer to Burgundy than it is to Nantes, and the grape for the reds is, unsurprisingly, the Pinot Noir. The region also includes Menetou-Salon, better known for its whites, but making reds as well, and Reuilly – and again, an awful lot of VDQS regions.

In general, Loire reds are not great wines. They are simple, uncomplicated, and slip down deceptively easily on a warm day. Dependent though they are on the quality of each vintage, they are just not the sort of wines to inspire learned discussions of vintages. Small growers abound, while few internationally-known big companies are involved in their export. The wines tend to be imported in small quantities, through specialists who love the wine, but cannot get the huge quantities they would need to make it a nationwide sales success. So much the better for people who like it as it is.

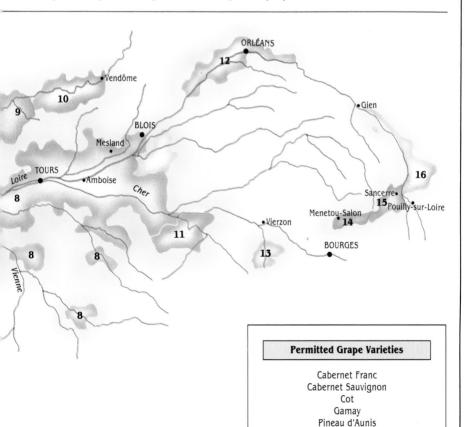

Permitted Grape Varieties

Cabernet Franc
Cabernet Sauvignon
Cot
Gamay
Pineau d'Aunis
Pinot Gris
Pinot Meunier

Anjou and Saumur are equally famous for their châteaux and their rosé wines, but while the châteaux continue to draw the crowds, year after year, the rosé is, well, fading. Rosé wine is just not as popular as it used to be, and so the growers have been turning their attention to the question of what else to do with all those red grapes that make the pink wine. The obvious answer is to make red wine. Production of red has risen, and along with the quantity, the quality has gone up too.

The problems associated with red wine making in the Loire are typically those of any northern region. Basically, it is a question of ripeness. The climate in this part of the Loire is temperate, but the Cabernet and Gamay grapes still do not achieve the sugar levels that they do further south where they get more heat from the sun. And as well as being fairly light in alcohol (which can be an advantage in these health-conscious times) they also tend to be light in colour. The traditional solution to this was a long maceration on the skins, to leach out every drop of colour, but this created its own problems. Colour is extracted in the early stages of the fermentation process; later, what you mostly get is tannin, and often too much of it. As a result, the winemakers' efforts to produce deep coloured reds could, in poorer years, result in lean, hard wines that were not at all the sort of gulpable fruity glassfuls that people wanted.

Advances in vinification have changed things. A shorter maceration of around three to five days, rather than ten or 12 days, avoids too much tannin, while the use of rotating drums which maintain the fermenting must at the right temperature while mixing the skins gently with the liquid, ensures plenty of colour and fruit. Another method is to bubble nitrogen through the fermenting must to mix in the skins – a technique more suitable for smaller scale wineries. The effect is similar: more fruit, more colour, more aroma, but less tannin. Sometimes the must is heated, too, to get the fermentation off to a quick start, because again, colour is extracted from the skins early in the process.

The main red grape in these parts is the Cabernet. Most of it is Cabernet Franc, but there is some Cabernet Sauvignon as well, and some Pineau d'Aunis. The characteristic grassiness and blackcurrant fruit taste of the Cabernet is nicely apparent in the wines. Vintages are important this far north, and in cool summers the wines can be unpleasantly high in acidity. But when the weather gets it right, the results can be delicious.

The basic ACs are Anjou and Saumur, and both come in pink and white forms as well as red. Saumur-Champigny is a cut above either, with a little more concentration, a little more depth – but again, steer clear of the off years. Saumur-Champigny is nearly all Cabernet Franc, and comes from a small region squeezed between the left bank of the Loire and the Saumur appellation. The soil in this eastern part of Anjou-Saumur is mostly a hard chalk called *tuffeau*, which is solid enough for caves to have been cut from it. Drive along the Loire and you will see such caves cut into the rock face, many of these actually fully equipped and furnished as dwellings and inhabited.

Apart from the Cabernet-based wines, there is also Anjou-Gamay. The Gamay is a less stylish grape than the Cabernet, but if you forget about stylishness and instead think in terms of *macération carbonique* and young, fresh, Beaujolais-type wine, you will find some good bottles. It is worth bearing in mind that Beaujolais is quite a long way further south, and further inland, than Anjou, and so the Gamay from Anjou will be a lighter wine altogether. But sometimes that is no bad thing.

Right: *Harvesting Gamay grapes in the Loire region. Gamay from Anjou resembles Beaujolais in style, especially if a touch of* macération carbonique *has been used in its production.*

Anjou-Saumur Wines

Grapes	Cabernet Franc, Cabernet Sauvignon, Gamay and Pineau d'Aunis.
Taste	The Cabernet-based reds have the blackcurranty grassiness of the grape about them, plus a lot of freshness. Anjou-Gamay tastes, not surprisingly, like Beaujolais, but is generally a bit lighter.
Value	Good when compared with the more fashionable Sancerre Rouge, not so good if the benchmark is *petit château* claret or even some Beaujolais.
Ageing potential	The usual advice is "drink young". The better vintages, though, will keep for several years.
Recommended producers	Paul Filliatreau; Château de Chaintre; Maurice Rebeilleau; Domaine des Roches Neuves; Château de Targe; Vignerons de Saumur; Les Caves de la Loire; Bouvet-Ladubay; P Tijou; Château de la Roche.
What to look for on the label	The grape name will in some cases be stated on the label. But mostly check the name of the appellation, because there are so many in the Loire, with similar names but different flavours. Cabernet d'Anjou, for example, is not a red at all, but a sweetish rosé.

The red wines of Chinon and Bourgeuil are light in colour and alcohol, coming from this far north, but providing that the winemaker knows how to go about extracting all the fruit and ripeness from the grapes, they can be delicious. Bourgeuil is often the earthier of the two, and sometimes the longer-lasting wine, while Chinon has finesse and elegance, and is the more approachable wine early on.

The grapes are the same for both: mostly Cabernet Franc, with up to 20 per cent Cabernet Sauvignon permitted, although often this is not grown. Most Bourgeuil, and Chinon too, is a blend from the various areas within the appellation. There are eight communes within the Bourgeuil region, including St-Nicolas-de-Bourgeuil, which has its own separate appellation. The soil is different in the St-Nicolas-de-Bourgeuil area, somewhat sandier, hence the distinction. Bourgeuil in general has three soil types, each of which introduces its own character in the wine: flat, sandy areas where vines are grown on what patches of gravel there are; sand mixed with gravel, for bigger wines; and clay and limestone on south-facing slopes with plenty of sun and not much rain, which produce lean, firm wines that keep well.

Chinon also has its variations. The 17 communes that are included in the AC cover areas of flat sand and gravel; areas of clay and gravel for wines with more depth; and the most favoured, the *coteaux* – clay and lime slopes or plateaux, which encourage roundness and fruit in the wines. Again, blends of wines from different areas are the norm, although it is possible to find single-vineyard examples.

When we look at the other appellations besides Chinon and Bourgeuil, it is soon evident that the grapes involved are far more

---

Touraine and Eastern Loire Wines

Grapes	Cabernet Franc, Cabernet Sauvignon, Cot, Pinot Meunier, Pinot Noir, Pineau d'Aunis and Gamay.
Taste	All these are relatively light wines, but the Cabernet-based ones have plenty of grassy raspberry fruit (which can taste stalky in poorer years), and the Gamay wines can be as attractive as Beaujolais. Freshness and crispness are among their stronger points. The Pinot Noir wines have good fruit, combined with quite high acidity and plenty of bite.
Value	Fairly good for Touraine wines, because they are little known outside the region. However, few Loire wines these days are particularly cheap, and red Sancerre is frankly poor value.
Ageing potential	Chinon and Bourgeuil can be drunk the year after the vintage, but in good years (and particularly if they are among the weightier examples of wines) they will keep five years or more. Red Sancerre is usually best drunk young, though in better years it may warrant three or four years' ageing.
Recommended producers	Couly-Dutheil, especially their Clos de l'Echo; Plouzeau et Fils; Audebert et Fils; Charles Joguet; Olga Raffault; Raymond Raffault; Jean-François Olek; Lamé-Delille-Boucard; Aimé-Boucher; Joel Taluau; the Confrérie de Oisly et Thésée; Henri Marionnet; Jean Vacheron; Henri Nather; Vincent Delaporte; André Dezat; Michel Thomas.
What to look for on the label	There may be a grape variety stated, usually Gamay or Cabernet, if the wine is made entirely from that grape. There are few single vineyard wines and a few brand names, but most wine from, say, Bourgeuil, will be called simply after the name of the appellation.

varied. Not just Cabernet Franc and Cabernet Sauvignon can be grown for red AC Touraine, but also Cot, Pinot Meunier, Pinot Gris, Pineau d'Aunis and Gamay. The latter, ever-popular and, when from Beaujolais, pretty expensive, is often undercut in price by Gamay de Touraine. Of the other varieties, the better wines tend to come from Cabernet, with the lesser grapes making, not surprisingly, lesser wines.

Certain towns are allowed to add their names to that of Touraine, and thus have their own separate appellations. Amboise is one of these, and the appellation of Touraine-Amboise covers eight communes. Touraine-Mesland is further east, and produces some good reds, including some attractive Gamays.

The visitor has to head north to reach the Coteaux du Loir, which is not a misprint but a region centred on the Loir river, a tributary of the Loire. Twenty-two communes make up the appellation and the main grapes are the Pineaux d'Aunis, with Cabernet, Gamay and Cot also grown. The wines are appealing, but so little is grown that exports are not really a practical proposition.

Continuing up the Loire, we reach Sancerre, where red wines only form less than one sixth of the total wine production of the area. But for some reason, red Sancerre has suddenly become fashionable, especially in smart Parisian restaurants, even though, on the whole, the white is better. Partly this is because the Pinot Noir vines are not always planted in the best places – indeed, sometimes they are in the worst, on land that was considered unsuitable for Sauvignon. North-facing slopes, for example, are not exactly ideal for red grapes this far north. There are, of course, exceptions, and it is the exceptions that make the decent Sancerre Rouge.

But exposure to the sun is not the only quality factor. The soil is another, and there are three basic types: the slopes around Chavignol are chalky; stony soil predominates on the lower slopes around Bué; and clay and chalk in the Ménétréol area. There are 14 communes in all, including Sancerre itself, and vineyard holdings per grower are small, in an area which is in itself one of the smallest of the Loire appellations.

With the Pinot Noir grape still surviving in Sancerre, one might imagine that some red wines would emerge from Pouilly-sur-Loire just across the river. But in fact this appellation is totally white, and to find more reds one has to go to the west side of Sancerre, to Menetou-Salon. Here we find the same grape, a very similar wine, but lower prices because fashion has yet to discover it. The soil is mostly chalky, and the climate can be better than in Sancerre, with consequent better ripening conditions for the Pinot Noir.

To travel south-west to Reuilly is to leave the Loire totally behind. There is a river there, flanking the vineyards, but it is the Arnon, a tributary of the Loire, and it is a smaller proposition altogether. The reds are few and far between, made from the Pinot Noir and Pinot Gris grapes, and from soil that is limey and not so very unlike that of Chablis.

Of the VDQS areas, Cheverny has not been VDQS all that long, and the grapes are typical Loire: Cabernet Franc or Cabernet Sauvignon, Gamay and Pinot Noir or Cot. Quality is high, and the wines are best drunk young. The same goes for red Coteaux du Vendômois, from Pinot Noir, Cabernet, Gamay and Pineau d'Aunis. They are best drunk early. Valencay grows Cabernet Franc, Cabernet Sauvignon, Gamay, Cot and Pineau d'Aunis, but production is small.

Moving further into central France, the VDQS areas are numerous, but hardly important. The biggest production is of Côtes d'Auvergne, which come under the general heading of Loire wines, although they bear more resemblance to Beaujolais. Vin d'Orléanais is attractive, but little exported, and Côtes Roannaises, too, is drunk mostly locally. The Gamay is the only grape here. Saint-Pourçain-sur-Sioule is made from Pinot Noir and Gamay, and resembles Beaujolais if the latter is dominant in the blend; Gamay, too, is grown for Côtes du Forez. The same grapes make Coteaux du Giennois and Châteaumeillant, with the addition of Pinot Gris for the latter.

Below: *Cask ageing of red Chinon wine in the cellars of the long-established firm of Maison Couly-Dutheil.*

avoie and the Jura are not great red wine producing areas. Most of the grapes grown on these hillsides are white, and it is the whites that have built up the areas' reputations. Nevertheless, the reds are worth a closer look (even if you have to go to France to look at them closely – few are exported) because they are so different from the other AC reds of France. In the Jura, to be sure, the Pinot Noir grape appears, but so do Trousseau and Poulsard; in Savoie, Gamay and Pinot Noir are both grown, but the wine you should make an effort to seek out is that made from Mondeuse.

The Jura is, geographically, fairly close to Burgundy and Beaujolais, but it looks very different. The terrain is mountainous rather than hilly, and the climate of cold winters, often wet summers and long, warm autumns, means that only those slopes that will catch as much sunshine as possible are planted with vines. Even there, the vines are grown only between 250m and just under 500m altitude. Yields are fairly low – 40hl/ha for Arbois, for example – the spring frosts often contributing to this scarcity. Given the climate, it is perhaps not surprising that the Pinot Noir from here is light, with the weightier wines coming from the Trousseau. Poulsard grapes, which are grown only in the foothills of the Jura mountains, in the Revermont area, do not possess much colour, and the result is often more rosé than red.

ACs and their Red Wine Production (1986 vintage in hectolitres)		
Arbois Arbois Pupillin	}	(23,021)
Côtes du Jura (7,596)		
Vin de Savoie (30,315)		

The soil is generally clay, with a lot of limestone in the south, and marl in the AC of Arbois. Thirteen communes are included in this appellation, and the three red grapes can be blended or made as varietals; the commune of Pupillin has its own AC of Arbois Pupillin. The other AC for reds is Côtes du Jura, in the south, where the minimum alcohol content of the wine is just 10°.

The wine picture in Savoie is, like that in the Jura, dominated by white. The reds are AC Vin de Savoie, the region's biggest AC. The Gamay was imported from Beaujolais after phylloxera, but Mondeuse had been growing here long before that, and is still popular. Pinot Noir is also grown, and 20 per cent white grapes (the main ones grown are Chasselas, Chardonnay, Aligoté, Jacquère and Altesse) may be added at fermentation stage. However, this seldom happens.

Certain communes have the right to put their names on the label of AC Vin de Savoie: they justify the privilege by lower yields (35hl/

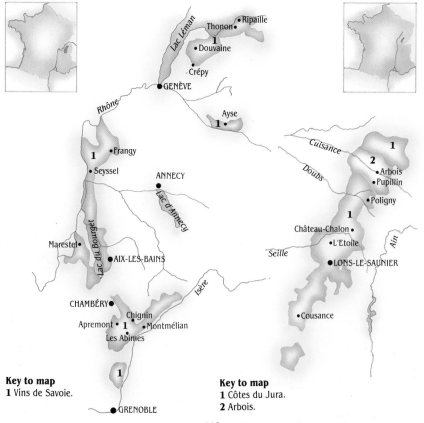

Key to map
1 Vins de Savoie.

Key to map
1 Côtes du Jura.
2 Arbois.

Above: *Vines on the slopes of Savoie grow in a climate that is cool, with summers that are often wet. Only the sunniest slopes are suitable for viticulture and yields are quite low.*

ha) and higher alcohol (9.5° minimum). These communes are: Chautagne; Montmélain; Chignin; Chignin-Bergeron; Ripaille; Apremont; Abymes; Ayse; Jongieux; Charpinnat; Marignan; St-Jean-de-la-Porte; Ste-Marie-d'Alloix; Arbin; Cruet; and Saint-Jeoire-Prieuré.

When it comes to VDQS wines, as is the case with Vin de Savoie, 20 per cent white grapes can be added to the Pinot Noir, Gamay, Poulsard and Mondeuse that are grown for Bugey. Again, it does not necessarily happen. Varietal wines may be produced, in which case the label will state the grape. Cerdon sells wines under its own name, or puts its name alongside that of the better-known Bugey.

Jura and Savoie Wines

Grapes	Gamay, Pinot Noir, Mondeuse, Trousseau, Poulsard.
Taste	The Trousseau grape makes full-bodied wines with plenty of colour and tannin, and is often blended with Pinot Noir. The latter is recognisably Burgundian in style, though not in weight. Mondeuse has more fruit, and is big enough to stand up to strongly flavoured food.
Value	Arbois and Côtes du Jura are generally more expensive than Savoie, and there are better value wines to be found. But these wines have distinctive characters, and are worth paying a little more for, in order to experience.
Ageing potential	Mondeuse lasts the longest, needing several years to mature; Trousseau, too, needs time. The Gamay, on the other hand, is best drunk young, within a year or so of the harvest.
Recommended producers	(Jura) Henri Maire; Hubert Clavelin; Lucien Aviet; Jacques Foret; Roger Lornet; Désiré Petit et Fils; Rolet Père et Fils; (Savoie) Cave Coopérative des Vins Fins Cruet; J Girard; André Quénard et Fils.
What to look for on the label	If the wine is made from a single grape variety the label will generally say so, which is useful if you want to sample one of the oddites. Otherwise, look out for the communes allowed to sell wines under their own names, or to put their names alongside those of the AC.

ACs and their Red Wine Production
(1986 vintage in hectolitres)

Béarn (9,965)
Bergerac (236,613)
Cahors (183,247)
Côtes de Bergerac (30,049)
Buzet (75,258)
Côtes de Duras (43,361)
Côtes du Frontonnais (78,926)
Gaillac (53,843)
Irouléguy (3,898)
Madiran (54,171)
Pécharmant (12,708)

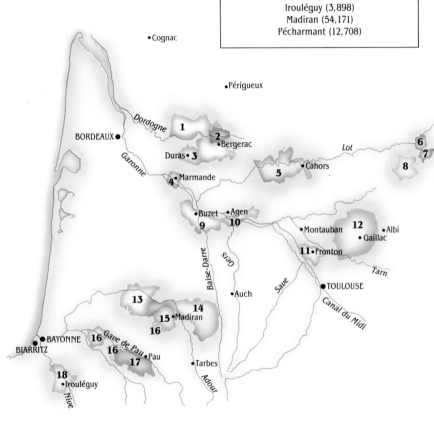

1 Bergerac.
2 Pécharmant.
3 Côtes de Duras.
4 Côtes du Marmandais.
5 Cahors.
6 Vins d'Entraygues.
7 Vins d'Estaing.
8 Vins de Marcillac.
9 Côtes de Buzet.
10 Côtes du Brulhois.
11 Côtes du Frontonnais.
12 Gaillac.
13 Tursan.
14 Côtes de St-Mont.
15 Madiran.
16 Béarn.
17 Jurançon.
18 Irouléguy

Permitted Grape Varieties

Abouriou
Cabernet Franc
Cabernet Sauvignon
Cinsault
Courbu Noir
Duras
Fer
Gamay
Jurançon Noir
Malbec
Manseng Noir
Mauzac
Merlot
Negret
Portugais Bleu
Syrah
Tannat

*T*he South-West is a catch-all term. It encompasses wines that are practically Spanish, so far into the Basque country is their area of origin, as well as those which would, were they a few kilometres nearer the Gironde, be blessed with the appellation of Bordeaux. It includes a number of wines which are pretty well unknown to the average drinker and a few which used to be very well known indeed but which have fallen from popularity. Some, like Cahors, have changed their style in recent years and are now making wines that are for immediate drinking, not just for keeping and admiring; others are using traditional grapes and methods to make wines that owe nothing to modern commercial tastes.

Basically they fall into two styles. There are the quasi-Bordeaux wines – Bergerac, Côtes de Duras, and Buzet in particular. Geographically, they are close to Bordeaux and they use the familiar Bordelais vines. The flavours are familiar, and there are a number of properties, particularly in Bergerac, that are busy producing reds that can sometimes beat the Médoc at its own game.

And then there are the others. The most commercially important vinous product south-west of Bordeaux is probably Armagnac, but on the edges of the Armagnac region, and scattered all around it, are areas like Madiran, Gaillac, and Béarn – the last of these being split into four separate parts. The grapes used in these wines might be the classics, like Cabernet, and there might even be some early-drinking Gamay, but chances are there will also be some local varieties that have been grown for centuries and which probably are used nowhere else in France.

Above: *Vineyards in Madiran. Some of the permitted grapes in this region are used nowhere else in France, and produce wines with a very distinctive character.*

That means, of course, that they are not commercial in style. They do not fit into the conventional pattern, and often are not produced in large enough quantities to be sold abroad, anyway. On top of this, buyers are generally conservative in what they buy. There are plenty of wine merchants who admire Madiran. Some of them have even tried to sell it. Most of them have given up, not because they cannot get supplies, and not because the wines are not good enough. It is simply that they are unknown, and while you can suggest to your customers that they might like to try this interesting little wine from south-west France, they are liable to look at the label, and then opt for a claret.

In the past the toughest of the red wines of the South-West were used to beef up the paler, weaker offerings from Bordeaux. That has all changed now. The appellation laws prohibit this sort of blending, while phylloxera devastated many of the vineyards, damaging the industry far more seriously than a mere market slump could ever have done. These days, too, the south-west of France is no longer the tourist centre that it once was; the world no longer flocks to Biarritz and Pau to spend the winter. This all means that the wines of the South-West are unfashionable and relatively little known at the moment. However, for the more adventurous there are many wines that are worth seeking out.

From the wine point of view, the only reason that Bergerac does not qualify as Bordeaux- is that the line had to be drawn somewhere. Certainly, in style the wines are lighter, but they are unmistakeably claret-like, and the classic claret grapes — Merlot, Cabernet Sauvignon and Cabernet Franc — are used, along with Malbec and Fer. Indeed, it would be surprising if this were not the case, since the Bergerac vineyards are an extension of the Libourne area: continue west along the D936 from the town of Bergerac, and before long you will find yourself in St-Emilion.

Given its proximity to St-Emilion, it comes as no surprise that the Merlot is the most popular grape for Bergerac's reds. When it goes into basic Bergerac it makes wine that is light in both colour and weight, needing only 10° alcohol to obtain the appellation; Côtes de Bergerac has to have 11°, and stands in rather the same relationship to plain Bergerac as does Bordeaux Supérieur to basic Bordeaux.

The best red of the region, however, is Pécharmant. A small area on the right bank of the river Dordogne, this region only grows Cabernet Sauvignon, Cabernet Franc, Malbec and Merlot to make its AC reds, and the results are quite different from the "petit Bordeaux" style of Bergerac. They are bigger, more deeply coloured wines with at least 11° alcohol, and generous fruit, and they need several years' ageing. They are more expensive than Bergerac, but well worth it; this is a region that, so far at least, is sticking to making the sort of wines it knows best, and very good they are too.

To the south of Bergerac, and near Bordeaux's Entre-Deux-Mers region, lies the Côtes de Duras. In fact it is an extension of Entre-Deux-Mers much in the same way that Bergerac is of St-Emilion, and the wines are

light, Bordelais in style, and made from the Bordeaux varieties of Cabernet Sauvignon, Cabernet Franc, Malbec and Merlot. Cabernet Sauvignon predominates, with around 60 per cent of the vineyard area being planted with this. The wines are pleasing, but have yet to attract international attention in the way that the reds of Bergerac are beginning to do. Quite a lot of them are made to be soft and fruity with the aid of *macération carbo-*

Below: *The Merlot grape is popular in Bergerac, making a light wine in style.*

nique. The soil in the Côtes de Duras is limestone and clay, the former being typical of white wine areas; the whites of the region are certainly better known than the reds, but the latter are worth seeking out for their round fruit and attractive rusticity.

Much bigger in style are the reds of Buzet. This region, just to the north of Armagnac, was badly hit by phylloxera but the gravel and chalky clay slopes were replanted and yield Cabernet Sauvignon, Cabernet Franc, Malbec and Merlot grapes for tannic, long-lived wines. The bulk of the area's production comes from the local Coopérative des Producteurs Réunis, and is matured entirely in oak – though not necessarily new oak. This sort of treatment of course produces wines that are different from the norm for country wines, but as well as being distinctive, Buzet reds are approachable. The co-op's top wine, Cuvée Napoleon, is particularly good.

The notable VDQS wines of this area are Côtes du Marmandais and Côtes de Bruhlois. Since Côtes du Marmandais is largely red, and squeezed in between Entre-Deux-Mers, Buzet and Duras, the natural wine for it to produce would be a Bordeaux style. Obligingly, it does so, but only up to 50 per cent of the wine has to come from the Bordelais varieties of Cabernet Sauvignon, Cabernet Franc and Merlot. The other half (at least) has to use Gamay, Syrah, Malbec, and the local varieties Fer and Abouriou. The resulting wine is soft and fruity, light and well-balanced. So if you have ever wondered what Abouriou tastes like, Côtes du Marmandais could be your best chance of finding out. To the south-east, the Côtes de Bruhlois is a more recent promotion to VDQS: the wines have good fruit and colour, and are typical country wines.

Below: *A maître de chai of the Buzet co-op assessing the colour of the wine.*

Bergerac, Buzet, Pécharmant and Côtes de Duras Wines

Grapes	Cabernet Sauvignon, Cabernet Franc, Merlot, Malbec, Fer.
Taste	Given the grape varieties, it is not surprising that the wines from this area resemble claret. Generally they are well-rounded, with generous fruit, and often can be quite light. The biggest wines come from Pécharmant.
Value	Often very good. They tend to be cheaper than Bordeaux, perhaps because of their lack of fame, but the quality can be equivalent.
Ageing potential	Best drunk within a few years of the vintage. Pécharmant is the main exception, but even this is not a wine for long-keeping.
Recommended producers	(Bergerac) Clos la Croix-Blanche; Château la Jaubertie; Château de Panisseau; Château Puy-Servain; Château la Raye. (Pécharmant) Cave Coopérative de Bergerac; Château de Tiregand; Domaine du Haut-Pécharmant. (Côtes de Duras) Domaine de Ferrant; Domaine de Durand. (Buzet) Coopérative des Producteurs Réunis; Domaine de Versailles.

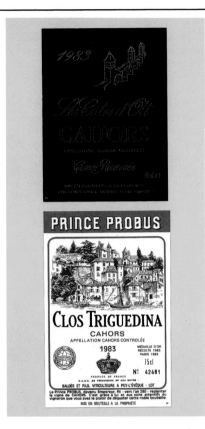

ahors used to be known as the "black wine": it is still often referred to in that way, but nowadays it is not such an accurate description. Cahors can be beefy, tough, and dark in colour, but compared with its earlier style, it is now a lightweight. The traditional type of Cahors was ultra long-lived – 80 years old and still going strong was perfectly possible, and wine that lives that long takes a fair while to mature. But few drinkers these days, brought up on Beaujolais Nouveau, want to buy wine for their as yet unthought-of grandchildren. So in recent years Cahors has become more accessible.

The predominant grape is still the Auxerrois (alias Cot or Malbec) with some Tannat, Merlot and Jurançon. Seventy per cent of the blend in fact has to be Auxerrois, and the percentage can be higher; Merlot and Tannat are not permitted to exceed 20 per cent each even though the Merlot might be presumed to have a softening influence: Tannat tends to make rather hard wine. Jurançon is being used less and less. In 1990 it will be limited to ten per cent, and there are some who favour phasing it out altogether. Wine made from it is apt to fade away very quickly after the malolactic fermentation has taken place, and that is not much use even for modern lighter-style Cahors.

Cahors' delimited vineyards are set in some of the most beautiful scenery in France, a wonderful blend of richness and arid rockiness. The region is situated to the south-east of Bordeaux and north of the city of Toulouse, in an area which has yet to be discovered by many tourists. It is a quiet, traditional place, the sort of wine region where you would expect to find growers tending their own smallholdings of vines, and then taking their grapes to the local co-opérative at vintage time. Such indeed is the case: the co-op at Parnac is big, modern and accounts for much of Cahors production. But there are also some enterprising growers

bottling under their own labels – and in some cases, with some enterprising thoughts on what those labels should say. Georges Vigouroux at Château de Haute-Serre, for example, decided that his vineyards were in a better spot than most in Cahors, so he started calling his wine "Coteaux de Cahors". The authorities and the *Repression des Fraudes* did not like it, but so far they have not stopped him

Below: *Cahors vineyards at Pescadoires during the severe winter of 1984-5. Such snow is rare in these regions.*

Cahors Wines

Grapes	Auxerrois, Tannat, Merlot, Jurançon.
Taste	Cahors still tend to be fairly big wines, to be taken seriously, and with considerable tannin when young. Some are lighter than others but these days the really long-maturing "black" wines are a thing of the past. Look for rich blackberry fruit with a smoky, tarry edge – and tannin.
Value	These are by no means the cheapest of the country wines of the South-West, but they are among the best, and the most international in style.
Ageing potential	This depends very much on the style. Four to six years is a good rule, but many can be drunk earlier.
Recommended producers	The co-opérative at Parnac, which uses a number of different labels; so look for the name Les Côtes d'Olt, often in small print at the bottom of the label. Château de Chambert; Clos la Coutale; Clos de Gamot; Domaine de Gaudou; Château de Haute-Serre; Domaine Lou-Camp-del-Saltre; Clos Triguedina; Château St-Didier-Parnac; Domaine de Paillas; Château Cayrou.
What to look for on the label	Most wines come from the co-opérative at Parnac; otherwise look out for the wines of an individual producer.

from using the term, and now other growers have followed suit and started using it, too.

The dry stony tablelands of Cahors, with their clay soil, and the lower alluvial terraces, are well-sheltered and have a climate that is remarkably reliable: they tell you that it never rains, for example, at the equinoxes. Most of the vineyards are near the river Lot, which meanders through the middle of Cahors. However, where the alluvial soil is too rich, no vines are planted.

Fermentation still lasts for a fairly long period: 15 to 21 days is the norm, and temperature-controlled fermentation has been the best technological news that Cahors has had in a long time. 28 to 30° is the usual fermentation temperature now, and, to prevent too much tannin in the wine, from 1988 all grapes are to be destalked before pressing. The alcohol content, though, is not as high as one might expect for such big wines: a minimum of 10.5° is required, and a maximum of 13° is allowed.

Below: *In the cellars of Château St-Didier-Parnac. The style of Cahors as a whole has lightened over recent years.*

aillac has some of the oldest vineyards in France; some claim that they predate those of Bordeaux. But Bordeaux need not be too worried about them because, older or not, at the moment they do not pose much of a threat to the supremacy of the Gironde. It has to be said, in fairness, that Gaillac growers are not trying simply to ape the Bordeaux style. Bordelais grapes are grown there, but only alongside some very little known varieties indeed, and the menu of grapes available means that red Gaillac can be found in a number of different styles.

At their best the reds have lots of ripe, peppery fruit and an individual character that comes partly from all those strange grapes. But a fair chunk of the production is in the hands of the local co-operatives, and while co-ops may make perfectly sound wine, it is seldom particularly exciting. There are, though, some good individual growers who care sufficiently about what they make to produce the sort of Gaillac on which reputations could be built.

The vineyards fall into several sectors: the Premières Côtes for whites, the Hauts Coteaux (on the east bank of the Tarn) and Cordais areas, and the vineyards on the plain. The red wine is produced where gravel soil occurs. Varieties like Cabernet Sauvignon, Cabernet Franc and Merlot are familiar, but they are in a minority, being used alongside Jurançon Rouge, Portugais Bleu and Mauzac. At least 60 per cent of the wine must be made from the far more esoteric varieties of Negrette, Fer, and Duras, plus Gamay and

Gaillac Wines

Grapes	Jurançon Rouge, Portugais Bleu, Mauzac, Negrette, Fer, Duras, Gamay, Syrah, plus Bordelais varieties (see text).
Taste	The wide variety of grapes available means that a number of styles of Gaillac are produced. The better reds have good, ripe, peppery fruit.
Value	Good Gaillac is good value. There is an awful lot of Gaillac that is not particularly exciting, but with the right grower you should be in luck. Côtes du Fronton, too, is not expensive – although it could seem so once you have added on the air fare to Toulouse you need in order to taste it.
Ageing potential	The reds are quite firm but not as long-lived as they used to be. However, styles vary considerably, and the longevity of the wines depends very much on the style of their producer.
Recommended producers	(Gaillac) Domaine Jean Cros; Domaine de Labarthe; Château de Rhodes; Domaine Clement Termes; Mas d'Aurel; Domaine des Bouscaillons; Mas Pignou. (Fronton) Château Bellevue la Forêt; Domaine de la Colombière; Château Cransac; Domaine de Baudare; the co-operative at Villaudric.
What to look for on the label	It is very much a question of finding a good grower whose style you like, and sticking with him.

Syrah. A certain amount of carbonic maceration has found its way into the area, so some of the reds are made to be drunk early, even as *primeurs*.

The winemaking has changed over the years, and not just with the advent of Cabernet Sauvignon and carbonic maceration. In the past (going back quite a long way) long ageing in both barrel and bottle was considered essential for red Gaillac. Thankfully that is no longer the case – whoever would want to treat a country wine like that these days?

To the west of Gaillac lies the smaller region of Côtes de Fronton. The production is not huge, and most of it gets drunk locally, which is rather a shame, since it is a red worth seeking out. It has only been AC since 1975 and again the grape names take some getting used to: Negrette accounts for up to 70 per cent of the blend, with Mauzac, the increasingly popular Gamay, and Cabernet Sauvignon, Cabernet Franc, Malbec, Syrah and Cinsault making up the rest. The wines

are well structured, with silky ripe fruit, and can last three or four years if the temptation to drink them young is avoided.

To the north-west of Gaillac are found the VDQS Vins d'Entraygues et du Fel; Vins d'Estaing and Vins de Marcillac. Cabernet Sauvignon is grown for all of them albeit as part of a selection of grapes: Cabernet Franc, Fer, Gamay, Merlot, Pinot Noir, Negrette, Jurançon Noir for the first two, and Merlot, Jurançon Noir and Gamay for the third. Vins de Marcillac are the biggest, most rustic of the three, the other two are much lighter. Nearer Fronton lies Lavilledieu, made from at least 35 per cent Negrette, plus Gamay and the other indigenous varieties: Jurançon Noir, Fer, Picpoul, Mauzac Noir.

Below: *The old and the new: on the right is Marcillac producer Laurens-Teulier's open wooden vat where the ripest grapes are pressed by foot; below it is a conventional modern horizontal press.*

Most wines are produced in just one region, and if you look at a map there it will be, outlined, named and delimited. Béarn, however, is different: there are four Béarn-producing areas, all separate from one another, and two of them (Madiran and Jurançon) produce other delimited wines as well. If this sounds surprising, remember that this is the Basque country, and things are surprising here.

The first, most northerly, Béarn, is next to the Armagnac region, and much of it, on the map, is liable to be labelled Madiran, with just a couple of small patches of land on its south-western edge noted as Béarn. The reason is that while the Madiran area is, strictly speaking, part of the Béarn area, Madiran wine is by far the better known of the two (although that is not saying a great deal).

To the south-west of Madiran, just below the town of Pau, lies Jurançon. That, too, is a part of Béarn, and adjoining its north-western edge is a piece of land that may only make Béarn, rather than Béarn and/or Jurançon.

The final chunk of Béarn (further to the north-west) may produce only wine labelled as that, so is rather less confusing than the other areas. Whites and rosés are made as well, the rosés probably being the best; the reds are full bodied, traditional in style and with all the character of the region. Cabernet Sauvignon and Cabernet Franc are grown, along with Tannat (which can comprise a maximum of 60 per cent of the wine), Manseng Noir, Fer and Courbu Noir. This part of the world includes the Gave valley, the soil of which is gravelly. The Gave river itself splits a little to the west of the two southerly Béarn regions; to the north is the Gave de Pau, which runs through the town of Pau while the Gave d'Oloron winds its way just to the south of the region.

Probably the best red of this part of the south-west is made in Madiran. Tannat is the

Above: *The up-to-date chais at Château d'Arricau-Bordes. The Tannat and* Cabernet grapes for its Madiran wine are *vinified in stainless steel.*

Béarn, Madiran and Irouléguy Wines

Grapes	A wide variety are available including Tannat, Manseng Noir, Fer, Cabernet Sauvignon, Cabernet Franc, and Courbu Noir (see text for regional varieties).
Taste	Styles vary, with Béarn at the lighter end, Madiran the weightiest, and Irouléguy somewhere in the middle. The last two have attractively spicy fruit and full flavour.
Value	These are quite good value country wines; it is a pity that they are so difficult to find in export markets.
Ageing potential	Madiran is best kept for a few years; the others can be drunk quite young.
Recommended producers	(Béarn) Cave Cooperative de Bellocq; (Irouléguy) Cave Cooperative d'Irouléguy; (Madiran) Producteurs de Plaimont; Lafitte Père et Fils; Vignerons Réunis du Vic-Bilh; GAEC Vignobles Laplace; Domaine Barrejat; André Dufau Père et Fils.

main grape here and, as its name suggests, it gives plenty of tannin to the wine. It can be so tough when young that it has to spend 20 months softening in wood before it may be bottled, and it is still quite long lived after that. The Tannat grape is generally held to be the secret behind Madiran's individual style, and there are those who say that too much Cabernet detracts from the character of the wine. Others maintain that the vineyards used to be predominantly Cabernet, and that the Tannat was introduced for the sake of its higher yields. Perhaps a comparison of two varietal styles is the way to choose which you prefer. The other permitted grapes are Cabernet Franc and Fer.

Further to the south-west, right on the border with Spain, lies Irouléguy. Where the vineyards actually straddle the border, on the Spanish side the area is known as Chacoli. The names of the French wine-making communes here sound as ancient as anyone would wish: St-Jean-Pied-de-Port; St-

Above: Château d'Arricau-Bordes in the south-west of the Madiran area has been extensively restored by its present owners, Henri and Gilbert Terradot.

Etienne-de-Baïgorry; Anhaux; Jaxu. The Tannat and Fer make spicy, often tannic reds. Cabernet Sauvignon and Cabernet Franc are also used, and they are being planted now rather more than the indigenous varieties. But the Tannat must still form 50 per cent of the blend. All the wines come from the local co-operative, and have an alcohol level between the minimum of 10° and the maximum of 14°. To the north of Madiran lie the VDQS districts of Tursan and Côtes de St-Mont. Both resemble Madiran in miniature, with Tannat forming the major part of both. Both Cabernets are also grown, but with the addition of Merlot for Côtes de St-Mont, and Fer for Tursan. Both wines are quite solid; most come from the co-op in Plaimont.

LANGUEDOC-ROUSSILLON

Languedoc-Roussillon comprises France's biggest vineyard: 40 per cent of France's wine production comes from here. It is densely planted and the hot, dry terrain is noted for producing wines that are more remarkable for their quantity than their class. Certainly, quite a lot of the notorious French wine lake derives from this part of the country. However Languedoc-Roussillon also produces a large percentage of France's AC wine.

Clearly much more is going on here than just the industrial production of *gros rouge* for sale in returnable bottles. The trend is towards better quality; even in France, people are drinking less cheap wine and the over-production problems of the EEC at the lower end of the market are huge. The option of growing other crops often is not available to the *vigneron* in Languedoc-Roussillon, for the simple reason that parts of the region are so arid that nothing will grow there except vines and olives. So, in the circumstances, the only alternative was to start making better wines.

The first step was better vines. Most of the region is still given over to Carignan, and Carignan seldom makes exciting wine. But more and more varieties are now appearing: the Syrah, for example, that produces top class wine in the uncompromising climate of the Northern Rhône valley; the Mourvèdre, which adds structure and tannin to the wine; the Grenache, which makes a wine that is rich and round, though not necessarily for long-keeping. And, surprise, surprise, Cabernet Sauvignon, Cabernet Franc and Merlot. Cabernet does well in California, runs the argument, so why not in the Midi? The overall effect of these new plantings has been to lift the quality of the wines, but the mere fact that growers want to plant them, and want to produce better wines, must in itself affect

Key to map
1 Banyuls.
2 Collioure.
3 Côtes du Roussillon.
4 Rivesaltes.
5 Côtes d'Agly.
6 Maury.
7 Fitou.
8 Corbières.
9 Minervois.
10 St-Chinian.
11 Faugères.
12 Coteaux du Languedoc.
13 Costières du Gard.

their methods of production. Once you start experimenting with different vines, you look again at your winemaking, or even at whether it is worth your while bottling your wine yourself, rather than simply carting your grapes to the local co-op.

So new winemaking methods have been making themselves felt. *Macération carbonique*, popular in neighbouring Provence, is being used to produce maximum fruit and freshness from the often unpromising Carignan, and the current market preference for more flavour and less alcohol is reaching even the more conservative producers.

Languedoc-Roussillon has been obtaining tangible rewards for all those efforts for some years now. The original AC areas were Fitou and Collioure. In 1983 St-Chinian was promoted, the following year Minervois became AC, and then Corbières, too, was upgraded. Apart from the most recent promotions of a handful or two of previously VDQS areas, the other ACs are the Côtes du Roussillon and Côtes du Roussillon-Villages, of which Latour-de-France and Caramany have their own appellations. At the eastern end of the region, Faugères is also AC.

Then there are the *vins doux naturels* (VDN). These are a Roussillon speciality, and Grand Roussillon is the most general appellation. More specific appellations are Maury, Banyuls, Rivesaltes and Côtes d'Agly. All these may be red. There are others too, but although calling a Muscat vdn "white" may seem to be stretching the definition of the colour, it is made from white grapes.

Above: *A sun-baked Coteaux du Languedoc landscape near Roujan, to the north-west of Pézenas. Wine production throughout this region is very high.*

Permitted AC Grape Varieties	
Carignan	Picpoul
Cinsault	Syrah
Grenache	Terret Noir
Mourvèdre	

Major ACs and their Red Wine Production (1986 vintage in hectolitres)
Faugères (54,420)
St-Chinian (67,233)
Fitou (80,307)
Corbières (635,577)
Minervois (252,594)
Collioure (6,585)
Côtes du Roussillon (305,075)
Côtes du Roussillon-Villages (93,118)

*T*he Minervois has not been AC territory for very long, but for some while before its promotion in 1984 people were saying it was the most promising area in this part of the Midi. Now it has made the AC grade, and people are still saying it. The wines have got potential, and now its a question of their becoming better known. As they do, they will presumably become more expensive – this has happened so far with practically every wine that has become popular – but for the moment, Minervois is in that happy position (for the buyer) of being both cheap and good.

The area itself is fairly large, although not on the same scale as Corbières, which is separated from Minervois by the valley of the Aude. On the southerly, Corbières side of the Aude begin the first hills of the Pyrénées; on the Minervois side the hills represent the earliest signs of the Massif Central. Vines are planted not just on the hillsides, but also on the gravel soil alongside the river. Gravel is generally fine for vines, but in Minervois it is the hillside vines that are the best. Here the soil is basically limestone, but there are areas too of stones or schist. The vineyards are separated into five basic areas. The eastern plain, with its comparatively rainy climate, produces light reds; on the flat land near the Aude, the opposite is the case; hot dry weather conditions produce fuller wines. To the north, where the hills begin, the wines keep longer, and in the north-east corner, where the climate is at its most uncompromising, the wines are the real keepers, well-structured and tough when young. In the western part of the region the rainfall is greatest and the wines the dullest.

Apart from these natural geographical divisions, there are two distinct types of red produced in Minervois: the traditional type is the bigger, richer wine, designed for keeping, and sometimes these days given some ageing in oak *barriques* to help it on its way. The other extreme involves the *macération carbonique* approach: making light, fresh reds for early drinking. Both have their place in the Minervois scheme of things and in any case some areas are simply better equipped by nature to produce a certain type of wine.

The list of grapes used for Minervois contains few surprises. The Carignan normally forms at least 50 per cent of a wine, with the Grenache, Syrah, Mourvèdre and Cinsault making up the balance. With little experiment possible for the AC wines, however, growers can plant a greater variety of vines if they choose (as many do) to make *vin de pays*. That means they can try out Cabernet or other varieties of the south-west of France, in addition to the usual Meridional grapes. In the future it seems quite probable that Malbec will join the list of recommended varieties for the AC wines.

At the moment, most of the production of Minervois is in the hands of the co-operatives. That is commonplace in the Midi. The next stage, perhaps, is to see more growers doing it themselves.

Above: *The town of Minerve in Minervois. Different regions in Minervois produce different styles, but all tend to be rich and fairly rustic.*

Minervois Wines

Grapes	Basically Carignan, Cinsault, Syrah, Mourvèdre and Grenache (for other varieties, see text).
Taste	All that Carignan gives Minervois reds plenty of concentration, but perhaps because of the other grapes, there is plenty of fruit there as well. They are firm, spicy wines, and altogether softer and lighter if *macération carbonique* has been used in their production.
Value	At the moment they are good value and should remain so for a while yet.
Ageing potential	The light variety should be drunk young, while the more traditional type needs five, maybe six years in bottle to come round.
Recommended producers	Château de Gourgazaud; Domaine Barroubio; Domaine de Mayranne; Domaine de la Lecugne; Domaine des Homs; Domaine de la Senche; Château du Blomac; Château de St-Julia; Domaine Meyzonnier; Château de Paraza; Jacqueline Le Calvez; Marceau Moureau et Fils; co-operatives at Les Coteaux de Pouzols-Minervois; St-Jean de Minervois; La Vigneronne.
What to look for on the label	There is often little on the label to indicate the style of the wine; one called "*cuvée tradition*" might be a light, *macération carbonique* wine, for example. Sometimes wines that have been aged in wood will state the fact on the label.

Corbières is huge. It embraces the largest delimited area in Languedoc-Roussillon, spreading for mile after mile over parched hills from the coast practically to Carcassonne. These days it is AC. Fitou has long been so, but does not boast a real area all to itself: instead it consists of nine communes within the Corbières region, which were given the AC long before the rest of Corbières because of the superior quality and greater longevity of their wines. The nine are: Cascastel-des-Corbières; Tuchan; Paziols; Villeneuve-les-Corbières; Treilles; Fitou; Leucate; Caves and Lapalme. Quite widely separated though they are, they are all in the southern part of the Corbières region, and the wine they make under the Fitou appellation is entirely red.

One reason why Fitou ages well is its high proportion of Carignan – at least 70 per cent of the blend must consist of this grape. This is somewhat unfashionable now: elsewhere Carignan is being replanted by less neutral varieties that make more easily approachable wines. But Fitou, with age, is approachable enough, helped by the fact that it has to spend 18 months in wood before it gets bottled. The part of the blend that is not Carignan may be Cinsault, Grenache, Syrah and Mourvèdre, which gives the growers a certain amount of flexibility.

Corbières does not need the ageing that Fitou does, but even so it is a big, chunky wine. Carignan predominates in the vineyards, but much of the blend can come from Cinsault, Grenache, Picpoul, Syrah, Mourvèdre and Terret Noir, as well as from Carignan. In addition to this greater variety, carbonic maceration is being used to give

Corbières and Fitou Wines

Grapes	Carignan, Cinsault, Grenache, Mourvèdre and Syrah.
Taste	The best Corbières are big, meaty, rich wines with good concentration of flavour; Fitou is still more concentrated, with greater tannin, and a darker colour.
Value	Fitou is fairly expensive for a Midi wine, but often worth it; Corbières is less expensive, although prices vary tremendously.
Ageing potential	Fitou, once bottled, is best aged for five or six years before drinking; Corbières can be enjoyed earlier, even a year after the vintage if of a fairly light style. Others will improve for a few years.
Recommended producers	(Fitou) Château de Nouvelles; co-ops at Tuchan; Villeneuve-les-Corbières; Fitou; Paziols; Cascastel. (Corbières) Château de la Baronne; Château l'Etang des Colombes; Domaine de Mandourelle; Château des Ollieux; Château Les Palais; Georges Bertrand; co-ops at Embres-et-Castelmaure; Paziols; Cucugnan (Château de Queribus); Ribaute; Villeneuve-les-Corbières; Cap Leucate at Leucate; Cascastel; St-Martin at Roquefort-des-Corbières.
What to look for on the label	As in Minervois, many labels give frustratingly little help to the consumer, and styles vary considerably. Most of the wines that are exported are, however, very well-made.

the wines all the round fruitiness possible.

Ninety-two communes are covered by the Corbières AC, some of the better ones being Fabrezan, Bizanet, Montséret, Boutenac, Lagrasse and the high-up Complong. The Fitou-producing villages can also produce Corbières, so long as the wine conforms to the right set of rules.

With such a large area covered by the AC, it is not surprising that the soil of Corbières is diverse. The hills are basically limestone, but there are also patches of schist, sandstone and marl. The unifying feature is the climate, which is, quite simply, hot. Rainfall is low, and practically non-existent in the summer. Even the rivers, normally a moderating factor on the climate of a vineyard region, are apt to dry up in the hottest weather. The strong dry winds – the Mistral, Tramontane and Cers – do not help, either, and are a hazard to the wine grower, causing damage to the vines, as well as drying out the soil. Sea breezes tend to cool things down a little, and bring some humidity, but it is still a climate that is, at least potentially, unpleasant and difficult for the vine grower.

The areas of La Clape and Quatourze, previously VDQS, are now AC: La Clape wine is based on Carignan and can be exclusively so, although other grapes are usually added.

Above: *Fitou comes from a rocky, uncompromisingly arid landscape where, because of the climate and the nature of the soil, yields are lower than in many theoretically finer wine regions. The AC is for red wine only, and it must, under* appellation contrôlée *regulations, age in wood for 18 months before bottling.*

Quatourze too, is a big wine, made from a similar blend of grapes and often high in alcohol. The more recent AC of Costières du Gard also deserves a look. The grape varieties, are familiar, Carignan can form half the blend at the most, with the other half coming from Syrah, Mourvèdre, Grenache, Cinsault, Terret Noir and Counoise.

Notable VDQS wines include those from the Côtes de la Malepère to the west of Carcassonne, made from Cinsault, Cot and Merlot, no one of which may form more than 60 per cent of the blend, plus Grenache, Syrah, Cabernet Franc and Cabernet Sauvignon. The results are fruity, and fairly light. And to the north of Carcassone is grown Cabardès, which is best drunk young. The grapes are the Carignan (but only up to 30 per cent), Grenache, Syrah, Mourvèdre, Cinsault, Cabernet Sauvignon, Fer, Merlot and Cot.

The most southerly vineyards in France are in Roussillon. On their eastern side is the Mediterranean; to the south rise the Pyrénées. And to reach the tiny AC area of Collioure, you have to squeeze your way between the two, and somehow still manage to stay in France. Collioure is right on the coast, and runs alongside the Spanish border for part of its length. It makes red wines that have been AC since 1949. They are never going to set the world alight because they are not produced in sufficient quantity – the total production is only about 3,000hl per year. They are rich, concentrated wines made with very little Carignan, a rarity here. At least 60 per cent must be Grenache, plus Cinsault, Mourvèdre and Carignan.

To the north of Collioure is the altogether larger expanse of Côtes de Roussillon and Côtes de Roussillon-Villages. These areas stretch over hillside and plain right to the edge of the Corbières AC. It is no longer fair merely to think of them as being one of the springs that fill the wine lake. *Macération carbonique* is increasingly popular here, which produces fruity wines rather than merely beefy ones; and while Carignan is still dominant in the vineyards, Grenache, Mourvèdre and Cinsault are being increasingly planted. The Villages area, in the north and around the valley of the River Agly, is the best part. Two of the villages have their own appellation, Caramany and the somewhat grandly-named Latour-de-France. Côtes de Roussillon-Villages wines must have 0.5° alcohol more than basic Côtes de Roussillon, and they generally represent a step up in quality.

Leaving Roussillon and going north to the Hérault *département*, St-Chinian makes reds only, and makes a lot of them – some 14 million bottles a year, in all. The area is quite substantial in size, though dwarfed by nearby Minervois, and the schistous soil, with some limestone in the south, produces wines that are stylish and not too heavy. Again, the Carignan has been losing ground to more exciting varieties, and while it may form up to half the blend, Grenache and Cinsault are being grown more and more. Most of the vineyards are on the hillsides, facing the sea, and the moderating effect this has on the local climate improves their quality.

St-Chinian's neighbour, Faugères, makes the bigger, meatier red of the two. The soil is poor and schistous, and the Carignan is dominant, though Cinsault and Grenache are gaining ground. The hillsides on which the vines are grown are steep, and again, this helps produce grapes of a higher quality.

Recently there has been a spate of promotions from VDQS in Languedoc-Roussillon and included in these is the Coteaux de Languedoc, with 11 communes inside its boundaries that have the right to put their own name to their wines. Lots of advances are being made here, so expect to see them promoted to AC in their own right sooner or later. The Coteaux de St-Christol area, near the town of Lunel, is enclosed by the Coteaux de Languedoc, and produces light wines for

Below: *A typical landscape in the Coteaux de St-Christol. The wines it produces are quite light in style.*

Roussillon Wines

Grapes	Principally Carignan, Cinsault, Grenache and Mourvèdre.
Taste	Look for rich plummy fruit from all these ACs, perhaps lifted by some *macération carbonique*. Collioure is the most concentrated, Faugères and St-Chinian stylish, and Côtes de Roussillon, if less distinctive, usually reliable.
Value	All except Collioure are inexpensive because of the large quantities produced. Collioure, as well as being higher priced, is rarely seen – in fact little finds its way out of the region.
Ageing potential	All except the biggest wines (the richest Collioures, the tougher Faugères, for example) should be drunk fairly young. That is, within three years of the vintage.
Recommended producers	(Collioure) Celliers des Templiers; Domaine du Mas Blanc. (Côtes de Roussillon and Côtes de Roussillon-Villages) Les Vignerons de Terrats; Salvat Père et Fils; Coopérative de St-Paul-de-Fenouillet; Coopérative de Pezilla-la-Rivière; Luc-Jérôme Talut; Ets Nicolas; Domaine de Canterrane; les Vignerons Catalans; Cazes Frères; Château l'Esparrou; Henri Limouzy; Coopérative Espira-de-l'Agly; Cave Coopérative de Latour-de-France; Cave Coopérative Lesquerde; Francis Bomzoms. (Faugères) Cave Coopérative de Faugères; Jacques Pons; Château Haut-Fabreges; Cave Coopérative de Laurens. (St-Chinian) Alain Jougla; Château Coujan; Domaine des Calmette.
What to look for on the label	Some producers have not yet got used even to putting the vintage date on the label, so do not expect many other indications of style. It is probably best to stick with a producer whose wines you like.

early drinking from typical grape varieties. Close by, and also within the Coteaux de Languedoc boundaries, is the Coteaux de Vérargues, where Carignan still rules but where other varieties are being planted. Nearby St-Drézéry makes only red, mostly from Carignan, but in small quantities; Coteaux de la Méjanelle uses the classic Languedoc varieties to make a full, concentrated wine that can be kept. Pic-St-Loup is lighter and fresher and fairly reliable.

St-Georges d'Orques, to the west of Montpellier, uses a high proportion of Cinsault and Grenache to produce wines that are stylish and improve with keeping, and Montpeyroux adds Syrah and Mourvèdre to the blend for deep coloured, characterful wines. St-Saturnin, as well as typically Languedoc reds, makes the "*vin d'une nuit*" – a very pale red made by leaving the skins on the juice for just one night. It is rather less exciting than its name might suggest.

*V*in doux naturel (vdn) – that is, a sweet wine that is fortified with spirit to arrest its fermentation – has acquired fame and fortune in the shape of the white Muscat de Beaumes de Venise from the Rhône, but that wine's sudden burst of fashionablility has not, as yet, spread to its red cousins. Nor, really, is it likely to: these largely Grenache-based wines are an acquired taste for outsiders, and acquired tastes take time and patience to develop.

Most red *vins doux naturels* come from Roussillon, with the exception of the Rhône's Rasteau. The method of production is common to all: the grapes are picked late, when they are over-ripe and often shrivelled, with a greatly concentrated sugar content. This should be, in fact, some 252g of sugar per litre of must. Not all this sugar is fermented into alcohol: the term *vin doux naturel* itself refers to the natural sweetness of the wine. The fermentation is stopped while considerable sugar is left in the wine, by the addition of grape brandy. This brandy is neutral in character and flavour, since its function is simply to fortify the wine.

All this sounds very much like the way port is made, but there are differences. For one thing, less spirit is added to *vins doux naturels*: over half the alcohol in port comes from the added brandy, while in *vin doux naturel* the proportion is much less, and represents only a tenth of the volume as opposed to a quarter in the case of port.

The end result must be a wine with an actual alcohol content of 15 to 18 per cent alc/vol, a sugar content of 45g per litre or more, and a total alcohol content (that is, the sum of the actual alcohol and the potential alcohol represented by the sugar) of 21.5 per cent or more.

Some *vins doux naturels* can be sold after a few months, but the Grenache-based ones must be aged in barrel or in 30-litre glass containers known as *bonbonnes*. If aged in

Above: *Roman terracing on the slopes behind Collioure and Banyuls. The AC of Banyuls covers vdn from both communes.*

Below: *The sea forms the natural boundary to some Banyuls vineyards. Not far to the south is the Spanish border.*

barrel they are topped up, as they evaporate, with younger wines. In this, the winemaking is similar to the way sherry is produced. With ageing, they acquire a flavour which is most kindly described as "distinctive".

The term for it is the Spanish word *rancio*, and depends on the oxidation of the wine for its tang. Any resemblance to port stops short of the taste.

The general appellation for *vin doux naturel* from Roussillon is Grand Roussillon, but as ever there are individual appellations. Banyuls and Banyuls Grand Cru come from the area that produces Collioure, right on the border with Spain. As well as the commune of Collioure itself, the appellation Banyuls includes the communes of Banyuls-sur-Mer, Port-Vendres and Cerbère.

Yields for vdn have to be low by law, but in Banyuls it is hard to imagine them being anything else but low. The schistous soil is thin, the hillsides steeply terraced, and work in the vineyards is by hand. Most of the ageing of the wine involves exposing it to the sun, whether the wine is in barrel or glass bottle. Some, however, are kept away from the air with great care, and the resulting wines, known as *rimages*, keep all their young fruitiness of flavour and aroma. Wines with the Banyuls Grand Cru appellation, though, must be aged in wood for 30 months.

The other two appellations for red *vins doux naturels* are Rivesaltes and Maury. The former is becoming known for its Muscat *vin doux naturel*, but Grenache is also made this way, and in Maury Grenache Noir is the only grape grown for its vdn.

Roussillon Vdn Wines

Grape	Principally Grenache.
Taste	Hard to pin down, but these wines have flavours of raisins, coffee, plums and cooked fruit. The added alcohol should not be felt as a spirity burning sensation. When aged for a long time they acquire the madeira-like flavour termed *rancio*.
Value	*Vins doux naturels* are fairly expensive, but it should be remembered that they are for drinking in small quantities, as dessert wines.
Ageing potential	Red *vins doux naturels* will last 10-20 years or even longer: the older, the better for aficionados.
Recommended producers	(Banyuls and Banyuls Grand Cru) Cellier des Templiers; Cave Coopérative l'Etoile; Domaine du Mas Blanc. (Rivesaltes) Cave Coopérative d'Aglya; Cazes Frères; Domaine de Garria; Château du Jau; Cave Coopérative de Paziols; SCV de Pollestres; Vignerons de St-Vincent; SCV les Vignerons de Terrats; Cave Coopérative d'Argeles; Château l'Esparrou; Château de Rey. (Maury) SCV les Vignerons de Maury; Jean-Louis Lafage; Domaine du Mas Amiel.
What to look for on the label	The word *rancio* might appear, but if it does not, that does not mean that the wine is definitely not *rancio* in style. Indications of age are often given, sometimes in actual years, often by such phrases as "*hors d'age*" or "*Vieille Réserve*".

PROVENCE

Provence's climate, while ideal for people, is less well suited to vines. Hot, relentless summer sun means high sugar levels in grapes that have been exposed to it all season, and consequent high alcohol levels in the wines. The terrain is rocky and craggy, with shallow soil that gets just as baked as the grapes. On top of the heat and the aridity, there is also the Mistral, a wind that can tear whole branches off vines, in spite of all the rows of cypresses planted everywhere to try to moderate its force. All in all it is not surprising that historically the wines have not been all that good.

However, all that is changing. Winemaking in the region is now being compared to California in its willingness to innovate and exploit new technology. Controlled temperature fermentation is taking over; growers want fruit, freshness and flavour in their wines, and, just as importantly, they want less alcohol and tannin, and often less colour. The hot fermentation and long maceration on the skins that produced the tired, tannic reds of the past are now rejected by all who aspire to serious winemaking.

The better estates are training their vines along wires, instead of as bushes, to encourage both higher yields and better quality. Wherever you go, too, you will find organic vineyards – estates where no chemical fertilisers or pesticides are used. That is one area in which Provençal growers have an advantage over more northerly regions – fungus diseases just do not thrive in the dry air, so *vignerons* can survive without fungicides in a way that the Bordelais, for example, simply could not. The otherwise harsh conditions for vines mean that the best winemakers treat their grapes as well and as carefully as anywhere in France – some will even say better. Harvesting machines are often eschewed because of potential damage to the grapes which could cause oxidation before the crop even arrives at the winery, especially if harvesting is taking place in heat of 30° or 35°C.

Apart from the winemaker himself, what separates the good from the mediocre in Provence? Soil, partly, but also the microclimate. The same blend of grapes can produce widely differing styles of wine in places that are not all that far apart. The humidity of the soil, and its ability to retain the little residual moisture, is important too.

Provence is, of course, rosé country. Roughly two-thirds of the wine made there is pink, a little is white, and about 30 per cent is red. The grapes are the usual southern mishmash but Mourvèdre and Syrah, both quality

Key to map
1 Coteaux des Baux-de-Provence.
2 Coteaux d'Aix-en-Provence.
3 Palette.
4 Cassis.
5 Bandol.
6 Côtes de Provence.
7 Bellet.

vines, are increasing their share of the vineyard in many estates, and the ubiquitous Cabernet Sauvignon, the most successful traveller of them all, is pretty well established. Some estates, indeed, are making what are intended to be Bordeaux-style wines. They are not much cheaper than Bordeaux, either: prices have always been fairly high in Provence, and show few signs of declining. It is one reason why the wines are not seen very much on export markets. Also, Provence does not on the whole produce wines for ageing. With certain exceptions, they are best drunk young and chilled, just as if they were rosé, or Beaujolais Nouveau. And the good, innovative growers are capitalising on the fact that the reds are often at their best like this to make them even fresher and fruitier, sometimes with more than a touch of *macération carbonique* to help matters along in this direction.

Below: *Most Provençal vines are Gobelet-trained although some growers are using other methods to promote higher quality.*

Permitted Grape Varieties

Braquet
Cabernet Sauvignon
Calitor
Carignan
Cinsault
Folle Noir
Grenache
Mourvaison
Mourvèdre
Pinot
Plant d'Arles
Roussanne du Var
(not permitted after the 1986 vintage)
Syrah
Tibouren

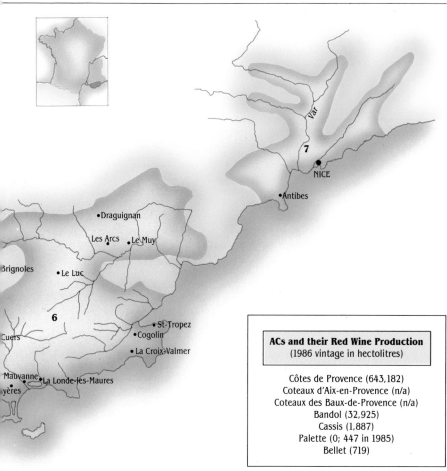

ACs and their Red Wine Production
(1986 vintage in hectolitres)

Côtes de Provence (643,182)
Coteaux d'Aix-en-Provence (n/a)
Coteaux des Baux-de-Provence (n/a)
Bandol (32,925)
Cassis (1,887)
Palette (0; 447 in 1985)
Bellet (719)

Until 1977, the Côtes de Provence was VDQS, and quite rightly so, in the opinion of most people. A few estates were making wines that stood head and shoulders above the rest, but the general level was ordinary. Then the whole area was upgraded to AC in one fell swoop. Some said this was a result of politics at the INAO; some said the wines by then really were good enough. Now, there is less doubt. The wines have come on by leaps and bounds, and even though the Côtes de Provence is remarkably large for a single AC area, the overall level is rising.

One of the main changes caused by the promotion relates to the proportion of the grape varieties used. Five "principal" varieties are allowed, and must comprise 70 per cent of a blend. These are Carignan, Cinsault, Grenache, Mourvèdre and Tibouren. Of these, the Carignan has been reduced to a maximum 40 per cent – it used to be so widely planted that when AC rules were first introduced the maximum had to be fixed at 70 per cent. Its popularity was based largely on its ability to produce large and reliable yields, but the wines do not keep, and they certainly do not give structure to a blend the way the Syrah and Mourvèdre do.

Of the secondary varieties, the Cabernet Sauvignon is firmly ensconced, of course, and adds a touch of elegance to the wines, even though it is not such a heavy cropper here as some of the more traditional vines. Which is grown depends, also, on where an estate is situated in the rambling Côtes de Provence. St-Tropez is in the region, but so is the valley of the Argens, to the north-west, and so is a border of land around Bandol, on the Mediterranean coast to the west. There is a fair bit of clay in the soil in the stretch from Toulon to St-Raphael; near the coast in the

Massif des Maures, the soil is largely sandstone. Mourvèdre does well here, liking the heat, and Cabernet Sauvignon generally does best where the climate is a little cooler: often it is planted at 250m above sea level or higher. Sometimes vineyards are even planted – heresy of heresies – facing north. Château Grand' Boise does this; it gets fruit, but not too much alcohol in its wines and that is what Provence is all about now.

One thing the Côtes de Provence winemakers do not have to worry about too much is consistency. There are few wine regions in Europe where differences between vintages do not matter at all, but in Provence growers are unlikely to have their crop devastated by

Côtes de Provence Wines

Grapes	Mourvèdre, Cinsault, Grenache, Carignan, Tibouren, Cabernet Sauvignon and Syrah.
Taste	The newer style is less tough, less tannic, and lower in alcohol, with lots of ripe raspberry or blackcurrant and herbs fruit: best drunk chilled.
Value	They *are* expensive for their quality.
Ageing potential	Generally best drunk young, or within a couple of years of the vintage. They seldom keep successfully much longer.
Recommended producers	Domaines Ott; Château Grand' Boise; Domaine St-André de Figuière; Château Minuty (especially Cuvée de l'Oratoire); Les Maitres Vignerons de la Presque'ile de St-Tropez; Domaine des Bertrands; Domaine Gavoty; Château Montaud; Château Boisseaux-Vannières; Domaines des Féraud; Domaine de la Croix; Château de Roux; Domaine de Curebeasse; Billette de Provence Listel.
What to look for on the label	The vintage date (for youth); some single varietal wines are sold under such titles as Cuvée (or Cépage) Cabernet Sauvignon.

Above: *Typical vineyards in the Côtes de Provence; winemaking in this region is improving by leaps and bounds.*

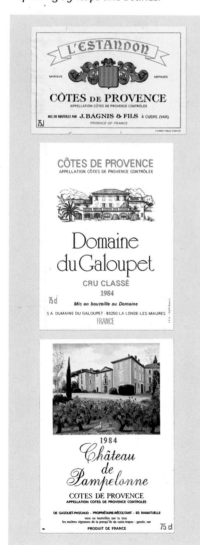

late frost, or early autumn gales, as they might in more northerly regions, and looking at the vintage date on the bottle is mostly important insofar as it ensures you get the youngest wine available.

Notwithstanding all the improvements that have been going on in the vineyards, better grape varieties and better training, the real revolution is in the winery. The fermentation time is shorter than it used to be (eight to 12 days is pretty average for reds) and some properties make two types of red, a traditional *cuvée* that is heavy on Mourvèdre and will keep in bottle for a time after having had a few months' ageing in large oak casks at the winery, and a lighter wine, often involving *macération carbonique* in its vinification and based on varieties like Cinsault and Grenache. Typically, *macération carbonique* wines have a pinky purply colour when young, smell of boiled sweets (or bubblegum), and do not last in bottle beyond a year or so. Côtes de Provence examples are no exception if they are pure *macération carbonique* products, but often they are a mixture, with a bit of *macération carbonique* wine added to the blend to lift it and make it immediately attractive to drink. In any case they are generally higher in alcohol than Beaujolais Nouveau.

There is no proper classification system in the Côtes de Provence. Despite this, 12 properties bear the words *Grand Cru Classé* on their labels. The reason for this is simply that they invented it. Quite properly, it should be stressed: these 12 got together when the Côtes de Provence was upgraded to AC status and determined their own system of classification based on the property name, not on the price of the wine over a century ago, as in Bordeaux, or the individual patch of vineyard, as in Burgundy. Officially, it does not mean a lot. In practice, a lot of the *crus classés* actually make rather good wine.

*W*hen the Côtes de Provence area was upgraded to AC in 1977, it joined four other Provençal ACs (Bandol, Bellet, Cassis and Palette), all of them small, relatively little known abroad, and rather expensive. They were generally recognised as producing classier wine than their immediately neighbouring vineyards and that, even with all the recent promotions, still holds true today.

It is particularly true of Bandol, which is regarded as the most serious AC in Provence. A strip of land surrounding it on three sides (the fourth side is bounded by the Mediterranean) is Côtes de Provence AC, but Bandol itself has just the right microclimate, soil and exposure for its high slopes to make the sort of red that needs ageing and which is at its best after a couple of years or so.

Above: *Domaine de Terrebrune in Bandol. This appellation produces the most serious red wine in Provence.*

The AC area includes the communes of Bandol itself, together with La Cadière d'Azur, Le Castellet, Sanary, and parts of Evenos, St-Cyr-sur-Mer, Ollioules and Le Beausset. Rainfall is low, about 650mm a year, and the land is arid, although breezes off the sea help to moderate the southern heat. The soil is generally calcareous and stony, and the vineyards are planted on terraces (known as *restanques* locally) supported by dry stone walls; behind them the ground rises to oak-and-pine covered hills on which the sun beats down all summer. The Mourvèdre grape loves this sort of treatment although it does not produce very high yields – the overall maximum yield for the appellation is 40hl/ha. What it does give is higher alcohol. The wine is well-structured, though tending to toughness if unblended with softening grapes like Grenache, and has a piney, herby taste redolent of the land; it is capable of considerable depth.

All this makes Bandol a much more interesting wine than most of its neighbours. It has to contain at least 50 per cent Mourvèdre by law, and usually has more, 60, 70 or even 80 per cent. The rest can be Carignan, Pecoui-Touar, Tibouren, Syrah and Pinot, in any desired combination. As well as these, up to 20 per cent of the total volume can be white grapes, as long as both colours are vinified together. Adding white grapes can make a wine lighter, but in Bandol it is the Mourvèdre that dominates the taste.

The other legal requirement is that the wine must be aged for 18 months in oak casks before release for sale. It might be aged more, if the vintage is a particularly tannic, tough one, and needs the softening that oak can give, and many producers will tell you that their wine needs several years in bottle as well, before it starts to show at its best. The vines are trained on wires, and picking, inevitably in such terrain, is by hand. Fermentation times are quite long (up to 15 days) and extraction of colour and tannin from the grapes is high.

The same blend of grapes, though without the minimum requirements for Mourvèdre, and with a few older Provençal varieties, are grown in Palette, to the north. Palette is

Provençal AC Wines

Grapes	(Bandol) Mourvèdre (50 per cent), Grenache, Cinsault, Mourvaison, Carignan, Pecoui-Touar, Tibouren, Syrah, Pinot. White varieties (up to 20 per cent of volume): Clairette, Ugni Blanc, Colombard, Frontignan, Malvoisie, Doucillon, Sauvignon.
Taste	Bandol is the best known, with a flavour of piney, herby fruit and a good blackcurranty backbone that comes from the Mourvèdre. Château Simone from Palette is distinctive, with a degree of toughness but quite good depth. Cassis and Bellet, if they can be found, tend to dullness.
Value	Expensive. Production is low, and yields quite small.
Ageing potential	Good for Bandol, which can safely be left in bottle for two to three years. Palette will also keep; drink the other two young.
Recommended producers	(Bandol) Domaine de Frégate, Moulin des Costes; Domaine de l'Hermitage; Château Vannières; Domaine Tempier; Mas de la Rouvière; the co-op Moulin de la Roque. (Palette) Château Simone. (Bellet) Château de Bellet; Château de Cremat. (Cassis) Domaine de la Ferme Blanche; Clos Ste-Magdeleine; Mas Calendal.
What to look for on the label	Bandol will call itself either Bandol or Vin de Bandol; the two names mean the same.

situated right next to the town of Aix-en-Provence, in the middle of the Coteaux d'Aix. The soil, again, is calcareous, and the wine needs some ageing to show well. Not too much, though: the major producer is Château Simone, whose reds can begin to taste tired after five years or so.

Heading south to the coast again, we come to the small port of Cassis. The scenery here is some of the most stunning in the region, but the wines, it has to be said, are generally less impressive. Mostly they are white or rosé: the production of red is small, and the usual Provençal mixture of grapes is grown for them.

The last of the original appellations is Bellet, and today it is probably the most obscure of the lot. It is situated just behind Nice, and the wines are fairly well known in the restaurants of that town. But the quantities produced are low, and whites and rosés tend to dominate. It is also pretty highly priced, and not a wine that you are likely to find outside the immediate region.

Below: *Bandol must by law be aged in oak casks for 18 months before bottling and sale. Here we see wine maturing in cask at Domaine de Terrebrune.*

The Coteaux d'Aix-en-Provence and the Coteaux des Baux-de-Provence are the most recent Provençal promotions to Appellation Contrôlée. They are worth looking out for: some of the most reliable wines in the Midi come from here. Geographically they are close together, with the Coteaux d'Aix extending north, south and east of the city of Aix-en-Provence, and the Coteaux des Baux further west in the dramatic scenery of the Alpilles mountains. The centre of the Coteaux des Baux is the village of Les Baux itself, a medieval fortress which was once the haunt of troubadours.

The VDQS regions of this part of France are almost as well-known as the ACs – in fact more so than some of them. The Côtes du Lubéron produces ripe, fruity wines from the same grapes as are grown in the Côtes du Rhône – the wines of Domaine Val Joanis are particularly good. The Coteaux de Pierrevert produces mostly rosé, but a few reds from Cinsault, Carignan and Grenache. A more important region, red-wise, is the Coteaux Varois, which uses the same grapes, plus Mourvèdre, Alicante and Aramon, but also Cabernet Sauvignon and Syrah.

The soil is basically chalky, and the landscape of the Coteaux d'Aix is mostly a little gentler than that of the Coteaux des Baux. The grape varieties grown in both are similar, and AC status for the Coteaux d'Aix has meant that the amount of Cabernet Sauvignon in the wines has had to be reduced from a maximum of 60 per cent in VDQS days, first to 50 per cent, then to 40 per cent, and perhaps then to 35 per cent. So what, one might think? It is not Bordeaux, after all, and they have plenty of other grapes to use instead.

However, the reason the reduction in the permitted proportion of Cabernet Sauvignon matters so much in this instance is that a number of growers in the Coteaux d'Aix have

Above: *The view from the ruined fortress of Les Baux is one of the most dramatic that France's wine regions can offer. The area attracts thousands of tourists, but the dependable wines of the Coteaux des Baux have yet to be fully discovered by the public at large.*

Coteaux d'Aix and Coteaux des Baux Wines

Grapes	Grenache, Cinsault, Mourvèdre, Carignan, Counoise, Cabernet Sauvignon.
Taste	There are some big, ripe wines in the Coteaux d'Aix that can taste startlingly like claret, as well as lighter, herbier ones from both districts. With the proportion of Cabernet Sauvignon coming down, the flavour of the first kind can be expected to change somewhat.
Value	With AC status recently achieved, the price of most of the wines is likely to rise.
Ageing potential	Good for the big, Bordeaux-type wines. Many of the others are intended for early drinking, preferably chilled.
Recommended producers	(Coteaux d'Aix) Château de Fonscolombe; Château Vignelaure; Domaine de la Cremade; Domaine de Paradis; Château la Coste; Domaine les Bastides; Château du Seuil. (Coteaux des Baux-de-Provence) Mas Sainte-Berthe; Domaine de Trevaillon; Château Estoublon; Mas de la Dame; Mas du Cellier; Domaine des Terres Blanches; Domaine de la Vallongue; Mas de Gourgonnier; Domaine des Lauzières.

themselves made rather a speciality of it. Estates like Château du Seuil used all the Cabernet Sauvignon they could in their wines, while stressing that they were not just producing a Bordeaux copy: the soil, the climate, the ripeness of the grapes, all made the difference. Then on the other hand there is Château Vignelaure, whose owner, Georges Brunet, sold the famous Bordeaux Château La Lagune to come south, and who has ever since been telling the world very firmly that his wine is not merely a claret copy, but "more Bordeaux than Bordeaux". In the bad old days the château owners of the Gironde used to mix in a shot or two of Hermitage or some other Rhône wine to beef up their more feeble offerings, and Georges Brunet has happily (and legally) been blending Grenache and Syrah with his Cabernet Sauvignon to make a super-claret. This explains why he (and others) are not too happy about having their *cépages* altered. The best solution would seem to be to increase the amount of Syrah in the wines to keep the blackcurrant flavour, but nobody pretends that the overall taste of the wine will remain the same after such a procedure.

The methods of winemaking in these areas are commendably "serious". Temperature-controlled fermentation, facilities for de-stalking, and stainless steel vats are commonplace on the better estates, and, inevitably, the wood controversy has taken hold. At Vignelaure they say proudly that the wine touches only steel and wood before it is bottled, and its time in the wood can be quite long – 18 to 20 months is usual, while a tough vintage may spend longer. At Château du Seuil, however, wood is no longer used – "too many good wines are spoilt by wood," they say.

In the Coteaux des Baux, the first experiments with new oak *barriques* are beginning. It is an innovative area, if a more obscure one: few outside the region know of its wines, yet the handful of estates in the AC are making wine which deserves the appreciation of a wider audience.

But visiting the Coteaux des Baux on a day when the Mistral is howling down from the Alpilles can make one realise just how difficult winemaking in such an apparently idyllic region can be. The wind rips branches off the vines, the earth is dry and cracked, and the Grenache, one of the mainstay grapes of the south, can have such problems with *coulure* that in places where it is planted in quantity, the crop can be halved if the Grenache fails. New clones are being developed to solve this problem, but it is a common feature wherever Grenache is found, and a continuing problem for *vignerons* in this area.

Macération carbonique is an option here, as elsewhere, to produce light, soft, gulpable reds. It is sometimes used for just part of a blend, perhaps for the tougher, more tannic grapes like Mourvèdre, Syrah, Cabernet Sauvignon and Carignan, while the rest of the blend is given a classic vinification along well-established traditional lines.

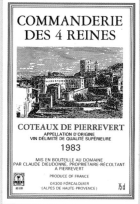

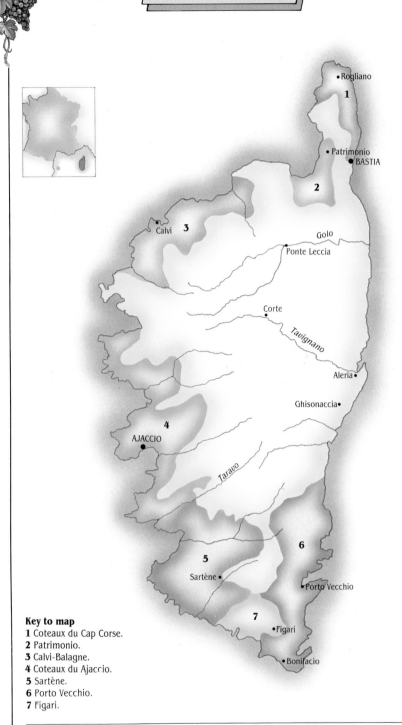

Key to map
1 Coteaux du Cap Corse.
2 Patrimonio.
3 Calvi-Balagne.
4 Coteaux du Ajaccio.
5 Sartène.
6 Porto Vecchio.
7 Figari.

When it comes to winemaking, life on an island can be problematic. All the items that winemakers need, such as machinery, presses, bottles, corks, labels, have to be bought and on a small island they are probably going to have to be shipped in, which is expensive.

On small islands, too, attitudes can be somewhat insular, and resistant to change. People admire the wine that is there simply because it *is* there, and has been for years. And since the locals are unable or unwilling to buy wines from elsewhere, new ideas are slow to filter through.

That is the bad news about Corsica. The good news is that things are beginning to change, and that there are some modern, innovative, enthusiastic winemakers who are able to exploit the best of what the island has to offer. Furthermore, these are the winemakers who are most likely to be exporting their wines in bottle.

Most Corsican wine, even so, is sold in bulk. Most, too, is blended into anonymous *vin de table* for filling returnable bottles in local French stores. And most of this, it has to be said, is not very nice. There is a *vin de pays*, with the seductive name of Ile de

Above: *Ajaccio is one of Corsica's AC regions and land may only be replanted with native grape varieties if the wines are to qualify as AC. Sciacarello and Niellucio are the classic varieties.*

Beauté, which can be good if properly made, and about ten per cent of the island's production is *Appellation Contrôlée*.

All wine so classified goes under the name of Vin de Corse, but within that broad term there are seven separate denominations. Some are better than others, but basically in Corsica quality depends on the winemaker.

The grape varieties are unfamiliar to the outsider: the two red vines considered classic

---

Permitted Grapes for AC vineyards

Carignan
Cinsault
Grenache
Mourvèdre
Niellucio
Sciacarello
Syrah
Vermentino (white)

ACs and their Red Wine Production
(1986 vintage in hectolitres)

Patrimonio
Ajaccio
Cap Corse
Calvi-Balagne
Sartène
Figari
Porto Vecchio
(Total: 74,104)

---

on the island are the Sciacarello and the Niellucio, the latter being a relative of the Sangiovese of Chianti country in Tuscany, the former probably having been brought to the island by the ancient Greeks. The two are generally blended together, often with the addition of Grenache, Cinsault, Mourvèdre, Carignan or Syrah. Cabernet Sauvignon and Merlot are making an appearance on the island, but as yet AC land may only be replanted with native grape varieties. That is an improvement on the days when an influx of *pieds noirs* from newly-independent Algeria arrived. Huge areas of totally unsuitable plain on the eastern side of the island were planted with equally unsuitable high-producing vines. Thankfully for the vinous future of the island (although it was presumably tough on the new immigrants) this form of winegrowing proved unprofitable, and much of this area has now been uprooted. Of those that survive, some attractive wines are made, and exported.

In the AC vineyards, before the approved native grape varieties are planted, the right clones have to be found. Clonal selection can do a fair bit towards upgrading some of these vineyards; another problem they face is an insect known as the Cicadelle de la Flavescance Dorée: an appealing name for a creature with less than appealing habits. The Cicadelle is a sort of mosquito that bites the woody parts of the vines and poisons them, so that the leaves turn black and the vines die. The answer is spraying, which is expensive, and needs to be undertaken on a large scale to be effective: some growers are now banding together to tackle the problem.

Even without such handicaps, yields would be fairly low. Machinery is of little use in some parts of the island, although where it is possible, growers are planting their rows of vines further apart – two metres between them rather than the traditional 1.6m – to allow room for tractors to work the soil.

Inevitably, the Corsican climate is hot. The wines are high in alcohol and, when made traditionally, tend towards the lean and austere – which is not what many consumers want to drink today. What usually happens is that the free-run juice in the vat of newly-picked grapes is run off. This can amount to as much as one-fifth of the total, and, coloured as it is with the skins of the black grapes, it goes to make rosé. Rosé made with free-run juice is good, but the red that is left behind is not automatically of similar quality. In Corsica's case, the high proportion of skins and pips to juice can result in red wines that lack fruit, and lack flesh on them. Allied to the traditionally somewhat careless winemaking, the results can be unattractive. So again, look to the winemaker. The best wines are properly made; they have fruit and balance and freshness, while still remaining quite powerful, and very individual.

*V*in de Corse, the label that covers all the AC wines on Corsica, does not have to bear any more specific name. A wine can be plain AC Vin de Corse, or if it comes from one of seven delimited regions on the island, can bear that name as well. Like all French wine regions, the rule is: the more specific the AC, the better the wine ought to turn out to be.

The oldest AC is Patrimonio, in the north; indeed it was the only AC on the island from 1968 until 1976. Niellucio, one of the grape varieties regarded as classically Corsican, is the backbone of the red wines. At least 60 per cent Niellucio is necessary for the AC, and the permitted yield is 45hl/ha. With the vineyards being as steep as they are, that yield is generally picked by hand. The soil in Patrimonio is chalky, which makes it good for vines: in fact it is the only AC area of chalk on Corsica. The minimum level of alcohol permitted under the regulations is 12.5°, which is the highest on Corsica.

The other classically Corsican grape is the Sciacarello. This is widely grown at Ajaccio, which as well as being the capital has its own AC region, on the west coast. The full name of the AC is Coteaux d'Ajaccio, which gives an indication of the sort of terrain. The height of the hills helps to keep the wine lighter than it might be otherwise. The growers believe that their wines are better than those of anywhere else on the island, although to outsiders' tastes, Patrimonio often has the edge.

To the south of Ajaccio lies Sartène, which again grows a lot of Sciacarello and Niellucio. This is where the Corsican nationalists have their base. The wines have a touch of elegance from the granite-based soil in which they are grown, and the minimum alcohol content is 11°. This same granite is found at Ajaccio, Figari, and Porto Vecchio, and at Figari again the Niellucio and Sciacarello dominate the blend. The land round here is particularly arid and inhospitable. The next AC as you head round the coast, Porto Vecchio, provides better wine. There is a degree of modernity in the winemaking here that is only creeping into some of the other regions. It is particularly interesting to see just how good the native grape varieties can be when they are handled properly, as they are here.

Plenty of vines are grown on the east coast, and some of it is AC, going under the basic name of Vin de Corse. Much of this comes from vineyards round Aléria and Ghisonaccia, and is unlikely to be particularly distinctive; elsewhere on the east coast the wine is more likely to be *vin de pays*.

As you head northwards up the east coast, the next individual AC you come to is Cap Corse, on the tip of the northern peninsula. The best known wines here are the sweet white Muscats, and little red is made. Those that do emerge are from the usual Corsican grape varieties of Niellucio and Sciarcarello, plus Grenache and other Southern varieties.

On the north west of the island is the region of Balagne, next door to Calvi and generally linked with it. The wines are deep coloured and big, made from the usual mix of grapes. The reds benefit from some ageing, but a year or two only, no more.

Like so many wine regions which are coming up in the world, Corsica's wines are a pretty mixed bunch at the moment. Northern drinkers are predisposed to like anything that comes from a region so inseparably linked in their minds with the good living of the south, and the wines are at last beginning to match up to the ideal. From now on things should only get better.

Right: *Vineyards at Sartène, an area in the valleys of the Rizzanese and Ortolo which has its own appellation. The soil is granite-based which makes these wines more elegant than some of their neighbours. Sartène produces mainly red and rosé wines based on Sciacarello, Grenache and Cinsault grapes.*

Corsican Wines

Grapes	Grenache, Niellucio, Sciacarello, Syrah, Mourvèdre, Carignan, Cinsault, Vermentino (white).
Taste	Good Corsican wines are full of the warm, ripe, spicy fruit of the south and may even have a touch of the scent of the *maquis* about them.
Value	Fairly expensive – but they are shipped in relatively small volumes, and are not that widely available.
Ageing potential	Some will keep for a year or two, but if in doubt, drink young.
Recommended producers	Domaine Peraldi; Domaine Martini; Domaine de Torraccia; Clos Nicrosi; Domaine Gentile; Domaine de Fontanella; Clos Marfisi; Domaine Capitoro.
What to look for on the label	Go for one of the delimited AC regions, rather than plain Vin de Corse: you are likely to get better grape varieties and possibly better winemaking.

COTEAUX CHAMPENOIS

Champagne makes some of the finest wine in the world – providing it has bubbles in it. Forget about the fizz, and drink it as still wine (for the purposes of this book, still red wine), and you have a bottle that, except in the hottest, ripest years, would in all honesty have been better as Champagne.

The name Champagne applies only to the sparkling white and rosé wine of the region. When the local product is sold as still wine, be it white or red, it may only call itself Coteaux Champenois. The term has been in use since 1974; before that the somewhat longer term "Vin Nature de la Champagne" was used.

One can understand the desire of the locals to have something red in their cellars as a change from the ubiquitous white and rosé, and most red Coteaux Champenois is drunk in the region. The grape is the Pinot Noir, so one would expect the wine to have something of the taste of burgundy about it. It does, but in most years there is just not enough sun for the Pinot flavour to come through as more than a faint echo of what it can be on Burgundy's Côte d'Or.

Viewed on its own merits, Coteaux Champenois is a light, strawberry-flavoured wine, best drunk chilled, and best not taken too seriously except in those years (1976 for example) when the sun blazed down for long enough really to put some ripeness into the grapes and produce a wine with the structure

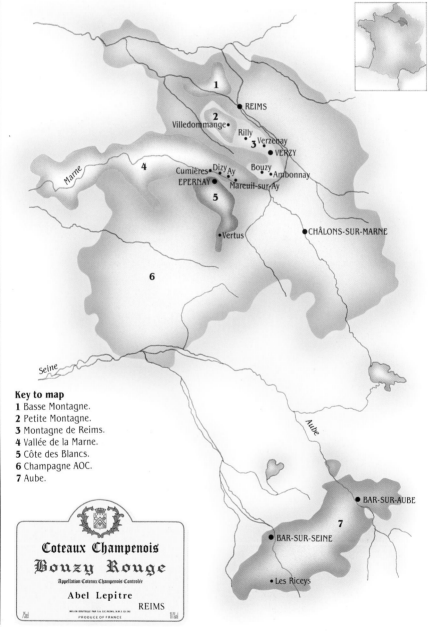

Key to map
1 Basse Montagne.
2 Petite Montagne.
3 Montagne de Reims.
4 Vallée de la Marne.
5 Côte des Blancs.
6 Champagne AOC.
7 Aube.

Coteaux Champenois
Bouzy Rouge
Appellation Coteaux Champenois Contrôlée
Abel Lepitre
REIMS
75cl
MIS EN BOUTEILLE PAR S.A. GC REIMS. N.M.1 321 342
PRODUCE OF FRANCE

Above: *The vineyards around the village of Bouzy produce most of the red Coteaux Champenois. It is, however, a difficult wine to make successfully because the sun seldom shines for long enough this far north to ripen the grapes properly.*

to age. Really good wines are made perhaps once a decade and decent ones slightly more often.

The vines are cultivated and the grapes picked just as if Champagne were the aim in view. But the first problem for the red wine maker in Champagne is colour. The *vigneron* is not looking for the intense black-purple colour of further south, but there is still a point at which a wine ceases to be red and becomes rosé. So the skins are left on the juice for as long as possible during fermentation to extract the maximum amount of colour, having been picked at their maximum ripeness. One to three years' ageing in cask before bottling is the norm.

The main Pinot Noir area of Champagne is the Montagne de Reims, and most red Coteaux Champenois comes from the commune of Bouzy, on the southfacing slopes of the Montagne. Dizy also produces some, as do Ay, Cumières, Ambonnay, Rilly, Villedommange and Verzenay, all on the Montagne de Reims. The soil is basically chalk, as it is throughout Champagne, and all these villages are rated as Grand Cru (except Villedommange, which is Premier Cru). In a time of shortage of Champagne, it would be possible to use red Coteaux Champenois for Champagne by blending it with still white wine to make rosé, and then starting a second fermentation in the bottle. But it would be a shame to do that with the best vintages of this unusual wine.

Coteaux Champenois Wines

Grape	Pinot Noir
Taste	Red Coteaux Champenois has a typically Pinot Noir flavour of strawberries, and generally little tannin. It is light and fresh, and is best drunk cool.
Value	Frankly poor. Quality for quality, there are better value wines produced in many a VDQS region of France.
Ageing potential	The best years, which come round infrequently, will age well and last several years. Otherwise, it is best drunk young.
Recommended producers	Bollinger; Barancourt; Laurent Perrier; Abel Lepitre; Georges Vesselle; Alain Vesselle; Jean Vesselle.
What to look for on the label	The wine from Bouzy generally has more body and richness than one from the other villages, although it varies from year to year. The name of the commune will often be stated on the label.

Above: *Pinot Noir, the grape from which Alsace reds are exclusively made.*

Key to map
1 Alsace.
Note: There is only one appellation here – that of Alsace. The wines are primarily distinguished by their grape varieties. Total red wine production in 1986 was 67,600hl.

*H*istorically Alsace has been one of the battlefields of Europe. At the moment it belongs to France, and has done so since 1918; between 1870 and 1918 it was German; before that French. But while the language is French, and the cooking and winemaking are French as well, the architecture is distinctly Germanic and so are the surnames. The people, indeed, stress that more than being either French or German, they are *Alsacien*.

With such a divided history, it is not surprising that Alsace has yet to establish its identity in the minds of the wine-buying public. The wines come in bottles that look more or less German (albeit taller and thinner). They are made from grapes that are also grown in Germany – but they taste French. Except that is for the Pinot Noir. All the rosés and reds are made from this grape, but while sounding French enough the wine lacks the colour, flavour and body associated with Burgundy where the grape is normally grown. Perhaps it is fairer to say that Alsace Pinot

Noir has the qualities of Burgundian Pinot Noir, but in miniature.

Alsace lies pretty far to the north. This is fine for growing Riesling, Gewürztraminer and so on (the vineyards actually lie further to the south than their equivalents in Germany), but Pinot needs that much more heat and sun, and while the south or south-east facing vineyards, planted on the foothills of the Vosges mountains, are sheltered from the wind, and sunny and dry, there is still not enough heat really to get the Pinot Noir producing its best.

That is not to say that the wines are unattractive. If what you want is a light red wine, then Alsace Pinot Noir, Coteaux Champenois, or the Loire ought to be your first thoughts. All the strawberry fruit of the Pinot Noir is present in these wines, plus high acidity and the ability to be drunk young. They are not wines for ageing, because they do not have the tannin or the structure to stand up to it.

All Alsace wine is identified primarily by the grape name. There is only one actual

Neither method, however, applies to Pinot Noir. In Germany it is possible to buy *spät-lese* (late picked) Pinot Noir wines, in which the fruitiness of the Pinot Noir is underlaid by a surprising sweetness, but they are rather an acquired taste.

Yields at the moment are high in Alsace: 80hl/ha is high by any standards. To cut that by half would increase the concentration and depth of the wine at a stroke, but it would also increase the price, and an Alsace Pinot Noir is not that easy to sell outside the region as prices stand now.

The traditional method of planting vines in Alsace is on terraces cut into the steep hill-sides, with the rows of vines running along the slopes. The disadvantage of this arrange-ment is that vines grown this way, even on a south-facing slope, do not get much sun on their backs. One grower reckons that by re-planting his vines in rows that run up and down the slopes rather than across, he can increase the Oechsle level (the measure of the sugar content) in his grapes by up to 10° Oechsle just by exposing them in this way to more sun. After fermentation a little wood ageing is used to develop the wine – only a few months, no more – before bottling. Such wood ageing that is given to Pinot Noir here is likely to be in old barrels. The taste of wood is not a traditional feature of Alsace wines, and where experiments with new wood are being carried out, they are likely to involve the white wines.

VDQS wines are not very important in the Alsace region, the only two being Côtes de Toul and Vins de Moselle. Pinot Noir is used for the red version of the former, although it is made less often these days, and Pinot Noir, Gamay and Pinot Gris for the latter.

appellation, that of Alsace, although since 1959 it has been possible to make *Vendange Tardive* wines, which are late picked, and *Sélection de Grains Nobles* wines, which are quite a step up the price ladder, as they are made with botrytised (noble rot) grapes.

Alsace Wines	
Grape	Pinot Noir.
Taste	Light in both flavour and tannin, with attractively strawberry-like fruit when good. When less good, they taste somewhat weak and acid.
Value	Fairly expensive, and not very easy to come by outside Alsace.
Ageing potential	Best drunk young. They can quickly lose their fruit if kept.
Recommended producers	Hugel are good for reds, but many houses ship little red wine. Other good Alsace growers, should you come across their Pinot Noir, are: Trimbach, Dopff & Irion, Faller Frères, Kuentz-Bas, Sparr, and among the many co-operatives, Turckheim.
What to look for on the label	Look past the label at the wine itself, if you can. A darker colour will tend to denote a slightly bigger wine than some of the very light reds that in fact are nearer rosé.

VINS DE PAYS

There is a wine lake in France and it is filled mostly by wine produced in the south of the country. There are also roughly 150 *vin de pays* regions in France, and they are concentrated in the south, too. Is there a connection? Well, no, not really. The liquid that fills the wine lake is the three-star *"gros rouge"* bought in returnable bottles from the local store and drunk, these days, almost exclusively by die-hard country people. The rest of the population is drinking less *vin de table* and more *appellation contrôlée* wine, and with the general desire for better quality on the part of the buyer has come an improvement in the quality, and the image, of much of the basic wine of France.

Vins de pays are the result of this general improvement in quality. The first moves towards this category were made in 1968, with a government decree that allowed various *vins de table* to be labelled with an indication of their geographical origin. In 1973 the conditions of production for such wines were defined more closely: the region, how great a yield from which grape varieties, the alcohol content and other technical details were fixed. And in 1979 came the finishing touch, with further definitions of these factors, and detailed rules for individual *vins de pays* being established.

Long before the name *vins de pays* had been thought of, there had been *Appellation d'Origine Simple* wines. These dated back to the early years of the appellation system, and were on a lower rung of the appellation ladder: the grape varieties and the regions had to be recognised, but little else. *Appellation Simple* came to an end with the decree of

Above: *Crushing Jurançon grapes in a vineyard near Mussidan in the Dordogne. Old-fashioned traditions such as this die hard in some of the country wine districts of France.*

1973, and was no great loss: they had never made much of an impact, and the *vin de pays* regulations were far better adapted to encourage quality by giving the growers a greater sense of identity and a better image.

So far, the idea is succeeding admirably. Advertising campaigns for *vins de pays* emphasise their qualities of honesty and rusticity (in the best sense) and, what is more, the wines are available at prices that look very cheap indeed beside some appellation wines.

With about 150 names to choose from, remembering all the regions is impossible. Luckily it is not necessary: some of them are highly unlikely to appear in your local wine merchant or supermarket, or indeed anywhere more than ten kilometres from the winery that produced them. However, others – Vin de Pays de l'Ardèche, for example – are fast making a name for themselves as sources of reliable everyday bottles.

All *vins de pays* fall into one of three broad categories, based, like all the French AC laws, on how closely the region is specified. At the base of the pyramid lie the three regional *vins de pays* names: Jardin de la France, which embraces the Loire region; Comté Tolosan, in the south-west; and Pays d'Oc, covering much of Provence, Languedoc-Roussillon and part of the Rhône valley.

More specific are the 45 departmental *vins de pays*. They bear the name of the *département* unless this has already been appropriated by an AC wine. And then there are some 92 *vins de pays de zone*, some of which cover a large area, like Charentais, while others are hardly more than a dot on the map – Caux in the Hérault, for example. The rules governing the production of the wines are stricter for the more specific regions, but all *vins de pays* must undergo the scrutiny of a tasting panel, and not all get through.

VDQS Wines

The category *Vin Délimité de Qualité Supérieure* was invented in 1949 and these wines form the second rank of quality, below AC wines but above *vins de pays*. Many VDQS wines have been promoted to AC, and for a while the policy was avowedly to phase out VDQS. However, that seems to be changing, and some areas have recently been promoted to VDQS from the ranks of the *vins de pays*.

The standard of VDQS wines is generally high, and the value is good, too. They can be considered in a general category of "country wines", a broad (and unofficial) term to include not only VDQS and *vins de pays* but also the lesser-known appellation wines. It is in this area that discoveries are to be made for anyone looking for good value and often innovative winemaking. If any reminder were needed that French wines have a greater variety of styles than almost anywhere in the world, these wines can provide it.

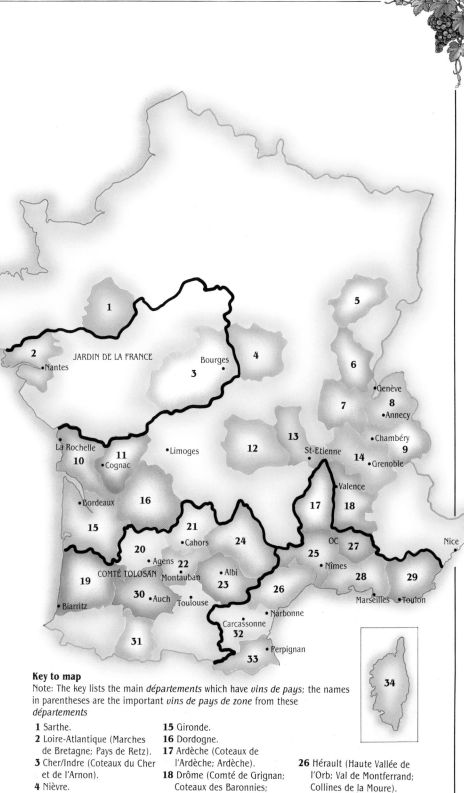

Key to map

Note: The key lists the main *départements* which have *vins de pays*; the names in parentheses are the important *vins de pays de zone* from these *départements*

1 Sarthe.

2 Loire-Atlantique (Marches de Bretagne; Pays de Retz).

3 Cher/Indre (Coteaux du Cher et de l'Arnon).

4 Nièvre.

5 Haute-Saône (Franche Comté).

6 Jura (Franche Comté).

7 Ain.

8 Haute-Savoie.

9 Savoie (Allobrogie; Balmes Dauphinoises; Coteaux du Grésivaudan).

10 Charente-Maritime.

11 Charente.

12 Puy-de-Dôme.

13 Loire (Urfé).

14 Isère.

15 Gironde.

16 Dordogne.

17 Ardèche (Coteaux de l'Ardèche; Ardèche).

18 Drôme (Comté de Grignan; Coteaux des Baronnies; Collines Rhodaniennes).

19 Landes.

20 Lot-et-Garonne (Agenais).

21 Lot (Coteaux des Glanes).

22 Tarn-et-Garonne (Coteaux du Quercy; St-Sardos; Coteaux et Terrasses de Montauban).

23 Tarn (Côtes de Tarn).

24 Aveyron (Gorges et Côtes de Millau).

25 Gard (Sables du Golfe du Lion).

26 Hérault (Haute Vallée de l'Orb; Val de Montferrand; Collines de la Moure).

27 Vaucluse (Principauté d'Orange).

28 Bouches-du-Rhône.

29 Var (Mont Caume; Argens; Les Maures).

30 Gers (Côtes de Gascogne; Condomois; Montestruc).

31 Hautes-Pyrénées (Bigorre).

32 Aude (Hauterive en Pays d'Aude; Haute Vallée de l'Aude; Val d'Orbieu; Vallée du Paradis).

33 Pyrénées-Orientales (Catalan).

34 Corsica (Ile de Beauté).

An abundance of *vins de pays*, and established AC areas, do not really go together. In Burgundy and Bordeaux there is a dearth of *vins de pays*, and the Loire is not exactly awash with them, either. In the south, on the other hand, and in Hérault particularly, the map is studded with still-unfamiliar names which are waging their battle against *vin de table* mediocrity. There is plenty of red made down there, but, surprisingly, a fair bit is produced in the great white wine area of the Loire, too. *Vins de pays* only make up about six per cent of the total Loire production (as against c. 14 per cent of total French production), and the largest (and probably the most often seen) Loire label is that of the Jardin de la France. This covers no less than ten *départements* and produces more than 20 million bottles in all, using all the red grapes that are permitted for AC wines in the Loire. They are best drunk young and cool.

Gamay is grown in the Coteaux du Cher et de l'Arnon (in the Quincy and Reuilly area) and Gamay and Cabernet Franc nearer the mouth of the Loire, in the Marches de Bretagne. Some Cabernet Franc also appears next door, in the coastal Vin de Pays de Retz, but this is predominantly white wine country.

The ten *départements* that make up the Jardin de la France area each have their own *vin de pays*, as do the *départements* of Nièvre and Sarthe which adjoin the Jardin de la France region, using Gamay and Pinot Noir in the former and Gamay, Cot and Cabernet Franc in the latter, which has the smallest production of all. And in the *département* of Loire itself, near the source of the river in central France, come the Vins de Pays d'Urfé, which somewhat resemble Beaujolais – not surprisingly, since Gamay as well as Pinot Noir is grown here.

All Bordeaux itself can offer in the way of red *vins de pays* is the small production of Vin de Pays de la Gironde, but most of this is white. The *département* of the Dordogne also produces some red, as does that of the Landes. To the north, some red *vins de pays* comes from the Charente and Charente Maritimes *départements*. Much more interesting are the *vins de pays* of the south-west of France. Here new, non-local grape varieties are often being planted, and since they are new, they have no right to adopt the ACs of the area. The red from Agenais can be quite tough, using as it does Bordelais grape varieties plus local types like Tannat, Fer, Bouchales and Abouriou.

Côtes de Gascogne wines come from the *département* of the Gers, in Armagnac country. It contains two other *vin de pays* regions, Condomois and Montestruc, the grape varieties being Tannat, Merlot and the two Cabernets in the former, and Jurançon Noir, Cot, Fer and Gamay in the latter, the Gamay helping to lighten the taste somewhat.

Next door to these is Saint Sardos, with its Syrah, Tannat and Cabernet-based wines, with the addition of Abouriou and Jurançon Noir – it is the Cabernet that makes the wines more supple here. And in the Coteaux et Terrasses de Montauban the soil produces light wines made from Cabernet, Gamay, Syrah

Above: *Co-operative cellars, such as this at Pic St-Loup in Hérault, can be among the most technically advanced in France.*

Right: *A large quantity of* vin de pays *is packed in bulk. The bag-in-the-box is becoming increasingly popular.*

and Tannat with some Jurançon Noir. Just to the north are the Coteaux du Quercy, from the Cahors area, which are made from Cahors grapes but with the addition of a fair amount of Gamay.

Some of the best country wines of the South West, however, come from the Côtes du Tarn. The grapes are mostly Gamay and Portugais Bleu, but often with some Syrah, Merlot and Cabernet in the blend: the results are reliable and attractive. Further to the north, just on the edge of the Lot departement, are the Coteaux de Glanes. Gamay and Merlot here produce nicely soft wines. Going further east one finds in Aveyron the splendidly-named Gorges et Côtes de Millau, based on Gamay, or Syrah, for two distinctly

Above: *These grapes, harvested at Reuilly in the Loire, are destined to become Jardin de la France vin de pays.*

different styles, and near the Pyrénées is Bigorre, producing red wines from Tannat and Cabernet Franc.

Some of these wines will be from individual growers, often farmers who have only started bottling their own wines comparatively recently. However, for *vin de pays* generally, the co-operatives are the main sources. That may change, if it becomes economically more worthwhile for growers to invest in making their own wines, but it will be a long time before that happens on a wide scale.

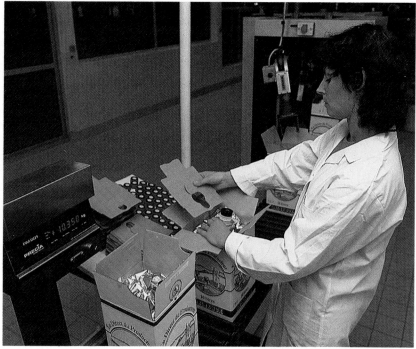

*I*n the eastern half of France the *vin de pays* picture is similar to that in the west – not much action in the classic regions, but the up-and-coming areas of the south absolutely bursting with them. Franche-Comté comes from further north, the *départements* of Haute-Saône and Jura to be precise, and mostly (within these *départements*) from the areas of Champlitte, Charcenne, and Offlanges. Most of the wine is white, but some reds are made from Pinot Noir and Gamay.

To the south, from Savoie, the Vin de Pays d'Allobrogie is also mostly white, with a little Gamay and Mondeuse for the red. A little more Gamay or Pinot Noir-based red comes from the Balmes Dauphinoises to the west (the word *balmes* is the local term for the rocky terrain), and there is also Gamay and Pinot Noir which is produced in the Coteaux du Grésivaudan.

Moving to the middle Rhône valley, the Collines Rhodaniennes produce largely red *vins de pays*, from Gamay and Syrah grapes. Where the *vin de pays* area intrudes into the Loire departement some Pinot Noir may be grown as well, as may Cabernet Franc and Merlot in the parts of the area which are in the *département* of the Isère. It is common to find the grape type mentioned on the label. Co-operatives are important here, particularly those at Tain-l'Hermitage, Saint-Donat, Saint-Desirat, and Péage-de-Roussillon, but around Tain-l'Hermitage and Chavanay there are also individual growers producing good *vins de pays*.

This area's southern neighbour is the *vin de pays* area of Comté de Grignan, where the

Below: *The Vignerons Ardéchois' bottling line at Ruoms. It processes about 125,000hl of* vin de pays *every year, as well as 218,000hl of* vin de table.

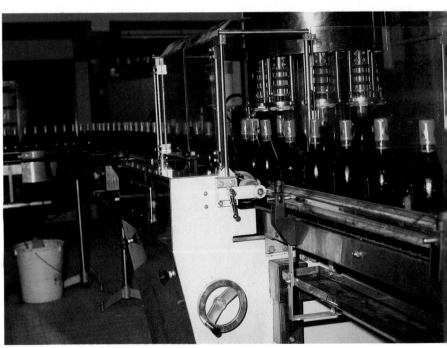

usual Côtes du Rhône varieties of Grenache, Carignan, Cinsault, Mourvèdre, Syrah and Alicante, are used for wines that must attain 12° alcohol. In the Ardèche, Vin de Pays de l'Ardèche comes from the whole *département*, and should not be confused with Vin de Pays des Coteaux de l'Ardèche, which covers the south of the *département*, and which produces wines that are, not surprisingly, similar in style. Some of the wines – from grapes such as Cabernet Sauvignon, Merlot, Gamay and Syrah – may be named on the label, or they may be blended into a more typical southern red with the usual local varieties. A typical southern blend of grapes, too, is used in the Coteaux des Baronnies together with Gamay, Merlot and Cabernet Sauvignon, for reds of a minimum of 11° alcohol. Côtes de Rhône varieties also go to make Vin de Pays de Principauté d'Orange. The most important co-operatives here are those at Sérignan and Sainte-Cécile-des-Vignes. The *départements* of the Drôme, Ain, Puy de Dôme and Vaucluse also have their own *vins de pays*.

The further south and west one goes after Avignon, the more *vin de pays* areas there are. The most important are the departmental Vin de Pays du Gard, of which two-thirds are red, made from Carignan, Cinsault, Grenache, Mourvèdre, and Syrah, plus other

Above: *The tranquillity of this vineyard in the Ardèche belies the technical sophistication of the industry that will vinify, bottle and market these grapes as Vin de Pays des Coteaux de l'Ardèche.*

local varieties and Cabernet Sauvignon and Merlot, Vin de Pays de l'Hérault, relying mostly on Carignan, with a large amount of Grenache, plus Cinsault, Mourvèdre and Syrah. And here, too, classic Bordelais varieties are being planted. In the Sables du Golfe du Lion Listel have the biggest wine estate in France, planted on ungrafted rootstock in the phylloxera-free sand.

Vin de Pays de l'Aude is made mostly from Carignan, with Grenache, Cinsault, Mourvèdre, with Bordelais varieties, and local grapes: look out for the companies of Nicolas and Chantovent here.

The *département* of Pyrénées-Orientales is also a large producer and contains, among others, the *vin de pays* zone of Catalan. Further east, in the Var *département*, the zones of Argens, Les Maures and Mont Caume use typical southern grapes. In Corsica there is only one *vin de pays*, the evocatively-named Ile de Beauté, which uses local Corsican varieties, plus some from the Southern Rhône, and Merlot and the Cabernets.

INDEX

All names of châteaux/vineyards are indexed, as well as names of wines, grape varieties, recommended producers, geographical regions, place names, and the illustrations. Figures in *italics* refer to illustration captions.

Note: St and Saint are followed by Ste and Sainte

A

AC *see* Appellation Contrôlée
Abouriou grape, 114, 117
Abymes, 113
d'Agassac, Ch, 40, 54
Aimé-Boucher, 111
Ajaccio, 143, *143*, 144
Aléria, 144
Alicante grape, 140
Aloxe-Corton, 74
Alsace, 148-9
    bottle, 22
    grapes, 149
    recommended producers, 149
Amiral de Beychevelle, 38
Amadieu, Pierre, 97
Ambonnay, 147
Ampeau, Robert, 76
Andron-Blanquet, Ch, 39, 40
Aney, Ch, 41
L'Angélus, Ch, 42, 59
des Anges, Domaine, 105
d'Angludet, Ch, 46
Anhaux, 123
Anjou, 106, 107, 108-09
    grapes, 109
    vintage chart, 33
Anjou Gamay, 107, 108
Anjou Rouge, 107
Anjou-Saumur, 106, 108-9
Appellation Contrôlée laws, 16-17, 98
Appellation d'Origine Simple, 150
Apremont, 113
Aramon grape, 140
Arbin, 113
Arbois, 112, 113
Arbois Pupillin, 112
Ardèche, 155
Argens, 155
d'Arricaud-Bordes, Ch, *122, 123*
L'Arrosée, Ch, 42
Arsac, 46
Artigue-Arnaud, Ch, 38
Les Arvelets, 76
Aubun grape, 89
Audebert et Fils, 110
Ausone, Ch, 42, *58*, 58, 59
Auxerrois grape, 118, 119
Auxey-Duresses, 78, 79
Aviet, Lucien, 113
Ay, 147
Ayse, 113
Azé, *17*

B

Bahans-Haut-Brion, Ch, 38
Balac, Ch, 41
Balagne, 144
Balestard la Tonnelle, Ch, 42, 59
Balmes Dauphinoises, 154
Bandol, 135, 138, 139
    grapes, 139
    recommended producers, 139
Banyuls, 125, 132, *132*, 133
    recommended producers, 133
Banyuls Grand Cru, 133
Banyuls-sur-Mer, 133
Barancourt, 147
Barbé, C, 63
de Barbe, Ch, 63
de Barjac, Guy, 94
de la Baronne, Ch, 128
Barrejat, Domaine, 123
Barroublo, Domaine, 127
de Barruol, Henri, 97
Barthex, Ch, 38
Barton family, 35, 49
Bas-Médoc, 44-5
    grapes, 44
    recommended châteaux, 44
    see also Haut-Médoc; Médoc
les Bastides, Domaine, 140
Batailley, Ch, 41, 53
de Baudare, Domaine, 120
Baudry, Ch, 38
Béarn, 114, 115, 122-3
    grapes, 123
    recommended producers, 123
Beau-Séjour-Bécot, Ch, 42
Beau-Site, Ch, 51
Beau-Site-Haut-Vignoble, Ch, 51
Beau-Mazaret, Ch, 38
de Beaucastel, Ch, 98
Beaudot, Mme Veuve Joseph, 70
Beaujolais, *13*, 27, 68, *84*, 84, *86*, 86-7
    grapes, 84, 86, *87*
    recommended producers, 86
    vintage chart, 31
Beaujolais Nouveau, *25*, 82, 84, 85, 86

Beaujolais Supérieur, 86
Beaujolais Villages, 86
Beaumes de Venise, 102
Beaumont, Ch, 39, 40
de Beaumont family, 52
Beaumont-Moteaux, 93
Beaune, 74, 75
Beaune Les Marconnets, 69
Beauregard, Ch, 60
Beauréard, Domaine, 98
Beauséjour Duffau-Lagasosse, Ch, 42
Beausite, Ch, 40
Le Beausset, 138
La Bécade, Ch, 41
Bégadon, 45
Bel-Air-Marquis d'Alègre, Ch, 46
Bel-Orme, Ch, 40
Bel-Orme-Tronquoy-de-Lalande, Ch, 54
Belair, Ch, 42, 59
Belgrave, Ch, 41, 54
Bellegarde, Ch, 38
Bellet, 135, 138, 139
    grapes, 139
    recommended producers, 139
de Bellet, Ch, 139
Bellerive, Ch, 41
Bellerose, Ch, 38, 41
Bellevue, Ch, 42
Bellevue la Fôret, Ch, 120
Bellevue-Laffont, Ch, 38
Belloy, Ch, 64
Bergat, Ch, 42
Bergerac, 32, 115, 116
    grapes, 117
    recommended producers, 117
    red wine production, 114
Berliquet, Ch, 42
Bernard, Guy, 91
de la Bernardine, Domaine, 98
Berthet, Paul, 105
Berthet-Rayne, Père et Fils, 105
Les Bertins, Ch, 41
Bertrand, Georges, 128
des Bertrands, Domaine, 136
Berzé le Chatel, *82*
Beychevelle, Ch, 25, 38, 41, *48*, 49
Bigorre, 153
Billette de Provence Listel, 136
Bizanet, 129
Blaignan, 45
Blayais, 62
Blaye, 35, 37, 62-3, *63*
    grapes, 63
    recommended châteaux, 63
du Blomac, 127
Boisgrand, Dom 38
Boisseaus-Vannières, Ch, 136
Boisset, Jean-Claude, 73
Bollinger, 147
Bomzoms, Francis, 131
Bonneau du Martray, Domaine, 75
Bonneau-Livran, Ch, 41
Bonnes Mares, 71
Bordeaux, 27, 28, 34-65
    bottle, 22
    classifications, 38-9, 40-1
    grapes, 35, 44, 46, 49, 51, 54, 57, 59, 60, 63, 64
    prices, 24, 35
    second labels, 32, 38-9
    vintage chart, 30, 35
    vins de pays, 152
    see also Bas-Médoc, Blaye, Bourg, Canon-Fronsac, Fronsac, Graves, Haut-Médoc, Listrac, Margaux, Médoc, Moulis, Pauillac, Pomerol, St-Emilion, St-Estèphe, St-Julien, Sauternes
Bordelais grapes, 120
Le Boscq, Ch, 41, 51
Le Bosquet des Papes, 98
Bouchard Aîné, 81
Bouchard Père et Fils, 76
Bouquet de Monbousquet, 38
Bourboulenc grape, 98, 100, 101
Bourdieu-la-Valadu, Ch, 64
Bourg, 35, 37, 62-3
    grapes, 63
    recommended châteaux, 63
Bourgeais, 62
Bourgeuil, 32, 106, 110
    red wine production, 107
Bourgneuf-Val-d'Or, 68
Bourgogne Grand Ordinaire, 66, 68
Bourgogne Passe-Tout-Grains, 66, 68
Bourgogne rouge, 66, 68
des Bouscaillons, Domaine, 120
Bouscaut, Ch, 42, 57
du Bousquet, Ch, 63
Boutenac, 129
Bouvet-Ladubay, 109
Bouzy, 147, *147*
Boyd-Cantenac, Ch, 40, 46
Branaire-Ducru, Ch, 40, 49
Brane-Cantenac, Ch, 38, 40, 46
Braquet grape, 135
La Bressandes vineyard, 74
Le Breuil, Ch, 41
La Bridane, Ch, 41, 49
Brillette, Ch, 40
Brochon, 70
Brouilly, 86, 87

Broustet, Ch, 39
Brulescaille, Ch, 63
Brunet, Georges, 55, 141
Bugey, 113
Burgundy, 27, 66-87
    bottle, 22
    Grand Crus, 71, 73, 74
    grapes, 66, 67, 70, 73, 76, 79, 81, 83, 86
    prices, 67
    red wine production, 66
    vintage chart, 31
    see also Beaujolais, Côte Chalonnaise, Côte de Beaune, Côte de Nuits, Mâconnais
Buxy co-operative, 83
Buzet, 115, 117, *117*
    recommended producers, 117
    red wine production, 114
By, Ch de, 41
de Byonne, Ch, 83

C

Cabardès, 129
Cabernet d'Anjou, 109
Cabernet Franc grape, *37*
    Bordeaux wines, 35, 36, 44, 46, 49, 51, 53, 54, 57, 58, 59, 60, 62, 63, 64, 65
    Languedoc-Roussillon, 129
    Loire wines, 106, 107, 108, 109, 110, 111
    South-West wines, 114, 116, 117, 120, 121, 122, 123
Cabernet Sauvignon grape, 16, *36*
    Bordeaux wines, 35, 36, 44, 46, 49, 50, 51, 52, 53, 54, 57, 58, 59, 60, 62, 63, 64, 65
    Languedocc-Roussillon, 129
    Loire wines, 107, 108, 109, 110, 111
    Provence wines, 135, 136, 139, 140, 141
    South-West wines, 114, 116, 117, 122, 123
La Cadière d'Azur, 138
Cadaujac, 57
Cadet-Piola, Ch, 42
Cahors, 114, 115, 118-19
    grapes, 119
    recommended producers, 119
Les Caillerets, 76
Les Cailloux, 98
Cairanne, 96, 102
Calitor grape
    Provence wines, 135
    Rhone wines, 100, 101
des Calmette, Domaine, 131
Calon-Ségur, Ch, 39, 40, 51
Le Calvex, Jacqueline, 127
Calvi, 144
Calvi-Balagne, *143*, 144
de Camensac, Ch, 41, 54, 55
Camus Père et Fils, 70
Canon, Ch, 42, 59
Canon de Brem, Ch, 64
Canon-Fronsac, 64
Canon-la-Gaffelière, Ch, 42, 59
Canteloup, Ch, 51
Cantemerle, Ch, 41, 54, 55
Cantenac, 46
Cantenac-Brown, Ch, 40, 46
Cantereau, Ch, 38
de Canterrane, Domaine, 131
Cap Corse, *143*, 144
Cap de Mourlin, Ch, 39, 42
Cap Leucate, 128
Cap Léon Veyrin, Ch, 41
Capbern, Ch, 40
Capbern-Gasqueton, Ch, 51
Capitoro, Domaine, 145
Caramany, 125, 130
carbonic maceration *see* macération carbonique
Carbonnieux, Ch, 42, 57
Carbanieux, Ch. 41
La Cardonne, Ch, 39, 40, 44, 45
Carignan grape
    Corsica wines, 143
    Languedoc-Roussillon wines, 124, 125, 126, 127, 128, 129, 130, 131
    Provence wines, 135, 136, 138, 139, 140, 141
    Rhône wines, 100, 101, 103, 104, 105
de Carles, 64
Carmenère grape, 35, 37
Les Carmes-Haut-Brion, Ch, 57
Caronne-Ste-Gemme, Ch, 38, 40, 54
Cascastel, 128
Cassevert, Ch, 38
Cassis, ↓35, 138, 139
    grapes, 139
    recommended producers, 139
de Castel Oualou, Domaine, 101
Le Castellet, 138
Castéra, Ch, 41, 44
Catalan, 155
Cave des Quatre Chemins, 103
Cave Coopérative d'Aglya, 133
Cave Coopérative d'Argeles, 133
Cave Coopérative d'Irouléguy, 123
Cave Coopérative de Bellocq, 123
Cave Coopérative de Bergerac, 117
Cave Coopérative de Die, 104, 105

Cave Coopérative de Faugères, 131
Cave Coopérative de Latour-de-France, 131
Cave Coopérative de Laurens, 131
Cave Coopérative de Paziols, 133
Cave Coopérative des Vins Fins Cruet, 113
Cave Coopérative l'Etoile, 133
Cave Coopérative Le Cellier des Templiers, 105
Cave Coopérative Lesquerde, 131
Caves, 128
Caves Coopératives, 18, 105
Les Caves de la Loire, 109
Cayrou, Ch, 119
Cazes Frères, 131, 133
Les Cellier des Dauphins, 105
Cellier des Templiers, 131, 133
Cerbère, 133
Cerdon, 113
Certan, Ch, 60
Certan de May, Ch, 60
Certan-Giraud, Ch, 60
Chacoli, 123
de Chaintre, Ch, 109
de Chambert, Ch, 119
Chambert-Marbuzet, Ch, 38, 41
Chambertin, 69, 71
Chambolle-Musigny, 70, 71
Champagne bottle, 22
Les Champans, 76
Champet, Emile, 91
Champlitte, 154
Champy Père et Cie, 75
Chanos-Curson, 93
Chanson Père et Fils, 67, 75
Chante-Cigale, Dom, 98
Chante-Perdrix, 98
Chanut Frères, 86
La Chapelle, 93
Chapelle-Chambertin, 71
Chapoutier, M, 90, 91, 93, 93, 94, 98
chaptalisation, 12, 13, 67
Charcenne, 154
Chardonnay co-operative, 83
Charente, 152
Charente Maritime, 152
Charentais, 150
Charmes-Chambertin, 71
Charpinnat, 113
Chassagne-Montrachet, 78, 79
Chasse-Spleen, Ch, 40, 54
Château-St-André, 97
du Château St-Roch, Domaine, 101
Châteaubourg, 111
Châteaumeillant, 111
Châteauneuf-du-Pape, 33, 89, 98-9, 99
   grapes, 98
   recommended producers, 98
   red wine production, 89
Chatelet, Ch Le, 42
Chatillon-en-Diois, 104-5
   red wine production, 89
Les Chaumes, 74
Chautagne, 113
Chauvenet, F, 73
Chauvin, Ch, 42
Chavanay, 154
Chave, Jean-Louis, 93, 94
Chavignol, 111
Chénas, 86, 87
Cheval-Blanc, Ch, 42, 43, 58, 59
de Chevalier, Domaine, 42, 57, 57
Cheverny, 111
Les Chevrets, 76
Chignin, 113
Chinon, 32, 106, 110
   red wine production, 107
Chiroubles, 86, 87
Chol et Fils, 91
Chusclan, 96, 102
Cinsault grape
   Corsica wines, 143, 145
   Languedoc-Roussillon wines, 125, 126, 127, 128, 129, 130, 131
   Provence wines, 135, 136, 137, 139, 140
   Rhône wines, 89, 96, 97, 98, 103, 104, 105
   South-West wines, 114, 121
Cissac, Ch, 39, 40, 54
La Citran, Ch, 40, 54
de Clairefont, Ch, 38
Clairette de Die, 104
Clairette grape, 96, 97, 98, 100, 101, 139
Clape, Auguste, 94
La Clape, 129
La Clare, Ch, 41
claret, 24, 25, 35
de Clargy, Ch, 100, 101
Clarke, Ch, 39, 41
Clavelin, Hubert, 113
Les Clefs d'Or, 98
Clement Termes, Domaine, 120
Clerc-Milon-Rothschild, Ch, 41, 53
Clergets, 70
Clinet, Ch, 60
Clos de Béze, 71
Clos de Gamot, 119
Clos de l'Echo, 110
Clos de l'Oratoire, Ch, 42
Clos de la Bousse d'Or, 76
Clos de la Roche, 71
Clos de la Tournelle, 39
Clos de Lambrays, 71
Clos de Tart, 70, 71
Clos de Vougeot, 72, 73
Clos des Jacobins, Ch, 42
Clos du Margins, 39

Clos du Monastère, 39
Clos du Mont-Olivet, 98
Les Clos du Roi vineyard, 74
Clos Fourtet, Ch, 42, 59
Clos la Coutale, 119
Clos la Croix-Blanche, 117
Clos la Madeleine, Ch, 39, 42
Clos Labère, 38
Clos Marfisi, 145
Clos Nicrosi, 145
Clos-René, 60
du Clos Renon, Ch, 38
Clos St-Denis, 71
Clos St-Jean, 79
Clos St-Martin, Ch, 42
Clos Ste-Magdeleine, 139
Clos Toulifaut, 39
Clos Triguedina, 119
La Closerie, Ch, 41
La Closerie-Grand-Poujeaux, Ch, 54
La Clotte, Ch, 42
La Clusière, Ch, 42
Collines Rhodaniennes, 154
Collioure, 125, 130, 131
   grapes, 131
   recommended producers, 131
   red wine production, 125
Collogne, 93
Colombard grape, 139
Colombier-Monpelou, Ch, 38, 40
de la Colombière, Domaine, 120
Les Combes vineyard, 74
La Commanderie, Ch, 39
Complong, 129
Comté de Grignan, 154
Comté Tolosan, 150
Condomois, 152
Confrérie de Oisly et Thésée, 110
Connétable-Talbot, 38
Conquilles, Ch, 38
Conseillante, Ch, 60, 61
Coopérative de St-Paul-de-Fenouillet, 131
Coopérative de Pezilla-la-Rivière, 131
Coopérative Espira-de-l'Agly, 131
Corbières, 125, 128-9
   grapes, 128
   recommended producers, 128
   red wine production, 125
Corbin, Ch, 42, 59
Corbin-Michotte, Ch, 42
Cornas, 94-5
   grapes, 94
   recommended producers, 94
   red wine production, 89
Corsica, 142-5
   grapes, 143, 145
   recommended producers, 145
   red wine production, 143
   vins de pays, 155
Corton, 74, 75
Corton-Bressandes, 74
Corton-Grancey, Ch, 74, 75
Cos d'Estournel, Ch, 39, 40, 50, 51, 51
Cos-Laboury, Ch, 41, 50, 51
la Coste, Ch, 140
Costières du Gard, 129
Cot grape
   Loire wines, 107, 110, 111
   Languedoc-Roussillon, 129
Côte Baleau, Ch, 42
Côte Blonde, 90, 91
Côte Brune, 90, 91
Côte Chalonnaise, 68, 80-1
   grapes, 81
   recommended producers, 81
   red wine production, 66
Côte de Beaune, 69, 74-5
   Grand Crus, 74
   grapes, 75, 76, 79
   recommended producers, 75, 76, 79
   red wine production, 66
   villages, 66, 69
   vintage chart, 31
Côte de Brouilly, 86, 87
Côte de Nuits, 68, 70-3, 75
   Grand Crus, 71, 73
   grapes, 70, 73
   recommended producers, 70, 73
   red wine production, 66
   villages, 69
   vintage chart, 31
Côte d'Or, 8, 11, 68, 69, 71, 84
Côte Roannaise VDQS, 32
Côte Rôtie, 90-1, 91
   grapes, 91
   recommended producers, 91
   red wine production, 89
   vintage, 32
Coteaux Champenois, 32, 146-7
Coteaux d'Aix-en-Provence, 32, 135, 140-1
   grapes, 140
   recommended producers, 140
Coteaux d'Ajaccio, 144
Coteaux d'Ancenis, 106
Coteaux de Cahors, 118
Coteaux de Glanes, 153
Coteaux de la Méjanelle, 131
Coteaux de Pierrevert, 140
Les Coteaux de Pouzois-Minervois Coopératives, 127
Coteaux de St-Christol, 130, 130
Coteaux de Vérargues, 131
Coteaux des Baronnies, 155
Coteaux des Baux-de-Provence, 32, 135, 140, 140-1
   grapes, 140

recommended producers, 140
Coteaux du Cher et de l'Arnon, 152
Coteaux du Giennois, 111
Coteaux du Grésivaudan, 154
Coteaux du Languedoc, 125, 130
Coteaux du Loir, 32, 107
Coteaux du Quercy, 153
Coteaux du Tricastin, 104-5
   red wine production, 89
Coteaux du Vendômois, 111
Coteaux et Terrasses de Montauban, 152
Coteaux Varois, 140
Côtes d'Agly, 125
Côtes d'Auvergne, 111
Côtes d'Olt, 119
Côtes de Bergerac, 114, 116
Côtes de Bourg, 62
Côtes de Bruhlois, 117
Côtes de Canon-Fronsac, 64
Côtes de Castillon, 32, 35, 65
Côtes de Duras, 32, 115, 116-17
   recommended producers, 117
   red wine production, 114
Côtes de France, 65
Côtes de Gascogne, 152
Côtes de la Malepère, 129
Côtes de Provence, 32, 135, 136-7, 137
   grapes, 136
   recommended producers, 136
   red wine production, 135
Côtes de St-Mont, 123
Côtes de Toul, 149
Côtes du Forez, 111
Côtes du Fronton, 120, 121
Côtes du Frontonnais, 114
Côtes du Jura, 112, 113
Côtes du Luberon VDQS, 32, 140
Côtes du Marmandais, 117
Côtes du Rhône, 102-3
   bottle, 22
   grapes, 103
   recommended producers, 103
   red wine production, 89
   villages, 102-3
Côtes du Rhône-Villages, 89, 102-3
Côtes du Roussillon, 125, 130, 131
   red wine production, 125
Côtes du Roussillon-Villages, 125, 130, 131
   red wine production, 125
Côtes du Tarn, 153
Côtes du Ventoux, 104-5
   grapes, 105
   recommended producers, 105
   red wine production, 89
Côtes du Vivarais, 103
Côtes Roannaises, 111
Coubet, Ch, 63
Coufran, Ch, 38, 40
Coujan, Ch, 131
Couly-Dutheil, 110, 111
Counoise grape
   Provence wines, 140
   Rhône wines, 89, 98
La Cour Pavillon, 38
Courbu Noir grape, 114, 122, 123
La Couronne, Ch, 53
Coursodon, Pierre & Gustave, 94
Coustelle, Ch, 64
Coutelin-Merville, Ch, 40
Coutet, Ch, 42
Couvent des Jacobins, Ch, 42
Cowdray, Viscount, 52
Cransac, Ch, 120
de la Cremade, Domaine, 140
de Cremat, 139
Le Crock, Ch, 39, 40
La Croix, Ch, 38, 60
de la Croix, Domaine, 136
de la Croix-Millorit, Ch, 63
La Croix-de-Gay, Ch, 60
Croizet-Bages, Ch, 38, 41, 53
Croque-Michotte, Ch, 42
Crozes-Hermitage, 92-3
   grapes, 93
   recommended producers, 93
   red wine production, 89
Cruet, 113
Cubzaguais, 65
Cucugnan, 128
Cumières, 147
Curé-Bon la Madeleine, Ch, 42, 59
de Curé-Bourse, Dom, 38
de Curebeasse, Domaine, 136
Cuvée de l'Oratoire, 136

D

Damoy, Domaine Pierre, 70
Dassault, Ch, 42, 59
La Dauphine, Ch, 64
Dauzac, Ch, 38, 41, 46
Delaporte, Vincent, 110
Delas Frères, 91, 93, 94
Delorme, J-F, 81
Demereaulemont, Ch, 38
Depagneux, 86
Dervieux, Albert, 91
Descombes, Jean, 86
Desmeure Père et Fils, 93
Desmirail, Ch, 38, 40, 46
Dezat, André, 110
du Devoy, Domaine, 101
Dillon family, 57
diseases, 8-9
   coulure, 8, 30, 33, 36, 89
   millerandage, 8, 36

noble rot, 8
phylloxera, 8, 100
Dizy, 147
La Dominique, Ch, 42
de Doms, Ch, 39
Dopff & Irion, 149
Doucillon, 139
Drouhin, Joseph, 70, 75
Duboeuf, Georges, 13, 25, 83, 86
Ducru-Beaucaillou, Ch, 25, 38, 40, 48, 49
Dufau Père et Fils, André, 123
Duhart-Milon-Rothschild, Ch, 39, 40, 53
Dujac, Domaine, 70
Duplessis-Fabre, Ch, 41
Duplessis-Hauchecorne, Ch, 40
de Durand, Domaine, 117
Duras grape, 114, 120
Durfort-Vivens, Ch, 38, 40, 46
Duroche, 70
Dutruch-Grand-Poujeaux, Ch, 40, 54

E

EEC regulations, 40, 70
Embres-et-Castelmaure co-opératives, 128
l'Enclos, Ch, 60
Enclos de Moncabon, 38
Entre Deux Mers, 65
Les Epenots, 76
l'Esparrou, Ch, 131
l'Estagnol, Ch, 103
Estoublon, 140
de l'Estremade, Dom, 38
l'Etang des Colombes, Ch, 128
Ets Nicolas, 131
l'Evangile, Ch, 60, 61
Evôme, 93
Evenoz, 138

F

Fabrezan, 129
Faiveley, J H, 73, 81
Faller Frères, 149
Faugères, 125
    grapes, 131
    recommended producers, 131
    red wine production, 125
Faurie de Souchard, Ch, 42
Fayolle et ses Fils, Jules, 93
Fer grape
    Languedoc-Roussillon, 129
    South-West wines, 114, 116, 117, 120,
    122, 123
des Feraud, Domaines, 130
La Fermade, 101
de la Ferme Blanche, Domaine, 139
Ferrande, Ch, 39
de Ferrant, Domaine, 117
Ferraud, 86
Ferrière, Ch, 40, 46
La Ferté sous Jouarre, 23
Figari, 143, 144
Figeac, Ch, 38, 42, 59
Fieuzal, Ch, 42, 57
Filliatreau, Paul, 109
Fitou, 125, 128-9, 129
    grapes, 128
    recommended producers, 128
    red wine production, 125
Fixin, 70, 71
La Fleur Milon, Ch, 40
La Fleur-Pétrus, Ch, 60, 61
Fleurie, 86, 87
Fleurie, Caveau de, 86
Fleury, Vidal, 91
Florent de Mérode, Prince, 75
Folle Noir grape, 135
Fonpetite, Ch, 38
Fonpiqueyre, Ch, 41
Fonplégade, Ch, 42, 59
Fonréaud, Ch, 41, 54
Fonroque, Ch, 42, 59
de Fonscolombe, Ch, 140
Fonseche, Ch, 38
de Fontanella, Domaine, 145
de Fontarney, Dom 38
Fontesteau, Ch, 40
food and wine, 26-9
Foret, Jacques, 113
Fort Vauban, Ch, 41
Fortia, Ch, 98
Les Forts de Latour, 38
Fourcas-Dupré, Ch, 38, 40, 54-5
Fourcas-Hosten, Ch, 40, 54
Franc-Mayne, Ch, 42
de France, Ch, 38
La France, Ch, 41
Franche-Comté, 154
de Frégate, Domaine, 139
Fronsac, 35, 64-5
    grapes, 64
    recommended châteaux, 64
Frontignan grape, 139
frost, 11, 36, 67, 82

G

GAEC Vignobles Laplace, 123
Gaby, Ch, 64
La Gaffelière, Ch, 39, 42, 59
Gaillac, 114, 115, 120-1
    grapes, 120
    recommended producers, 120
Gallais-Bellevué, Ch, 38, 41
Gamay d'Anjou, 106

Gamay de l'Ardèche, 32
Gamay de Touraine, 32, 111
Gamay grape, 67, 69, 79, 84, 87, 108
    Burgundy, 66, 68, 81, 82, 83, 86
    Jura and Savoie wines, 84, 113
    Loire wines, 84, 106, 107, 108, 109, 110,
    111
    Rhône wines, 84, 104
    Provence wines, 84
    South-West wines, 114, 120, 121
La Garde, Ch, 57
de Garria, Domaine, 133
de Gaudou, Domaine, 119
Gavoty, Domaine, 136
Gazin, Ch, 60, 61
Geantet-Pansiot, E, 70
Geisweiler et Fils, 73
Gelin, Domaine Pierre, 70
Gentile, Domaine, 145
Gerin, Alfred, 91
Gervans, 93
Gevrey-Chambertin, 69, 70, 71
Ghisonaccia, 144
Gigondas, 96-7, 97, 102
    grapes, 97
    recommended producers, 97
    red wine production, 89
Gilles, Louis, 94
Girard, J, 113
Gironde vineyards, 55
Giscours, Ch, 40, 46, 47
Givry, 80, 81
Du Glana, Ch, 40
Gloria, Ch, 39, 49
la Gombaude, Ch, 38
Gorges et Côtes de Millau, 153
Gouge, Domaine Henri, 73
de Gourgazaud, Ch, 127
Gouroux, Henry, 73
Goureaux, Louis, 73
Grand Barrail, Ch, 63
Grand-Barrail-Lamarzelle-Figeac, Ch, 38,
    42, 59
Grand' Boise, Ch, 136
Grand-Canyon, Ch, 38
Grand-Corbin, Ch, 42
Grand-Corbin-Despagne, Ch, 42
Grand Duroc Milon, Ch, 38, 41
Grand-Mayne, Ch, 38, 42
de Grand Montmirail, Domaine, 97
Grand Moulin, Ch, 41
Grand-Pontet, Ch, 42
Grand-Puy-Ducasse, Ch, 38, 53
Grand-Puy-Lacoste, Ch, 41, 53
Grand Renouil, Ch, 64
Grand Roussillon, 125, 133
du Grand Tinel, Domaine, 98
de Grangeneuve, Ch, 38
de Grangeneuve, Domaine, 105
de la Grave, Ch, 63
Graves, 56-7
    classified wines, 42
    grapes, 57
    recommended châteaux, 57
    red wine production, 35
    vintage chart, 30
Graves de Vayres, 65
Les Gravilles, 38
Grenache grape, 33
    Corsica wines, 143, 145
    Languedoc-Roussillon wines, 124, 125,
    126, 127, 128, 129, 130, 131, 133
    Provence wines, 135, 136, 137, 138, 139,
    140, 141
    Rhône wines, 89, 96, 97, 98, 100, 101,
    103, 104, 105
Gressier-Grand-Poujeaux, Ch, 54
Les Grèves vineyard, 74
Greysac, Ch, 40, 44
Griotte-Chambertin, 71
Grippat, Jean-Louis, 93, 94
Grivelet, Domaine, 70
Grivot, Jean, 73, 73
Grivot, Veuve Gaston, 73
Gros Frère et Soeur, 73
Gruaud-Larose, Ch, 39, 40, 49
Guadet-St-Julien, Ch, 42
Guffens-Heynen, 83
Guigal, E, 91
de la Guyonnière, Domaine, 75

H

Hanteillan, Ch, 40
Harveys of Bristol, 52
Haut-Bages-Avérous, Ch, 38, 53
Haut-Bages-Libéral, Ch, 41
Haut-Bages Monpelou, Ch, 41, 53
Haut-Bailly, Ch, 39, 42, 57
Haut-Batailley, Ch, 39, 41, 53
Haut Brion, Ch, 38, 40, 42, 56-7
Haut-Canteloup, Ch, 41
Haut-Comtat, 103
Haut-Corbin, Ch, 42
Haut-Fabreges, Ch, 131
Haut-Garin, Ch, 41
Haut-Marbuzet, Ch, 39, 40, 51
Haut Mazeris, Ch, 64
Haut-Médoc, 40, 44, 55
    classified wines, 40-1
    red wine production, 35
    see also Bas-Médoc; Médoc
Haut-Padernac, Ch, 41
de Haut-Pécharmant, Domaine, 117
Haut-Prieuré, 38
Haut-Saroe, Ch, 39

Haut-Sarpe, Ch, 42
de Haut-Serre, Ch, 118
Haut Sociondo, Ch, 63
Hautes Côtes de Beaune, 66
Hautes Côtes de Nuits, 66
L'Héritier Guyot, 73
Hermitage, 32, 92, 92-3
    grapes, 93
    recommended producers, 93
    red wine production, 89
de l'Hermitage, Domaine, 139
des Homs, Domaine, 127
des Hormes, Ch, 38
Hospices de Beaune, 67, 74, 75
Hospices de Nuits, 73
Houbanon, Ch, 41
Hourtin-Ducasse, Ch, 41
Hudelot et ses Fils, Paul, 70
Hudelot-Noëllat, Alain, 70
Hugel, 149

I

Ile de Beauté, 142-3, 155
Institut National des Appellations
    d'Origine, 16
Irouléguy, 114
d'Issan, Ch, 40

J

Jaboulet, Paul, Aîne, 91, 93, 94, 97
Jadot, Louis, 75, 86
Jamet, Joseph, 91
Jardin de la France, 150, 152
Jasmin, Georges & Robert, 91
du Jau, Ch, 133
la Jaubertie, Ch, 117
Jaxu, 123
Jean-Blanc, 38
Jean Cros, Domaine, 120
Jean-Faure, Ch, 42
Jeandeman, Ch, 64
Jête, Louis, 86
Jongieux, 113
Joguet, Charles, 110
Jougla, Alain, 131
Juge, Marcel, 94
Juliénas, 86, 87
de Juliénas, Ch, 86
Les Jumelles, 91
Junayme, Ch, 64
Jura, 112-13
    bottle, 22
    recommended producers, 113
    red wine production, 112
Jurançon, 122
Jurançon Noir grape, 114, 118, 119, 121
Jurançon Rouge grape, 120

K

Kirwan, Ch, 40, 46
Kuentz-Bas, 149

L

Labarde, 46
Labarde, Ch, 38
de Labarthe, Domaine, 120
de Labat, Ch, 41
labels, 20-1, 31
Labégorce-Zédé, Ch, 46
Labory-de-Tayac, Ch, 38
Labouré-Roi, 73
La Labut, Ch, 38
Ladoix-Serrigny, 74
Lafage, Jean-Louis, 123
Lafite Père et Fils, 123
Lafite-Rothschild, Ch, 39, 40, 45, 50, 52,
    53
Lafleur, Ch, 60, 61
Lafleur-Gazin, Ch, 60
Lafon, Ch, 40, 54, 55
Lafon, Domaines des Comtes, 76
Lafon-Rochet, Ch, 41, 50, 51
Lagrange, Ch, 40, 49, 60
Lagrasse, 129
La Lague, Ch, 64
La Lagune, Ch, 40, 54, 55, 141
Lalande de Pomerol, 35, 61
Lamarche, Domaine Henry, 73
Lamarque, Ch, 40, 54
Lamarzelle, Ch, 38
Lamarzelle-Figeac, Ch, 38
Lamé-Delille-Boucard, 110
Lamothe, Ch, 40
Lamothe Bergeron, Ch, 41
Lamothe-Cissac, Ch, 38
Lamy, Hubert, 79
Le Landat, Ch, 41
Landon, Ch, 41
La Landonne, 91
Lanessan, Ch, 39
Langoa-Barton, Ch, 35, 40, 49
Laniote, Ch, 42
Languedoc-Roussillon, 124-33
    bottle, 22
    grapes, 125, 127, 128, 131, 133
    red wine production, 125
    see also Corbières; Fitou; Minervois;
    Roussillon
Les Languettes vineyard, 74
Lapalme, 128
Larcis-Ducasse, Ch, 42
Larivière, Ch, 41

Larmonde, Ch, 39, 42
Larnage, 93
Larose-Trintaudon, Ch, 54
Laroze, Ch, 42
Larrivet-Haut-Brion, Ch, 57
Lartigue de Brochon, Ch, 38, 41
Lascombes, Ch, 38, 40, 46
Lassalle, Crû, 41
Latour, Ch, 34, 38, 40, 52, 53, 53
Latour, Louis, 67, 70, 74, 86
Latour à Pomerol, Ch, 60
Latour-de-France, 125, 130
Latricières-Chambertin, 71
Laudun, 96, 102
Laujac, Ch, 40, 44
Laurens-Teuller, 121
des Lauzières, Domaine, 140
Lavalière, Ch, 41
Laville-Haut-Brion, Ch, 57
Lavilledieu, 121
de la Lecugne, Domaine, 127
Lemoyne-Nexon, Ch, 38
Léognan, 57
Léoville-Barton, Ch, 35, 40, 48, 49
Léoville-Las-Cases, Ch, 25, 39, 40, 48, 49,
    49
Léoville-Poyferré, Ch, 39, 40, 48, 49
Lepitre, Abel, 147
Leroy, 79
Lestage, Ch, 41, 54
Leucate, 128
Lidourie, Ch, 63
Limouzy, Henri, 131
Lirac, 100-1, 101
    grapes, 101
    recommended producers, 101
    red wine production, 89
Listrac, 44, 54-5
    co-operative, 54
    grapes, 54
    red wine production, 35
Liversan, Ch, 38, 39, 40, 54
Livran, Ch, 39
Lognac, Ch de, 39
Loire, 106-11
    bottle, 22
    grapes, 107, 109, 110
    red wine production, 107
    vins de pays, 152
    vintage chart, 32, 33
    see also Anjou; Saumur; Touraine
des Lônes, Domaine, 105
de Longue-Toque, Domaine, 97
Lornet, Roger, 113
Loron, 86
Lou-Camp-del-Saltre, Domaine, 119
Loudenne, Ch, 38, 40, 44, 45
Loumede, Ch, 63
La Louvière, Ch, 57
Lugny St Gennoux-de-Scisse, 83
Lupé Cholet et Cie, 73
Lussac-St-Emilion, 58
Lynch-Bages, Ch, 38, 41, 53
Lynch-Moussas, Ch, 41, 53

M

Malleret, Ch, 38, 40
Malmaison, Ch, 39
de la Maltroye, Ch, 79
MacCarthy, Ch, 40
MacCarthy-Moula, Ch, 39, 41
Maccabéo grape, 100, 101
macération carbonique, 28, 82, 84-5, 98,
    108, 116, 121, 125, 126, 130, 141
Mâcon, 82
Mâcon-Mancey, 82
Mâcon Rouge, 82
Mâcon Supérieur, 82
Mâconnais, 68, 82-3
    grapes, 83
    recommended producers, 83
    red wine production, 66
    villages, 69, 82
Madiran, 22, 115, 115, 122-3
    grapes, 123
    recommended producers, 123
    red wine production, 114
Magdelaine, Ch, 42, 59
de Magenta, Domaine du Duc, 79
Magnan-la-Gaffelière, Ch, 39
Maire, Henri, 113
Maison Couly-Dutheil, 110, 111
Maitre d'Estournel, 50
Les Maitres Vignerons de la Presque'île de
    St-Tropez, 136
Malartic-Lagravière, Ch, 42, 57
Malbec grape
    Bordeaux wines, 37, 44, 46, 49, 51, 53,
        54, 57, 59, 60, 62, 63, 64, 65
    South-West wines, 114, 116, 117, 120
Les Malconsorts, 72
Malescot-St-Exupéry, Ch, 40, 46, 47
de Malle, Ch, 39
Malvoisie grape, 139
de Mandourelle, Domaine, 128
Manseng Noir grape, 114, 122, 123
de Marbuzet, Ch, 38, 39, 40, 51
La Marche, Ch, 64
de Marcilly, 79
Les Marèchaudes vineyards, 74
Marey-Monge, Domaine, 73
Margaux, Ch, 15, 19, 39, 40, 41, 44
Margaux commune, 46-7
    grapes, 46
    recommended châteaux, 46

red wine production, 35
Marignan, 113
Marion, Domaine, 70
Marionnet, Henri, 110
Marquis d'Alesme-Becker, Ch, 40, 46
Marquis-de-Terme, Ch, 41, 46
Marsanne, Jean, 94
Marsanne grape, 92, 93, 94
Marshall, Domaines Tim, 73
Martillac, Ch, 57
Martinens, Ch, 40, 46
Martini, Domaine, 145
du Martiny, Dom, 39
Mas d'Aurel, 120
du Mas Amiel, Domaine, 133
Mas Blanc, 131
du Mas Blanc, Domaine, 133
Mas Calendal, 139
Mas de Gourgonnier, 140
Mas de la Dame, 140
Mas de la Rouvière, 139
Mas du Cellier, 140
Mas Pignou, 120
Mas Sainte-Berthe, 140
Matras, Ch, 42
Maucaillou, Ch, 54
Maufoux, Prosper, 79
Les Maures, 155
Maurice, Marc, 94
Maury, 125, 133
Mausse, Ch, 64
Mauvezin, Ch, 42
Mauvezin-Badette, Côtes, 39
Mauzac grape, 114, 120, 121
Mayne d'Artignan, Ch, 39
Mayne Vieil, Ch, 64
de Mayranne, Domaine, 127
Mazeris, Ch, 64
Mazeris Bellevue, Ch, 64
Mazis-Chambertin, 71
Médoc, 36, 48, 54, 55
    classified wines, 40-1
    classification, 38-9
    red wine production, 35
    vintage chart, 30
    see also Bas-Médoc; Haut-Médoc
Meffre, Gabriel, 97
Meffre, Roger, 97
Les Meix vineyard, 74
Méjan, Domaine, 101
Melon de Bourgogne grape
    Burgundy, 66, 68
    see also Muscadet
le Menaudat, Ch, 63
Menetou-Salon, 32, 107, 111
Ménétréol, 111
Mentzelopoulos family, 46
Mercurey, 80
Merlaut family, 54
Merlot grape, 30, 37, 47, 116
    Bordeaux wines, 35, 36, 44, 46, 49, 50,
        51, 52, 53, 54, 56, 57, 58, 59, 60, 61,
        62, 63, 64, 65
    Languedoc-Roussillon wines, 129
    South-West wines, 114, 116, 117, 118,
        119, 120
Meursault, 76, 78
Meyney, Ch, 39, 40, 51
Le Meynieu, Ch, 40
Meyzonnier, Domaine, 127
Michel, Georges & Veuve, 70
Michel, Robert, 94
Millet, Ch, 38
Minervois, 125, 126-7, 126
    grapes, 127
    recommended producers, 127
    red wine production, 125
Minuty, Ch, 136
La Mission-Haut-Brion, Ch, 25, 42, 57
Moillard-Grivot, 73
Mommessin, 70, 86
Monbousquet, Ch, 38
Mondeuse grape, 112, 113
Mongeard-Mugneret, 73
Mont Caume, 155
de Mont-Redon, Domaine, 98
Montabert, Ch, 38
Montagne de Reims, 147
Montagne-St-Emilion, 58
Montagny, 80
Montaud, Ch, 136
Montestruc, 102
Monthélie, 76, 77, 77
Monthil, Ch, 41
de Montille, François, 76
Montélain, 113
de Montmirail, Ch, 97
Montpeyrous, 131
Montrose, Ch, 24, 40, 50, 51
Montséret, 129
Morey-St-Denis, 71
Morgon, 32, 86, 87
Morin, Ch, 40
Moueix, J P, 61
Moulin-à-Vent, Ch, 32, 39, 40, 54,86, 87
Moulin d'Arvigny, 39
Moulin de Calon, 39
Moulin de Duhart, Ch, 39
Moulin de la Roque, 139
Moulin de St-Vincent, Ch, 39
Moulin des Carruades, Ch, 39
Moulin des Costes, 139
Moulin du Cadet, Ch, 39
Moulin-Pey-Labrie, Ch, 64
Moulin-Riche, Ch, 41
Moulin Rouge, Ch, 41

La Mouline, 91
Moulinets, Ch des, 39
Moulis, 44, 54
    grape varieties, 54
    red wine production, 35
Moureau et Fils, Marceau, 127
Mourvaison grape, 135, 139
Mourvèdre grape
    Corsica wines, 143, 145
    Languedoc-Roussillon wines, 124, 125,
        126, 127, 128, 129, 130, 131
    Provence wines, 134, 135, 136, 137, 138,
        139, 140
    Rhône wines, 89, 96, 97, 98, 100, 101,
        103, 104, 105
Mouton-Baronne-Philippe, Ch, 41, 53
Mouton-Rothschild, Ch, 37, 40, 52, 52, 53
    labels, 31
Muscadet, 68, 106
Muscardin grape, 89, 98
Musigny, 71

N

Naigeon-Chauveau et Fils, 70
de Nalys, Domaine, 98
Nather, Henri, 110
Néac, 35, 61
négociants, 19, 35, 67
Negrette grape, 114, 120, 121
Nenin, Ch, 60
de la Nerte, Domaine, 98
Niellucio grape, 143, 144, 145
Noëllat, Charles, 73
Noëllat, Henri & Michel, 73
de Nouvelles, Ch, 128
Nuits-St-Georges, 73

O

Offlanges, 154
Olek, Jean-François, 110
Olivier, Ch, 42, 57
des Ollieux, Ch, 128
Ollioules, 138
L'Oratoire, Ch, 42
L'Oratoire St-Martin, 103
Ordonnac, 45
Les Ormes de Pez, Ch, 40, 50
Les Ormes Sorbet, Ch, 40, 44
Ott, Domaines, 136

P

de Paillas, Domaine, 119
Les Palais, Ch, 128
Palette, 135, 138, 139
    grapes, 139
    recommended producers, 139
Les Pallières, Les Fils de, 97
Palmer, Ch, 25, 37, 40, 46-7, 47
Panigon, Ch, 41
de Panisseau, Ch, 117
Le Pape, Ch, 57
Pape-Clément, Ch, 42, 57
de Paradis, Domaine, 140
de Paraza, Ch, 127
La Parde de Haut Bailly, 39
Parent, Domaine, 76
Parnac, 118, 119
Pascal, 97
Pasquier, Jayer, 73
Pasquier-Desvignes, 86
Patache-d'Aux, Ch, 40, 44
Patrimonio, 144
Patrimonio grape, 143
Pauillac, 52-3, 44
    grapes, 53
    recommended châteaux, 53
    red wine production, 35
Pavell de Luze, Ch, 40
Pavie, Ch, 42, 59
Pavie-Decesse, Ch, 42
Pavie-Macquin, Ch, 42
Pavillon-Cadet, Ch, 42
Pavillon Rouge, 39
Pays d'Oc, 150
Paziols, 128
Péage-de-Roussillon *coopérative*, 154
Pécharmant, 116, 117
    recommended producers, 117
    red wine production, 114
Pecoui-Touar grape, 138, 139
Pédesclaux, Ch, 38, 41, 53
Pélaquilé, Domaine, 145
Peraldi, Domaine, 145
Pernand-Vergelesses, 74
Perrier, Laurent, 147
Perrière, Domaine de la, 70
Les Perrières vineyard, 74
Perroy, Ch, 39
Pescadoires, 118
Petit et Fils, Désiré, 113
Petit-Faurie-de-Soutard, Ch, 42
Petit Verdot grape, 35, 37, 44, 46, 49, 51,
    53, 54, 57, 59, 60
Petit-Village, 60
Pessac, 57
Pétrus, Ch, 25, 38, 60, 61
Peymartin, Ch, 39
Peyrabon, Ch, 25, 40, 54, 54
Peyrelebade, Ch, 39
de Pez, Ch, 39, 51
Phélan-Ségur, Ch, 38, 51
Philippe, Ch, 78
Pibran, Ch, 41, 53

Pic-St-Loup, 131, *152*
Picardin grape, 98
Pichon-Baron, Ch, 53
Pichon-Lalande, Ch, 40, 53
Pichon-Longueville-Baron, Ch, 40, 53
Pichon-Longueville-Lalande, Ch, 39, 53
Picpoul grape
    Languedoc-Roussillon wines, 125, 128
    Rhône wines, 89, 98, 100, 101
    South-West wines, 121
Pineau d'Aunis grape
    Loire wines, 106, 107, 108, 109, 110, 111
Pinet, Joseph, 103
Pinot grape, 135
Pinot Gris grape, 107, 110, 111
Pinot Meunier grape, 107, 110, 11
Pinot Noir grape, *68, 83, 148*
    Alsace wines, 148, 149
    Burgundy, 36, 66, 67, 68, 70, 73, 75,
    76, 79, 81, 82, 83
    Coteaux Champenois wines, 146, 147
Jura and Savoie wines, 113
    Loire wines, 107
    Rhône wines, 104
Plaimont, 123
Plant d'Arles grape, 135
Plantey-de-la-Croix, Ch, 39, 41
Plince, Ch, 60
Plouzeau et Fils, 110
La Pointe, Ch, 60
Pomerol, 10, 36, 38, 60-1, *61*
    grapes, 60
    recommended châteaux, 60
    red wine production, 35
    vintage chart, 30
Pommard, 76
Pomys, Ch, 51
Pons, Jacques, 131
Ponsot, Domaine, 70
Pont-de-l'Isère, 93
Pontac-Monplaisir, Ch, 57
Pontet, Ch, 41
Pontet-Canet, Ch, 41, 53
Pontoise-Caba~rus, Ch, 41
Port-Vendres, 133
Porto Vecchio, 143, 144
Portugais Bleu grape, 114, 120
Potensac, 45
Potensac, Ch, 38, 41, 44, 45
Pouget, Ch, 40, 46
Les Pougets vineyard, 74
Pouilly, 106
Poujeaux, Ch, 39, 41
Poujeaux-Theil, Ch, 54
Poulsard grape, 113
de la Pousse d'Or, Domaine, 76
Pradelle, Jean-Louis, 93
Premières Côtes de Bordeaux, 35, 65
prices of wines, 35, 67
Le Prieur de Meyney, 39
Le Prieuré, Ch, 42
Prieuré-Lichine, Ch, 38, 41, 46
Priourat, Ch Le, 39
Producteurs de Plaimont, 123
Protheau et Fils, François, 80, 81
Provence, 134-41
    bottle, 22
    grapes, 84, 135, *135*, 139, 140
    red wine production, 135
    see also Coteaux d'Aix; Coteaux des
    Baux; Cotes de Provence
Puisseguin-St-Emilion, 58
Puligny-Montrachet, 78
Pupillin, 112
Puy-Servain, Ch, 117

Q

Quatourze, 129
Quénard et Fils, André, 113
de Queribus, Ch, 128

R

Rabaud-Promis, Ch, 38
Raffault, Olga, 110
Raffault, Raymond, 110
Rahoul, Ch, 57
Ramage la Batisse, Ch, 41
Ramonet, André, 79
Rancio Rasteau, 105
Rapet Père et Fils, 75
de Raspail-Ay, Domaine, 97
Rasteau vdn, 89, 102, 105, 132, 133
Rausan-Ségla, Ch, 40, 46
Rauzan-Gassies, Ch, 40, 46
Rayas, Ch, 98
la Raye, Ch, 117
Rebeilleau, Maurice, 109
Redortier, Ch, 103
Les Renardes vineyard, 74
Réserve de la Comtesse, 39
Reuilly, 107, 111, *153*
de Rey, Ch, 133
de Rhodes, Ch, 120
Rhône, 27, 88-105
    grapes, 84, 89, 91, 93, 94, 97, 98, 101,
    103, 105
    red wine production, 89
    vintage chart, 32-3
    see also Châteauneuf-du-Pape; Cornas;
    Côtes du Rhône; Côtes du Ventoux; Côte
    Rôtie; Coteaux du Tricastin; Crozes-
    Hermitage; Gigondas, Hermitage; Lirac;
    St-Joseph

Ribaute, 128
Ricard, Claude, 56
des Richards, Domaine, 103
Richebourg, 72, 73
Rieussec, Ch, 38
Rilly, 147
Ripaille, 113
Ripeau, Ch, 42
Rivesaltes, 125, 133
Roaix, 102
La Roche-de-Glun, 93
de la Roche, Ch, 109
des Roches Neuves, Domaine, 109
Rochegude, 102
Rodet, Antonin, 81
Le Rognet-Corton vineyard, 74
Rolet Père et Fils, 113
Romanée, 73
Romanée-Conti, 72, *72*, 73
Romanée-Conti, Domaine de la, 24, 72, *72*
Romanée-St-Vivant, 72, 73
Romefort, Ch, 39, 41
Rondil et Fils, Gabriel, 101
La Roque, Ch, 39
La Roque de By, Ch, 41
de Roquefort, Ch, 39
Roquefort-des-Corbières, 128
Roquemaure, 100
de Roquemaure, Cave Coopérative, 101
Ropiteau-Mignon, Domaine A, 76
La Rose de Faurie, Ch, 39
La Rose Goromey, Ch, 39
La Rose Maréchal, Ch, 39, 41
La Rose Trintaudon, Ch, 41
de Rothschild, Baron Eric, 52
de Rothschild, Baron Philippe, 52
Rothy, Domaine Joseph, 70
Rouet, Ch, 64
Rouget, Ch, 38
Roumier, 70
Roure, Raymond, 93
Roussanne grape, 92, 93, 94, 98
Roussanne du Var grape, 135
Rousseau, Domaine, 101, 103
Rousset, Ch, 63
Rousset-les-Vignes, 102, 103
Roussillon, 130-3
de Roux, Ch, 136
Ruchotte-Chambertin, 71
Ruet, Jean, 86
Les Rugiens, 76
Rully, 80, 81, *81*

S

SCV de Pollestres, 133
SCV les Vignerons de Terrats, 133
SCV les Vignerons de Maury, 133
Sabatier, Jacques, 103
Sables du Golfe du Lion, Listel, 155
Sablet, 102
de Sablon, Domaine, 101
St-Amour, 86, 87
St-André de Figuière, Domaine, 136
St-Aubin, 78, 79
Saint-Bonnet, Ch, 41
St-Chinian, 125, 130, 131
    grapes, 131
    recommended producers, 131
    red wine production, 125
St-Christoly, 45
St-Christophe des Gardes, 58
St-Cyr-sur-Mer, 138
Saint-Desirat co-operative, 154
Saint-Donat co-operative, 154
St-Didier-Parnac, Ch, *119*, 119
St-Drézéry, 131
St-Emilion, *19, 43, 58,* 58-9
    classified wines, 42
    grapes, 59
    recommended châteaux, 59
    red wine production, 35
    vintage chart, 30
St Estèphe, 44, 50-1
    grapes, 51
    recommended châteaux, 51
    red wine production, 35
St Estèphe-la-Croix, Cru, 39
St-Etienne-de-Baigorry, 123
St-Etienne de Lisse, 58
St-Gemme, Dom du 39
St-Genies-de-Comolas, 100
St-Georges d'Orques, 131
St-Georges-St-Emilion, 58
St-Georges-Côte-Pavie, Ch, 42
St-Germain-d'Esteuil, 45
St-Gervais, 102
Ste-Hélène, Dom du, 39
St-Hippolyte, 58
St-Jacques, Ch, 39
St-Jean de Minervois, 127
St-Jean-de-la-Porte, 113
St-Jean-Pied-de-Port, 123
St-Jeoire-Prieuré, 113
St-Joseph, 27, 94-5, *95*
    grapes, 94
    recommended producers, 94
    red wine production, 89
de St-Julia, Ch, 127
St-Julien, 44, 48-9
    grapes, 49
    recommended châteaux, 49
    red wine production, 35
St-Laurent-des-Arbres, 100
St-Laurent des Combes, 58
St-Marc, Cru, 39

St-Martin, 128
St-Martin-sous-Montaigu, 80
St-Maurice-sur-Eygues, 102
St-Nicolas-de-Bourgueil, 106, 107
St-Pantaléon-les-Vignes, 102, 103
St-Pey d'Armens, 58
St-Pierre, Ch, 40, 49
Saint-Pourçain-sur-Sioule, 111
St-Roch, Ch, 39
St-Romain, 78, 79
Saint Sardos, 152
St-Saturnin, 131
St Sauveur, Domaine, 105
St-Sulpice de Faleyrens, 58
St Yzans, 45
Sainte-Cécile-des-Vignes, 155
Sancerre, 32, 106-7, 111
Sancerre Rouge, 107, 110, 111
Sansonnet, Ch, 42
Santenay, 78, 79
Les Santenots vineyard, 76
Sapin, 86
Sarasot, Ch, 41
Sarget de Gruaud-Larose, 49
Sarrou, 86
Sartène, 153, 144, *144*
Sauman, Ch, 63
Saumur, 106, 107, 108-9
    grapes, 109
    red wine production, 107
Saumur-Champigny, 106, 108
    red wine production, 107
Savigny-lès-Beaune, 74
Savoie, 32, 112-13, *113*
    grapes, 113
    recommended producers, 113
    red wine production, 112
Sciacarello grape, 143, 144, 145
Segonzac, 63
de Ségriès, Ch, 101
Ségur, Ch, 38
de Ségur, Ch, 39
Séguret, 102, 103
de la Senche, Domaine, 127
Sérignan, 155
La Serre, Ch, 42
de Seuil, Ch, 140, 141
Sigalas-Rabaud, Ch, 38, 39
Sigognac, Ch, 41, 44
Simone, Ch, 139
Siran, Ch, 38, 39, 46
Smith-Haut-Lafitte, Ch, 42, 57
Sociando-Mallet, Ch, 38, 41
de la Solitude, Domaine, 98
Sorrel, 93
Soudars, Ch, 41
Soussans, 46
Soutard, Ch, 39, 42
South-West, 114-23
    grapes, 114, 117, 119, 120, 123
    red wine production, 114
    see also Béarn; Bergerac; Buzet;
    Cahors; Côtes de Duras; Gaillac;
    Irouléguy; Madiran; Pécharmant
Sparr, 149
Les Suchots, 72
Syrah grape, *90*
    Corsica wines, 143, 145
    Languedoc-Roussillon wines, 124, 125,
    126, 127, 128, 129
    Provence wines, 134, 135, 136, 138, 139
    Rhône wines, 89, 91, 92, 93, 94, 96, 97,
    98, 100, 101, 103, 104, 105
    South-West wines, 114, 120, 121

T

La Tâche, 72, 73
du Taillan, Ch, 41
Taillefer, Ch, 39, 60
Tain co-operative, 93, 154
Talbot, Ch, 38, 40, 49
Talence, 56
Taluau, 110
Talut, Luc-Jérôme, 131
Tannat grape, 114, 118, 119, 122, 123
de Targe, Ch, 109
Tasta, Ch, 64
Tastevin, Chevaliers de, 72, 73
Tayac, Ch, 38, 41
Tempier, Domaine, 139
des Templiers, Ch, 39
de Tenon, Domaine, 97
du Terme, Domaine, 97
Terradot, Henri and Gilbert, *123*
Terrebrune, Domaine, *138, 139*
des Terres Blanches, Domaine, 140
Terret Blanc grape, 98
Terret Noir grape
    Languedoc-Roussillon wines, 125, 128
    Rhône wines, 89, 98
Terry-Gros-Caillou, Ch, 49
du Tertre, Ch, 41, 46
Tertre-Daugay, Ch, 42
Testut, Phillippe, 101
de Thalabert, Domaine, 93
Thenard, Baron, 81
Thévenin, Roland, 78, 79

Thomas, Michel, 110
Thomas-Bassot, 70
Thorin, 86
Tibouren grape, 135, 136, 138, 139
Tijou, P, 109
de Tiregand, Ch, 117
Tollot-Beaut, 75
des Tonnelles, Ch, 64
de Torraccia, Domaine, 145
Tortochot, Domaine, G, 70
La Tour Blanche, Ch, 39, 41
La Tour-Carnet, Ch, 40, 54
La Tour d'Aspic, Ch, 39
de la Tour d'Elyssas, 105
La Tour de By, Ch, 39, 40, 44, 45
de la Tour de Lirac, Domaine, 101
La Tour-de-Mons, Ch, 46
La Tour du Haut Moulin, Ch, 41
La Tour du Mirail, Ch, 41
La Tour-du-Pin-Figeac, Ch (Giraud-Bélivier), 42
La Tour-du-Pin-Figeac, Ch (Moueix), 42
La Tour-Figeac, Ch, 42, 59
Tour-Haut-Brion, Ch, 42, 57
La Tour Haut-Caussan, Ch, 41
La Tour-Martillac, Ch, 42, 57
La Tour Saint-Bonnet, Ch, 41, 44
La Tour Saint-Joseph, Ch, 41
Touraine, 106, 110-1
  grapes, 110
  recommended producers, 110
Touraine-Amboise, 106, 107, 111
Touraine-Azay-le-Rideau, 107
Touraine-Mesland, 106, 107, 111
Tourelles, Ch des, 41
Trapet, Domaine Louis, 70
des Travers, Domaine, 103
Treilles, 128
de Trevaillon, Domaine, 140
Trimbach, 149
Trimoulet, Ch, 42
Trois Croix, Ch, 64
Trois-Moulins, Ch, 42
Trollat, 94
Tronquoy Lalande, Ch, 41, 61
Troplong-Mondot, Ch, 42
Trotenoy, Ch, 60
Trottevieille, Ch, 42, 59
Trousseau grape
  Jura and Savoie wines, 112, 113
de la Tuilière, 97
Tuchan co-operatives, 128
Turckheim, 149
Tursan, 123

U
Ugni Blanc grape
  Provençal wines, 139
  Rhône wines, 100, 101

V
VDQS wines, 150
Vaccarèse grape,
  Rhône wines, 89, 98
Vacheron, 110
Vacqueyras, 102
Val Joanis, Domaine, 32, 140
Valençay, 111
de la Vallongue, Domaine, 140
de Vallouit, L, 91, 93, 94
Vannières, Ch, 139
Verdignan, Ch, 39, 41
Les Vergennes vineyard, 74
Vermentino grape, 143, 145
Vernay, George, 91, 94
Vernous, Ch, 41
de Versailles, Domaine, 117
Verset, Noel, 94
Verzenay, 147
Vesselle, Alain, 147
Vesselle, Georges, 147
Vesselle, Jean, 147
Viénot, Charles, 73, 75
La Vieille Ferme, 105
Vieux Château Certan, 60, 61
du Vieux-Lazaret, Ch, 105
du Vieux Micocoulier, Domaine, 105
du Vieux Télégraphe, Domaine, 98
Vieux Robin, Ch, 41
La Vigne au Saint vineyard, 74
Vignelaure, Ch, 32, 55, 140, 141
La Vigneronne, 127
Vignerons Ardéchois, 154
les Vignerons Catalans, 131
les Vignerons de Terrats, 131
Vignerons de St-Vincent, 133
Vignerons de Saumur, 109
Vignerons Réunis du Vic-Bilh, 123
Vignonet, 58
Vigouroux, Georges, 118
Villaudric co-operative, 120
de Villamont, Henri, 75, 86
Villedomange, 147
Villemaurine, Ch, 42
Villenave d'Ornon, 57
Villeneuve-les-Corbières, 128
Vin d'Orléanais, 111

Vin de Corse, 143, 144, 145
Vin de Savoie, 112, 113
Vin Délimité de Qualité Supérieure (VDQS), 150
Vin de Pays d'Allobrogie, 154
Vin de Pays de l'Ardèche, 150, 155
Vin de Pays de l'Aude, 155
Vin de Pays de l'Hérault, 155
Vin de Pays de Coteaux de l'Ardèche, 155
Vin de Pays de Principauté d'Orange, 155
Vin de Pays du Gard, 155
vin doux naturel, 29, 105, 125, 132-3
Vincent, Ch, 64
vines, 8-9, 8-11
  clonal selection, 9, 143
  cultivation, 8-11
  grafting, 8, 8
  pruning, 79, 87
  spraying, 43, 143
  training, 10, 135
Vins d'Entraygues et du Fel, 121
Vins d'Estaing, 121
Vins de Marcillac, 121
Vins de Moselle, 149
Vins de pays, 150-5
  VDQS wines, 150
Vinsobres, 102
vintage charts, 30-3
Viognier grape, 89, 90, 91
Visan, 102
Voarick, Michel, 75, 81
Vogüe, Alain, 94
Vogüe, Domaine Comte Georges de, 70
Volnay, 76, 77, 77
Vosne Romanée, 24, 72, 73
Vougeot, 73
Vray-Canon-Bouché, Ch, 64
Vray-Canon-Boyer, Ch, 64

W
wine and food, 26-7, 28-9
wine auctions, 25
wine buying, 22-5
  as investment, 24-5
wine drinking, 26-7
wine industry, 18-19
wine merchants, 22-3
winemaking, 12-15
wines and grapes, 8-9, 16

Y
Yon-Figeac, Ch, 42

Bibliography

Oz Clarke, Wine Factfinder and Taste Guide, Webster's/Mitchell Beazley, 1985
Oz Clarke, Webster's Wine Guide 1987, Webster's/Mitchell Beazley, 1987
Hubrecht Duijker, The Great Wines of Burgundy, Mitchell Beazley, 1982
Hugh Johnson's Wine Companion, Mitchell Beazley, 1983
Hugh Johnson, The World Atlas of Wine, 3rd edition, Mitchell Beazley, 1985
Anthony Hanson, Burgundy, Faber and Faber, 1982
John Livingstone-Learmonth and Melvyn C. H. Master, The Wines of the Rhône, Faber and Faber, 1983
L'Office National Interprofessionnel des Vins, Les Vins de Pays

David Peppercorn, MW, Bordeaux, Faber and Faber, 1986
David Peppercorn, MW, Pocket Guide to The Wines of Bordeaux, Mitchell Beazley, 1986
Jancis Robinson, MW, Vines, Grapes and Wines, Mitchell Beazley, 1986
Steven Spurrier and Joseph Ward, How To Buy Fine Wines, Phaidon/Christie's, 1986
Serena Sutcliffe, MW, Pocket Guide to the Wines of Burgundy, Mitchell Beazley, 1986
Serena Sutcliffe, MW, The Wines of France, Futura Publications, 1985
Serena Sutcliffe, MW, The Wine Drinker's Handbook, Pan Books, 1985
André Vedel (general editor), The Macdonald Guide to French Wines 1986, Macdonald, 1986

Picture Credits